Monetary Macroeconomics

Traditional monetary analysis has failed to explain monetary disorders and to provide a satisfactory solution. The main reason for this lies in the unsuccessful integration of money in the theories of relative exchange and in the confusion which still besets economists between money and credit. The majority of books concerned with monetary analysis are therefore either trapped in the neoclassical dichotomy between real and monetary variables, or incapable of distinguishing between the roles of monetary and financial intermediaries played by the banks.

The aim of this book is to provide the grounding for a new approach to monetary economics, based on the book-keeping nature of money. The main themes of macroeconomics are examined to show how we may improve our understanding through a thorough analysis of their monetary aspects. Money is the key element and its role is investigated in relation to value, prices, profits, capital and interest. Alvaro Cencini's analysis rejects the traditional, net asset definition of money, arguing that, despite appearances to the contrary, money is issued by banks as a mere numerical form. It is through its association with production that it is given its positive value, purchasing power. The resulting theory elicits a new understanding of the conditions behind today's monetary disorders and prescribes new remedies to cure them once and for all.

Alvaro Cencini is Professor of Monetary Theory and Monetary Economics at the Università della Svizzera Italiana and at the Centre for Banking Studies, Lugano, Switzerland. He is also founder and co-director of the Laboratory of Research in Monetary Economics. His previous publications include *Monetary Theory: National and International* (Routledge 1995) and *Inflation and Unemployment*, with M. Baranzini, eds (Routledge 1996).

Routledge international studies in money and banking

Monetary Macroeconomics

A new approach

Alvaro Cencini

London and New York

First published 2001
by Routledge
11 New Fetter Lane, London EC4P 4EE

Simultaneously published in the USA and Canada
by Routledge
29 West 35th Street, New York, NY 10001

Routledge is an imprint of the Taylor & Francis Group

© 2001 Alvaro Cencini

Typeset in Times by
Prepress Projects Ltd, Perth, Scotland
Printed and bound in Great Britain by
the University Press, Cambridge

British Library Cataloguing in Publication Data
A catalogue record for this book is available
from the British Library

Library of Congress Cataloging in Publication Data
Cencini, Alvaro.
  Monetary macroeconomics : a new approach / Alvaro Cencini.
    p.cm. – (Routledge international studies in money and banking ; 15)
  Includes bibliographical references and indexes.
    1. Monetary policy. 2. Money. 3. Macroeconomics. I. Title. II. Series.

HG230.3 .C398   2001
339.5´3–dc21   00-068032

ISBN 0–415–19569–1

Contents

Figures

Tables

Preface

In his foreword to *Money, Income and Time*, Lord Desai encouraged the reader to abandon firmly held beliefs, to open his mind to a new way of thinking about money. This is what I am asking readers to do once again. My aim is to show how a new monetary macroeconomic theory may be built through a critical approach to mainstream, axiomatic theories. The choice of authors quoted in the book is functional to this end, and does not pretend to be uncontroversial. Since, in my opinion, the construction of a consistent theory of economic reality takes precedence over a close textual reading, my main concern is neither to provide an exhaustive survey of the literature available on the subject nor to attempt yet another exegesis of the works of the great economists. The debate on whether an author actually meant this or that when she/he wrote a given sentence may be of interest to historians, but is irrelevant to my purpose. I apologise in advance for my 'somewhat' free interpretation of some texts in the hope that the reader will follow me in the quest for a thread that, from Adam Smith onwards, will lead us to a new approach to monetary macroeconomics.

This book is a modest contribution to the research programme elaborated at Fribourg, Switzerland, and Dijon, France, by Bernard Schmitt. Waiting for the publication of his latest manuscripts, I believe it is worth providing an introduction to his quantum theoretical approach, mediated through a critical reappraisal of the works of such famous economists as Ricardo, Marx, Walras, Wicksell and Keynes as well as through an uncompromising analysis of recent developments in monetary theory. Being well aware of the dangers inherent in any kind of dogmatism, I have endeavoured to show how each result conforms to logic and facts. Of necessity, proofs have not always been developed in detail, whereas any interested reader is invited to look for more extensive ones in Bernard Schmitt's and my own earlier publications. Although I have translated some quotations from Schmitt's published works into English, I have left others in French, so as to give the reader the genuine flavour of the original. Of course, the importance and nature of the various subjects dealt with in the book is such that much additional effort is needed in order to have them exhaustively investigated. If my work proves to be stimulating and thought provoking, it will have fulfilled its task. It is my hope that the reader will find it so despite its numerous imperfections, for which the author alone must be held responsible.

Acknowledgements

This book is the fruit of research conducted at the Centre for Banking Studies and at the University of Lugano and has greatly benefited from the interaction with my students there. I am grateful to them. My thanks also go to Bernard Schmitt, who has constantly encouraged me on the way and read the first draft of the manuscript. I am also much indebted to Sergio Rossi, whose reading of both manuscript and proofs always unveils unspotted errors. This book would never have reached the present linguistic standard without the help of Simona Cain; she has read through and polished its successive English versions with care and style. Nicole Martinez has always been generous with her time and skills; she has plotted all the figures and tables and provided bibliographical assistance. Both deserve my appreciation and warmest thanks.

Introduction

It is often implicitly assumed that economic events can be understood through direct observation. This may be one of the reasons why economic analysis is mainly carried out in microeconomic terms. Monetary analysis is no exception. Even though concepts such as income, saving, investment, interest and capital are mostly considered at the national level, they are almost inevitably arrived at through a process of aggregation of their microeconomic components. If, as is widely believed, macroeconomics were simply the result of such an aggregative process, microeconomic variables would be the only relevant object of enquiry of economic analysis. This would not imply, however, that economists are to limit their analysis to direct observation. In particular, this would not allow them to define money irrespective of its peculiar, immaterial nature. Even at the microeconomic level, money remains a numerical form issued by the banking system. One important point of our analysis is therefore the fact that monetary economics requires a thorough investigation over and above mere factual observation, centred on a clear understanding of the banking nature of modern money.

Another central point is the fact that, unlike what happens both in micro- and in traditional macroeconomic analysis, the concept of equilibrium is not made to play any fundamental role. Indeed, the very idea of a monetary equilibrium is at odds both with the banking nature of money and with the definition of money income. An equilibrium is a (more or less) stable condition in which distinct and opposite forces balance each other. Hence, a monetary equilibrium is a concept presupposing the existence of the demand for and supply of money as two distinct and opposite forces. But, if demand for and supply of money are to define two opposite forces, it is necessary that money exists independently of produced output. It is only in this case, and on condition that it had a positive value of its own, that money could be held as a net asset. The reader will recognise here the assumption made by neoclassical theorists and known in economic literature as the classical dichotomy. Now, modern monetary analysis shows that this dichotomy is an avatar of the old-fashioned conception of material money. Once it has been understood that money is issued as a simple numerical form, it is easy to see that its value is derived from its integration with current output. Thus, money income – the result of this integration – does not exist separately from current output. In fact, money income is current output and current output is money income, the two expressions describing the twin aspects of one and the same object. This being so, it should be clear that total supply (output) and total demand (money income) can no longer be considered as two autonomous entities. The very concept of equilibrium or conditional equality must therefore be replaced with that of identity. Similarly, we can no longer consider the supply of money income as distinct from its demand. As soon as a positive income appears in the economy, it is there to define a supply (of the current output that it is identified with) and an equivalent demand. Moreover, because of the banking nature of money, income is, from birth as it were, necessarily deposited within the banking system, which means that it is necessarily demanded (by the agents entered on the assets side of the banks' balance sheet) and supplied (by the agents entered on the liabilities side). Double-entry book-keeping is a rigorous instrument that leaves no room for hypothetical adjustments between supply and demand, and rings the toll for any analysis based on the concept of equilibrium.

The identity between money income and produced output affects the traditional distinction between micro- and macroeconomics. In fact, every single process of production gives rise to a new positive income (output) and must hence be considered as a macroeconomic event, even if it is carried out by a single unit of production. Under these conditions, it no longer makes any sense to consider the number or size of the economic agents as the discriminating criterion between micro- and macroeconomic events. A more rigorous principle, first proposed by Schmitt, consists in considering as macroeconomic all the events that modify the situation for the entire economic set-up and as microeconomic those events that, while modifying the situation of any number of economic agents, do not alter that of their set. As already mentioned, production is an example of a macroeconomic event, every new production giving rise to an income that increases the wealth of the whole economic set (as the concept of national income clearly suggests). On the contrary, even if it is carried out by a large number of income holders, the purchase of financial assets is a microeconomic transaction because it simply modifies the distribution of national income among economic agents without altering its amount.

Referring to the microeconomic theory of demand and supply, the theory of non-Walrasian price formation, the theory of efficient rationing and all the other theories that have recently been elaborated by mainstream 'model' economists, Morishima (1992: 167) has no qualms about considering them 'as examples of oversophistication which enrich the theorists' imaginary world'. The Japanese economist is right. Neoclassical economists have been developing over-sophisticated models with no bearing on the real world. Despite their increasing mathematical complexity, all these models suffer from the same shortcomings because they all stem from the same basic assumption, i.e. that economic theory is intrinsically axiomatic. The procedure proper to mathematics, and so often fruitfully applied to physics and other 'exact' sciences, has been extended to economics on the arbitrary assumption that economic events can be analysed in the same way as physical events. Now, contrary to what happens in physics, the economic system is entirely a man-made entity. This means that not even a single element of this system may be taken to be an axiom. But if everything must be explained starting from scratch, then economic analysis cannot result from the combination of a given number of assumptions according to a series of axiomatic relationships.

Debreu's analysis is one of the clearest examples of the path followed by most contemporary economists in their search for a rigorous theory capable of gaining respect from the followers of other, more famed, sciences. Mathematics is seen as a necessary requirement for rigour and seriousness, and its use is thought to be essential to economic theory even at the expense of its faithfulness to reality. 'Allegiance to rigor dictates the axiomatic form of the analysis where the theory, in the strict sense, is logically entirely disconnected from its interpretations' (Debreu 1959: x). A strange allegiance to rigour indeed, if it allows for the 'logical' severance of theory from its economic interpretation. Debreu does not seem to care about the fact that, by relying so much on mathematics, he is constructing an axiomatic theory that has nothing to do with reality. If successful, his exercise would provide a new field for mathematical application, but a field hopelessly removed from the real world of economics. In the first two chapters we shall try to show that, logically, the neoclassical attempt at determining relative prices through exchange is doomed to failure. Economics is a science in itself, capable of being as rigorous as any other exact science. Yet, it is not through the systematic use of mathematics and through axiomatisation that this end will be reached. It is logic that shows that relative prices are necessarily undetermined, and it is reality that forces us to recognise that the peculiar character of an economic system is money.

Now, money is a very peculiar 'object', which has too often been mistaken for a real good. As recent developments in banking theory have confirmed, it would be both anachronistic and wrong to take money as a material thing. This makes things clearer if not easier: money is an immaterial entity issued by banks every time they carry out a payment on behalf of their clients. Referring to the famous economic distinction between stocks and flows, we would say that money is a flow whose instantaneous circulation has a stock of income (or capital) as its object. Banks create the flow but not its object, which is closely related to production. This is to say that money and credit are not one and the same thing. To provide their clients with credit, banks need to back it with a positive deposit, i.e. with a positive amount of income or capital. Contrary to what happens for the creation of a simple flow (a numerical vehicle with no positive value), the income banks lend is not of their making. Correctly used, double-entry book-keeping does not allow for the creation of income independently of production. Thus, by creating money, banks simply provide the economy with a numerical *means* of payment, the object of the payment being derived from the association of money with current output.

The very nature of bank money is numerical. Real goods and services, on the other hand, are physical (albeit not necessarily material). What of production then? Is it a process of transformation taking place continuously or discontinuously in chronological time? From a physical point of view, it is. But this should not be an economist's main concern. It is from an economic point of view that economists must analyse production, and from this viewpoint production is the process by which physical output is given its monetary form. The association between money and output being the result of an (instantaneous) payment, production itself is an instantaneous event. Surprising as this may appear at first, it must be recognised that it is the only result consistent with the fact that physical goods and services are given their numerical form (money) only through the payment of their costs of production. Through a process of physical transformation, raw materials are given a new utility form, but it is through a payment that the newly manufactured objects are transformed into economic goods.

The economic nature of production emerges when referred to profits and their definition as a net surplus. Since Quesnay's contributions, profit has been identified with a surplus, produced either by nature (as maintained by the physiocrats), by labour (as claimed by the Classics) or by the process of production itself (Sraffa, Leontief and Pasinetti). The existence of a net product within a process of physical transformation is somewhat mysterious. If production is considered for its physical nature, there is no point in looking for a real surplus. Lavoisier's principle of transformation applies, and no positive difference can ever appear between outputs and inputs. A critical analysis of the attempt to identify profit with a net surplus leads us to choose between two reciprocally exclusive alternatives. Either we maintain that no net product can ever be formed in the economy (which is thus reduced to an infinite series of processes of physical transformation) or we claim that the whole output of any period is a net surplus. In the latter case, production is considered not as a physical process of transformation but as a truly economic event in which output acquires its original economic form. Quantum monetary theory stands by the latter alternative.

It is interesting to note that, by considering value as a relationship between goods and not as an intrinsic quality of goods, neoclassical economists have been able to avoid the metaphysical definition of profits. Giving up the search for a net surplus, they implicitly admit that their conception of relative prices does not allow for a net surplus. The necessary clearance of all markets follows from the equality between supply and demand at equilibrium. Moreover, even if equilibrium prices did not imply the clearance of all markets, stocks of unsold goods could not be defined as a net product. Their failure to be exchanged would deprive them of all value, so that it would be rather odd to consider them as a positive profit.

The conception of production as an instantaneous event referred to a positive and indivisible period of time (a quantum) is deeply rooted in the classical and neoclassical traditions, insofar as they rest on the numerical definition of money (Marx's form of value, Walras's *numéraire*), and in Keynes's project to build a monetary theory of production. As for the analysis of capital, the best insights are still to be found in the works of Böhm-Bawerk as well as of Ricardo, Marx, Wicksell, Keynes and Hicks. Thanks to their analyses, we know that capital is related to time, that it is real and monetary at the same time, that it is at the origin of interest and that its process of accumulation is at the heart of the capitalist mode of production. What has only recently been clarified is how capital may be accumulated either in harmony with or in opposition to the laws of monetary economics. As shown by Schmitt, the pathological process of capital accumulation has its origin in the way investment of profits is entered by banks into their double-entry book-keeping. This might sound strange to a newcomer, but will not come as a surprise to those who know that our economic reality is essentially of a book-keeping nature. What we still need to emphasise is the fact that monetary disorder is caused by a structural inadequacy of our systems of payment rather than by the behaviour of economic agents.

From a monetary point of view, economics is a science with its own logical laws. The aim of economic theory is to determine what these laws are and to show how they can be implemented. The analysis of capital provides a clear example of the way these laws work. In particular, it helps us to understand what devastating consequences may derive from a failure to abide by them. Let us take, for example, the law according to which an income is destroyed when it is spent for the final purchase of output. If the investment of profits takes place in such a way that profits are spent (on the labour market) for the final purchase of capital goods, the result is the formation of a new deposit. Instead of being destroyed, profits reappear in the form of wages and define a new deposit immediately available on the financial market. This sort of duplication is the sign of an anomaly that inevitably leads to inflation as soon as fixed capital goods enter the process of production and that amortisation is introduced to account for their wear and tear. One of the great merits of Bernard Schmitt is to have shown that, in its pathological state, the economic system splits up into three sectors, and that the more the third sector expands the greater the danger of deflation and unemployment. According to Wicksell's intuition, in the pathological state capital accumulates until it reaches a point where the natural rate of interest falls below the market rate. From then on, profits derived from amortisation can no longer be invested in the production of new capital goods, and this triggers a process that eventually leads to involuntary unemployment.

Ono puts it quite clearly: 'the current prosperity of neoclassical economics has led to the situation where even Keynesian phenomena such as unemployment and stagnation are analysed totally in the neoclassical equilibrium framework' (Ono 1994: 1). Of course, unemployment and stagnation are Keynesian phenomena only in the sense that they are at the heart of Keynes's theory. As pathological manifestations of our economic systems, they are no more Keynesian than neoclassical or neoricardian. The real problem is, therefore, that of establishing which theory is more appropriate to explaining the nature of these pathologies. Now, if there can be little doubt about the inadequacy of the analysis of stagnation proposed by those economists who attribute the shortage in effective demand to 'price–wage rigidities or market imperfections' (ibid.: vi) or 'even insist that workers are unemployed because of their own preference' (ibid.: vi), it is likewise hard to believe that unemployment and persistent stagnation can be explained in terms of equilibrium and speed of adjustment. If it is true that the rate of interest plays a role in the genesis of deflation, this cannot be shown by forcing Keynes's theory into a neoclassical framework, even if this is done by replacing two fundamental postulates of neoclassical analysis. The time has come to abandon the Walrasian approach and all the different neoclassical interpretations of Keynes's monetary analysis in order to get to the true origin of the anomalies that hamper the development of our economies.

As stated before, the aim of this book is to provide the elements for a new approach to monetary macroeconomics that is based on the book-keeping nature of money. The main subjects of macroeconomics are examined with the explicit purpose of showing how we may improve our understanding of these subjects by means of a thorough analysis of their monetary aspects. Money is the key element and its role is investigated in relation to value, prices, profits, capital and interest.

The first chapter deals with the problem of value. Since the Classics, this problem has been considered to be fundamental to the very existence of economics. If produced goods and services were to remain heterogeneous (as they are when considered merely from a physical point of view), economics would have no status as a science as it would lack a proper object of enquiry. To become homogeneous and be transformed into commodities, physical goods and services must be measurable by a common unit or standard of value. Money has traditionally played this function. Yet, there is still little agreement as to how money (particularly modern bank money) may become the standard of value. According to a widespread interpretation, classical and neoclassical authors share the belief that money is essentially a commodity chosen among other commodities to act as a general equivalent. Now, this material conception of money is far from being unanimously adhered to by the great classical and neoclassical economists. Marx's concept of form of value, for example, is close to Walras's concept of *numéraire* and they both refer to money as to a non-material entity, a numerical form whose fundamental role is to act as a numerical unit of account. The age-long debate on the existence and the nature of value in economics originates from lack of consensus as to whether value should be considered as a substance, a peculiar dimension of commodities (absolute value), or resulting from the measurement of commodities in terms of commodities (relative value). The analysis of bank money shows, however, that neither alternative is the right one. Instead, it is the combined intuition of Marx and Walras that leads to the correct definition of value. In the first chapter, the relationship between money and value is analysed through a critical reappraisal of the contributions of Smith, Ricardo, Marx, Walras and Keynes, as well as through the modern monetary approach underlying the works of Bernard Schmitt.

Chapter 2 is concerned with the relationships among money, prices and exchange. Although economists are unanimous in considering money as a means of exchange, most theories still lack a satisfactory explanation of the way in which money may become the general equivalent of produced output. Mainstream economics is based on the concept of relative exchange. In their most rigorous expression, neoclassical theories consider money as being perfectly neutral. Yet, the assumption of money neutrality is seriously challenged by a demand for commodities that is overdetermined. The smooth functioning underlying the traditional Arrow–Debreu Walrasian model is hindered by a series of restrictions

(Jevons's double coincidence of wants, budget balance constraint, monotone excess demand diminution, excess demand fulfilment). To overcome these difficulties, some economists have pleaded for the effective introduction of money and the financial market into general equilibrium theory. Their attempts are carefully analysed in this chapter, which ends by showing that their main shortcoming lies in the old-fashioned conception of money to which they are still anchored. The same conclusion applies to the traditional version of the quantity theory of money and to its determination of prices. An alternative solution is provided by quantum monetary analysis. As soon as money is conceived of as a pure numerical form, it becomes possible to move from the world of relative exchanges to the world of absolute exchanges. It is the nature of bank money that leads us towards this new conception of monetary transactions. Whereas the concept of relative exchanges subsumes a world in which money is essentially a commodity, that of absolute exchanges applies to a world in which money is a numerical standard issued by the banking system as a simple IOU (I owe you). In this chapter, we deal mainly with neoclassical general equilibrium analysis in both its Walrasian and monetary forms, and through its critical appraisal we show what changes are needed for economic theory to match monetary reality.

The third chapter looks at the relationship between money and credit and the role played by banks as 'money creators'. Money and credit have long been confused, partly because of the net asset definition of money and partly because money creation implies indeed a financial intermediation by banks. It is not easy, thus, to avoid considering the creation of money as a creation of credit. The analysis of the way in which money is issued by banks and integrated with physical output is once again fundamental in clarifying the relationship between monetary and financial intermediations. Although they take place simultaneously, these two operations are distinct; and so are their results. While money is a simple numerical vehicle allowing the flow of payments, credit implies a financial transfer of income. While money has no value of its own and can indeed be created, income derives from production and defines an absolute exchange between a real and a monetary deposit. Credit is concerned with the lending of such a deposit. It appears, thus, that the supply of credit must be kept distinct from that of money. The monetarist concept of money supply is ill-founded because, assuming money to be a positive asset, it confuses money with income. In fact, it is income that is a positive asset. The supply of credit is the supply of a positive amount of income and requires the existence of a bank deposit (a stock), whereas the supply of money refers to the capacity of banks to convey payments (flows) on behalf of their clients. By failing to distinguish clearly between these two functions (monetary and financial intermediations) carried out by banks, economists have been led to develop an anachronistic conception of money, inconsistent with its book-keeping nature and incapable of explaining the working of our monetary economies of production. As the recent evolution of banking and applied technology shows, it is no longer possible to conceive of money as a material medium of exchange. If money is a general equivalent, it is because it gives a numerical form to current output, and not because it has a positive value equal to that of the goods it is exchanged with.

Money and output enter an absolute, not a relative, exchange, and banks are the intermediaries through which the result of this absolute exchange is lent, spent or invested. It is only through a rigorous analysis of this double function of banks that we may hope to lay the foundations of a new monetary economics.

In Chapter 4, money is analysed in its relationship with production. Here again it is no mystery that economists have not reached agreement as to the way that this economic process must be conceived. Important differences remain, for example, between Keynesian and neoclassical authors, between those who consider production as a one-way process and those who analyse it as a circular flow. The role of money within this process has been thoroughly investigated in the past, and is still one of the most debated arguments of economic theory. French and Italian economists have recently enlivened a fruitful debate about the way that money may be associated with current production, and Morishima has provided a stimulating contribution to a new formulation of the general equilibrium theory, in which money and production are central elements. Thanks to these efforts, it has become clearer that, when considered as an economic process, production is a monetary (as well as a physical) phenomenon. Leaving the study of the physical properties of output to other experts, economists must centre their investigation on the monetary aspect of production. It is only by so doing that they can determine whether production is merely a physical process of transformation or whether it is also a process of creation, i.e. whether output is only a transformed input or a net product. Once again, the analysis of bank money makes it possible to reconsider the whole problem afresh, clearing the way for a new conception of production as an instantaneous process in which money and physical output become one and the same thing. The chapter considers the contributions of authors such as Smith, Keynes, Schumpeter, Schmitt and Morishima, and gathers together the elements for a monetary macroeconomic analysis of production.

Chapter 5 is devoted to the analysis of capital. All the concepts elaborated in the previous four chapters converge here to provide a theory of capital in keeping with the laws of bank money. Consistent with the method followed throughout this book, we start by considering the classical concept of capital and the main contributions provided by the economists who have analysed it. Among them, particular attention must be paid to the works of the Austrian school. According to the Austrian vision, capital is time and it involves command over current output. This view has been in part taken over by some neoclassical economists, who have come to consider capitalistic production as a process stretching over time. The concept of intertemporal prices is fundamental in the neoclassical approach; so is capital aggregation. However, the difficulties inherent in the problem of aggregation and in the need to derive the prices of capital goods from their own costs of production seriously undermine this approach. As Hicks clearly put it, capital is a twofold entity: monetary and real. To reduce capital to a collection of capital goods is seriously misleading. The Austrian view must be reassessed starting from a rigorous analysis of bank money and its relationship with time and current output. Although it is correct to relate capital to time, this relation is not the same with respect to circulating or fixed capital. The passage from one form of capital to the other implies the investment of profit and involves the definitive transformation of savings into a social capital. This process has recently been analysed by Schmitt and is the core of quantum monetary macroeconomics. This chapter is concerned with it as well as with a critical survey of the principal theories of capital.

Chapter 6 follows closely on from the analysis developed in Chapter 5. The determination of interest is part of the theory of capital and can be properly investigated only once the concept of capital has been clearly defined. A crucial question is whether or not interest is to be added to the value of current output, i.e. whether or not interest is an additional macroeconomic income. The answer is far from self-evident. Economists have usually answered in the positive without being really able to prove the correctness of their intuition. Of particular interest is the analysis put forth by Böhm-Bawerk. Even if his attempt is not entirely successful, his contribution is still fundamental. Following his distinction between interest related to loans on consumption (*Leihzins*) and interest related to capital accumulation (*Urzins*), it is possible to show that the accumulation of capital leads to the formation of a positive value independently of the physical productivity of capital goods. As in capital theory, time plays a central role in the determination of interest. Yet, the importance of time and the way it enters into the determination of interest can be fully perceived only if the process of capital accumulation is analysed in terms of the new theory of emissions. As the critical appraisal of the arguments elaborated by Marx, Böhm-Bawerk, Wicksell, Keynes, Hicks and Patinkin shows, the theory of interest is the target of the whole body of monetary macroeconomics. The origin of interest (*Urzins*) lies in the formation of macroeconomic saving, i.e. in the investment of savings and in their transformation into fixed capital. In this chapter, the relationship between money and interest is analysed in terms of capital accumulation, and a modern theory of interest and interest rate is derived from the critical assessment of the works of the authors mentioned above.

The last chapter is concerned with a concise survey of the main monetary disorders that hamper the further development of our economic systems. The traditional attempt to explain these disorders in terms of disequilibrium is challenged by the idea that disorder is caused by the failure of the present system of payments to comply with the logical rules of bank money. The transition from the microeconomic to the macroeconomic approach to monetary economics is marked by the need to reconsider the role played by the structure of monetary payments in the process of capital accumulation. It is argued that the time has come to shift attention from behavioural considerations to the working of the monetary structure underlying the whole economic activity. This does not mean, of course, that microeconomics has to be left behind. On the contrary, analyses referred to entrepreneurial decision and economic policy would continue to be elaborated in microeconomic terms. Yet, they would have to respect the logical framework represented by the laws of monetary macroeconomics. Economic agents should be totally free to make decisions, and microeconomic theory can help them towards choosing the most profitable ones. The absence of monetary disorders, however, does not depend on the nature of these decisions, but on the logical compliance of the system of payments with the laws of monetary macroeconomics. It is thus possible to tell apart the field that is proper to macroeconomics and that pertaining to microeconomic analysis. It is also possible to clarify the relationship existing between these two complementary approaches and to show that, contrary to a commonly held belief, macroeconomics cannot be arrived at through the simple aggregation of microeconomic variables. Macroeconomics is a science in its own merits. It defines a set of logical rules with which the system of payments (national and international) must comply if monetary disorders are to be definitively avoided.

1 Money, value and prices

The problem

From a purely physical point of view, produced goods and services are heterogeneous. It is the primary task of economics to make them homogeneous by determining a common unit of measure. It is therefore particularly surprising to read the following sentence in Hicks's *Capital and Time*: 'Physically, there could be many inputs and many outputs; by confining attention to their values we made them homogeneous, whatever their physical character. When we pass to the more strictly economic application, we lose that advantage' (Hicks 1973: 37). The Oxonian economist seems not to be aware of the fact that any economic application requires the existence of an economic system, and that no economic system can ever exist if commodities remain heterogeneous. What Hicks is claiming here is that an economic theory might be constructed on mere technological grounds. His attempt at so doing is based on growth theory and relies on the assumptions that 'all "original" inputs are taken to be homogeneous, and all final outputs homogeneous' (ibid.: 37). This is a curious way of proceeding. Having claimed that when we pass to the more strictly economic application we lose the advantage of making inputs and outputs homogeneous, is it legitimate to enter the world of economic application on the assumption that homogeneity can be taken for granted among the elements of each category? Hicks's approach is all the more unconvincing that he thinks of final output 'as standing for "consumption goods in general" ' (ibid.: 37).

Like the majority of his fellow economists, Hicks maintains that 'any bundle of goods can be treated as a single good, so long as the proportions in which the component goods are combined are kept constant' (ibid.: 144). Hence, variations in these proportions define variations in the specification of the single good. But, how can we measure these changes in specification? How can we establish a numerical relationship between two different single goods? The problem allows for no solution. This is so because each single good is a bundle of heterogeneous goods, which can only be described in each of its component parts without it being possible to express it in a single unit of measure. Every change in specification gives rise to a new single good that cannot even be compared with the others as each of them is made up of different proportions of different (and heterogeneous) component goods. Let us take a very simple example, and suppose that good I is made up of 3 tons of iron and 2 tons of wheat, while good II is composed of 2 tons of iron and 3 tons of wheat. What kind of relationship can we establish between good I and good II? Is good I greater or lesser than good II? It should be obvious to everybody that in order to answer these questions we have to make iron and wheat homogeneous. If we were able to reduce both iron and wheat to a common denominator, there would be no difficulty in expressing the relationship between our two single goods. Conversely, if iron and wheat remain heterogeneous, there are no possibilities of valuing good I in terms of good II, or vice versa.

A good example of the difficulty inherent in the heterogeneity problem is provided by Wicksell in his *Value, Capital and Rent*. Attempting to elaborate 'a definite theory of the value of goods' (Wicksell 1954: 153), he starts his analysis by assuming the existence of two economies producing two different goods, corn and linen. He assumes also that, in the first economy, 'wages, ground-rent, and capital-interest are all received in the form of goods, that is to say in corn, and the capital itself consists of corn' (ibid.: 153), while in the second economy they are all expressed in terms of linen. Then, if A, B and K are used to represent the number of wage-earners, the area of land and the capital, respectively, and if l, r and z stand for wages per worker, rent per hectare and interest per unit of capital, respectively, it is possible to 'express the quantities of goods which are produced every year in the two economies' (ibid.: 154) as follows:

$$\text{Corn-producing economy} \qquad A_1 l_1 + B_1 r_1 + K_1 z_1 \qquad\qquad (1.1)$$

$$\text{Linen-producing economy} \qquad A_2 l_2 + B_2 r_2 + K_2 z_2 \qquad\qquad (1.2)$$

The real problem arises when 'both economies are united *in a single economy*, so that the existing wage-earners, natural resources and capitals of both can now be used indiscriminately in the one or the other production of goods' (ibid.: 155). To account for a single economy, corn and linen are to be made homogeneous, and this is because their value can 'only be determined after having found out their prices' (ibid.: 155). Equations (1.1) and (1.2) can be written down only if their terms are all expressed in the same unit, which is obviously the case if wages, rent and interest consist only of corn or only of linen. When the two economies are transformed into sectors of one and the same economy, corn and linen must become the constituent parts of a single national output. The problem, therefore, is that of determining the value of each of them in terms of a common unit of measure.

The direct confrontation between physically heterogeneous goods is no basis for the construction of an economic theory. Now, in Hicks's analysis, we find also the elements of an entirely different approach to the problem. By taking labour as the sole input, he opens the way to the measure of goods in terms of labour or wage units. 'It would indeed have been equally possible to have taken the value of goods in terms of labour as our fundamental price-ratio, making labour the standard of value instead of goods. This is to say, we might have decided to work in terms of wage-units' (Hicks 1973: 38). As the reader will immediately recognise, the idea of making labour the standard of value can be traced back to the Classics, while that of measuring value in wage units is a cornerstone of Keynes's monetary theory. By contrast with the attempt to work out a solution in terms of value, Hicks's own choice, like that of Wicksell and of the majority of contemporary economists, is that of defeating physical heterogeneity through the determination of relative prices. Although the differences existing among the solutions proposed so far testify to the need for further theoretical progress, they also show the centrality of the problem of heterogeneity and the necessity of determining a common unit of measure for goods and services. 'It is overlooked that the magnitudes of different things only become comparable in quantitative terms when they have been reduced to the same unit. Only as expressions of the same unit do they have a common denominator, and are therefore commensurable magnitudes' (Marx 1976: 140–1).

Money and value

Money, value and labour

In the paper read at the Economic Club, November 1934, Hicks maintains that money is better understood and integrated in the real world if it is related to the theory of value. 'I should prefer to seek illumination from another point of view – from a branch of economics which is more elementary, but, I think in consequence better developed – the theory of value' (Hicks 1967: 8). He thus claims that the crucial problem is that of explaining why people choose 'to have money rather than other things' (ibid.: 10). Dismissing the traditional approach based on the concepts of velocity of circulation, natural rate of interest, and saving and investment relationship, he sets out to prove how money can have a positive marginal utility. His analysis is microeconomic and is mainly concerned with the factors influencing people's demand for money. Now, the problem is that the decision to hold money (for example in the form of bank deposits) cannot be considered as a demand for money. If I am the holder of a bank deposit of 100 units and decide not to spend or invest it, I cannot say that I am exerting a positive demand for 100 units of money because I already own a right on them. Moreover, although my decision might be motivated by one (or more) of the factors enumerated by Hicks, none of them can account for the effective value of money. In other words, if money did not have any positive value, people would never hold it. Hicks's factors play a role in the choice between different forms of investment and consumption. To hold money as a bank deposit is one of these forms of investment, but it is evident that if bank deposits had no value no choice would be possible. Neither investment nor consumption could be positive if money were valueless. The central point is therefore that of explaining the origin of the value of money. It is here that Hicks's suggestion to refer money to the theory of value becomes significant.

The Classics are the first to have worked out a detailed economic theory of value. Starting from the physical heterogeneity of real goods, they corroborate

Quesnay's intuition about the role played by human labour and make it the standard of value. 'Labour alone, therefore, never varying in its own value, is alone the ultimate and real standard by which the value of all commodities can at all times and places be estimated and compared' (Smith 1974: 136). Here, the difficulty lies not in the fact that human labour is taken as the unique source of value but in the attempt to transform labour into the standard of value. As alleged by Marx, as labour is the only source of value, it cannot itself have any positive value. 'Labour is the substance, and the immanent measure of value, but it has no value itself' (Marx 1976: 677). If labour has no value of its own, and if value is defined as 'embodied labour', it follows either that value itself does not exist or that it is not a material property of commodities. Thus, Marx is not entirely up to the mark when he claims that labour is a substance. If labour were a substance, it would itself have a value, and the measurement of value would be analogous to that of a physical dimension. Since it is logically inconsistent to claim both that labour is a substance and that it has no value proper, we have to choose between a physical and an immaterial conception of value. As is well known, the Classics have never definitively rejected the idea of value being a substance. The failure of Ricardo's search for an invariable measure of value and of Marx's attempt to reduce complex to simple labour is a clear proof that their choice was the wrong one. Ricardo was well aware that in order to explain changes in relative value we must express real values in terms of an 'invariable standard measure of value, which should itself be subject to none of the fluctuations to which other commodities are exposed' (Ricardo 1951: 43). The Anglo-Portuguese economist could not find any invariable standard of value, mainly because he was looking for a dimensional unit, a commodity of invariable value to which every other commodity is referred in much the same way as a distance is referred to as a standard unit of length called a meter. No such commodity exists, and Ricardo's problem is bound to remain unsolved as long as labour itself is considered a commodity. 'Labour, like all other things which are purchased and sold, and which may be increased or diminished in quantity, has its natural and its market price' (ibid.: 93). Although in Marx's analysis an important distinction is introduced between labour as such and the labour power (which is said to be the commodity through whose use value is created), the value and its standard are still thought of as physical dimensions. 'How, then, is the magnitude of this value to be measured? By means of the quantity of the "value-forming substance", the labour, contained in the article. This quantity is measured by its duration, and the labour time is itself measured on the particular scale of hours, days etc.' (Marx 1976: 129). What Marx seems not to be aware of is that time also is a physical dimension. His value is a substance (embodied labour time), and his standard of value a dimensional unit. But it is precisely because his conception of value is still dimensional that he finds himself caught in the same trap as Ricardo: the search for an invariable standard. It is true that physically heterogeneous goods cannot be made homogeneous on the basis of their use values.

The exchange values of commodities must be reduced to a common element, of which they represent a greater or a lesser quantity. This common element cannot be a geometrical, physical, chemical or other natural property of commodities. Such properties come into consideration only to the extent that they make the commodities useful, i.e. turn them into use-values.

(ibid.: 127)

Yet, it is also certain that labour time is no less heterogeneous than physical commodities. The multiple kinds of works exerted by individuals are fundamentally different, in quality as well as in quantity. Even the labours provided by different individuals working in the same branch and with the same qualification are in fact heterogeneous. Hence, the measurement of value in terms of labour time is as hopeless as that in utility terms.

Now, Marx claims also that value does not derive immediately from labour time. If this were the case, value could be expressed in labour certificates or 'labour money', individual labour being perceived directly as social. Marx unhesitatingly rejects the identification of labour time with money, an idea to which he refers as 'the shallow utopianism of the idea of "labour-money" in a society founded on the production of commodities' (ibid.: 189, note 1). Thus, despite numerous, deceptive appearances to the contrary, Marx refuses to adopt a dimensional measure of labour as the standard of value. It is not the fundamental relationship between output and labour that is questioned, but its expression by a dimension of time. Without the objective mediation of money, individual labour cannot be transformed into social, undifferentiated labour, making it impossible to identify value with labour time.

Having abandoned Ricardo's search for an invariable (dimensional) standard of value, Marx emphasises the social aspect of value and the need to express it by means of what he calls 'the form of money'. 'Everyone knows, if nothing else, that commodities have a common value-form which contrasts in the most striking manner with the motley natural forms of their use-values. I refer to the money-form' (ibid.: 139). Let us be as clear as possible. The expression of value form chosen by Marx shall not lead us astray. The problem is not that of analysing or describing the different forms that value could take (according to entirely accidental circumstances) with regard to exchange. For example, if a given commodity, say wheat, exchanges against iron instead of copper, this has no effect on the determination of the value of wheat, iron and copper. Differences in the physical terms of their exchange have no repercussion on their values, the form of which is that of a numerical 'general equivalent'. The value form appears therefore for the first time when physical output is transformed into an economic output, i.e. when physical goods are transformed into commodities. 'The product of labour is an object of utility in all states of society; but it is only a historically specific epoch of development which presents the labour expended in the production of a useful article as an "objective" property of that article, i.e. as its value. It is only then that the product of labour becomes transformed into a commodity' (ibid.: 153–4).

As a relationship between output and labour, value represents the only objective criterion of distinction between physical objects and commodities. Determined by the production process, value defines commodity and is simultaneously defined by it. Value and commodity are so closely linked as to define one another. Hence, output is a commodity because it has a value, which is tantamount to saying that the existence of output as a commodity is defined by the existence of its value. Now, value itself is defined by its social form of existence, a form that results from the same process that determines value. Social labour is therefore the source of value and its form. But how is labour related to the form of value? How can money become the economic unit of account of physical output?

Money, labour and wages

According to Marx, the social determination of value does not take place on the commodity market. The same process that accounts for the social expression of value accounts, simultaneously, for the substitution of money to physical output. What has still to be determined is the nature of this process. What we know already is that of necessity it takes place on the labour market. As the social expression of value is also the social expression of labour, the definition of value must coincide with that of social labour. Because of the physical heterogeneity of individual labour, labour time cannot be taken as the unit of measure of value. The solution implicit in Marx's analysis is to define social labour by resorting to its monetary measure: wages. The relationship output–labour becomes the social expression of value as soon as production takes place within a system of paid labour. 'Labour must directly produce exchange value, i.e. money. It must therefore be *wage labour*' (Marx 1973: 224). Wages are the social definition of labour, and are themselves expressed numerically in money terms. Hence, money defines goods through wages. The payment of wages is the transaction allowing for the social definition of labour and for the replacement of physical output by money.

It is through the rigorous investigation of the role played by money that Marx attains this result, which is openly in opposition to his analysis of the labour power. In fact, his distinction between labour and labour power does not take into account the need to express the value of commodities in money terms. As soon as it is established that value can be socially defined only through the mediation of money, that money is perceived as a form of value and that the identity between output and labour is defined in terms of wages, it is no longer possible to distinguish between labour and its power. Thus, if labour defines output and is itself defined by wages, wages necessarily define output in its totality. As the transformation of individual into social labour is granted by money wages, the labour power coincides with labour itself.

Labour is the prime cause of value. By defining total output, wages define simultaneously the totality of social labour. This is so much so that, as recognised by Marx, a value deprived of its social (monetary) expression is a value that cannot even exist. In Marx's analysis, wages respect a double constraint. They do not represent the price of labour – because it is not logically possible to consider labour as a positive commodity – and they allow for the social definition of output.

The modernity of Marx's analysis is highlighted by that of Keynes. Like the Classics, Keynes maintains that numerical comparison of physically heterogeneous output can be obtained by choosing the amount of employment associated with a given stock of capital goods as the standard of value. Perfectly aware of the difficulty related to the heterogeneity of labour itself, he avoids it by introducing the money wage as a unit of account. As rightly observed by Bradford and Harcourt, if wages were conceived of as the price of labour and if 'price is a non-numerical relation between a commodity and money' (Bradford and Harcourt 1997: 118), they would have to be expressed by some kind of wage index. But, 'if they are subject to residual vagueness in the same sense as price indices, then the labour-unit device is similarly infected and hence the quantity of employment so measured ceases to function as a precise numerical index for the quantity of total output' (ibid.: 118). Thus, in order for the wage unit to work as a homogeneous standard of value, it must not be considered as the price of labour. 'The alternative possibility is that Keynes did not view the wage as a kind of price' (ibid.: 118).

Now, even if it is true that 'for all the ingenuity and subtlety of Keynes's reasoning on the question of units, he ultimately failed to apply it consistently in *The General Theory*' (ibid.: 119), what really matters is to establish whether or not the expression of labour in wage units allows for its numerical measurement. If we refer back to Marx's claim that labour has no value itself (which necessarily follows from it being the source of value), we immediately get the idea that labour cannot be expressed in terms of a unit of value. We also realise at once that labour is not a commodity, and cannot therefore have a price. The conclusion is straightforward: wage units can only be the numerical expression of labour. Perfectly homogeneous, they give different kinds of individual labour a form that makes them comparable on a numerical basis. Of course, this is so if money itself is seen as a numerical form, and not as a commodity. In this respect, Keynes's distinction between money of account and money proper (which recalls the classical distinction between nominal and real money) is significant. In *A Treatise on Money*, he claims that 'money of account, namely that in which debts and prices and general purchasing power are *expressed*, is the primary concept of a theory of money' (Keynes 1971: 3). Thus, Keynes's money of account corresponds to our numerical form, while his money proper, which 'can only exist in relation to a money of account' (ibid.: 3), is the result of the association of the numerical form with its real content (current output). 'The money of account is the *description* or *title* and the money is the *thing* which answers to the description' (ibid.: 3). Current output is the 'thing' that is numerically expressed by money and that defines its real content.

Money and relative prices

Money, value and relative prices

Giving up the classical attempt to determine absolute values, neoclassical economists set to work to prove that commodities can find their unit of measure through their direct exchange on the commodity market. For these authors, prices are subject to variations due to supply and demand; they are generated by exchange and are, therefore, essentially relative. As for value, this concept is not investigated in any particular way, and is usually referred to as that of relative prices. In *Capital and Time*, Hicks deals with this subject, although rather briefly, and maintains that 'value must always be reckoned in terms of something – money, a particular good chosen as standard, or a bundle of such goods (money deflated by a price-index number)' (Hicks 1973: 152). Almost immediately, Hicks shifts his interest from value to the problem of measuring goods in real (non-monetary) terms, and seems to suggest that measuring goods in value or real terms amounts to the same thing as, in both cases, they are valued at constant prices. 'We are accustomed to measuring *real* output by valuing output at constant prices; or, what is approximately the same thing, deflating the money value of output by an index of output prices' (ibid.: 152). However, since in neoclassical theory money is a standard chosen among real goods, the money value of output is determined as an equilibrium (relative) price resulting from the simultaneous solution of a general equilibrium system (GES). A problem arises then as to how any particular solution can be chosen as the value of reference. At various moments in time, relative prices are different, but at each particular moment there is only one set of equilibrium prices. What is the set to which 'constant prices' must be referred to? Because production varies continuously in time (always according to neoclassical theory), and because supply and demand are also free to vary continuously, in a given period of time there can be an infinite number of successive sets of relative prices that clear the markets (each of them at different instants). The problem is present even when there are no changes in the quality of produced goods, i.e. even when there are no index number difficulties. Now, it might be claimed that, although every set of relative (equilibrium) prices can be chosen as a reference, this high degree of arbitrariness has no serious consequences as long as, the choice being made, the set of reference remains unaltered. Let us grant this. It is true (at least under specific conditions) that prices could mathematically be kept constant with respect to this particular set by using an appropriate index number, but we would have no criterion for defining value univocally and for distinguishing it from relative prices.

Of course, most neoclassical theorists do not believe value to be a necessary requisite for the determination of a system of homogeneous prices. Yet, it cannot be denied that the search for an invariable unit of value is not due to conceptual confusion, but to the 'necessity to measure in *logically satisfactory* terms the value of the real aggregates used as *determinant* quantities in the theory' (Garegnani 1972: 8). The problem is well known. If the commodity used as general equivalent in a system of relative prices is subject to variations in price, the whole system is modified without it being possible to establish to what extent the variation in relative prices is caused by the change in the cost of the general equivalent. Let us suppose, for example, that the commodity used as general equivalent (money) is produced by labour alone and that, because of a variation in the demand for and supply of labour, wages increase. The cost of our standard will increase, and so will the cost of production of all the other goods produced by labour. Relative prices will be influenced by these variations, of course, but we will never be able to work out whether their change is ultimately due to them more than to other possible factors of variation in the demand and supply exerted by consumers and producers. As clearly perceived by Ricardo, this problem relates to the difficulty of reconciling the determination of (absolute) value with that of relative prices. If real goods were exchanged according to their values – determined, for example, in terms of incorporated units of labour – then absolute values and relative prices would be perfectly consistent. Conversely, if prices vary with the variation of the ratio between wages and profits, it is impossible to determine a constant unit of measure allowing for a consistent determination of absolute values and relative prices. If relative prices were derived from absolute values, there would be no reason to worry about variations in the rate of profit. However, since relative prices are considered to be determined somehow independently of absolute values, the rate of profit becomes a key variable. 'The ratio according to which commodities are exchanged depends on the rate of profit and can only be determined simultaneously with it' (ibid.: 20).

Hence, our main concern here is the logical possibility (or impossibility) of determining relative prices directly, without having recourse to absolute values. As shown by Schmitt (1996), relative prices remain undetermined if real goods are not expressed in purely numerical terms. Let us consider the exchange between two real goods, a and b. Before a given quantity of good a is effectively exchanged against another quantity of good b, the two commodities are made to vary, one with respect to the other, until their respective owners agree on a common rate of exchange. If we suppose that the quantity of good b can vary continuously with respect to a given quantity of good a (a very strong assumption indeed, which never applies in the real world), we may expect that such an agreement will be reached sooner or later. Analogously, if it is the quantity of good a that is made to vary continuously with respect to a quantity of good b, which is supposed to remain fixed, the process of adjustment may in fact lead to an equilibrium. However, if both goods a and b are varying continuously, it immediately appears that their relationship is bound to remain undetermined unless they are assimilated to pure numbers. It is only in this case, in fact, that the ratio determined by the continuous variation of one quantity with regard to the other (maintained fixed) is not substantially modified when the second is also made to vary continuously. Mathematically, the ratio $1/n$ is equal to the ratio x/nx, where n is any number in the series of real numbers and x is a numerical coefficient. On the contrary, from an economic point of view, the ratio a/nb is not equal to the ratio xa/xnb (a and b being real goods) as it is obviously not indifferent for an economic agent to exchange 1 unit of good a against n units of good b, or x units of a against xn units of b. The introduction of numbers into general equilibrium analysis (GEA) is thus of paramount importance. It is not surprising, therefore, that Walras himself felt the necessity of providing a technical solution for the transformation of real goods into pure numbers.

Money as a numéraire

According to Walras, there is no such a thing as absolute value. He rejects the metaphysical idea held by the Classics that value is a particular substance of goods. In particular, he refuses to consider value as a dimension; the only concept that he is prepared to accept being that of 'rareness'. 'To be sure, behind relative value, there is something absolute, namely the intensities of the last wants satisfied or the *raretés*. These *raretés*, which are indeed absolute and not relative, are nevertheless subjective or personal and not physical or objective. They are in us and not in things' (Walras 1984: 188). Thus, value is no longer conceived of as a substance but as a mere relationship. The *numéraire* is then introduced not as a unit of value, but as a numerical quantity of the commodity chosen as a standard. 'Our standard of measure must be a certain quantity of a given commodity and not the value of this quantity of the given commodity' (ibid.: 188). Even if it is true that Walras defines the *numéraire* as a commodity, it is possible to argue that his own conception of (relative) value calls for another definition. The passage from dimensional to relative value requires in fact the transformation of the standard of measure into a pure number. As the word *numéraire* so well indicates, the standard must essentially be a numerical one. When Walras claims that 'the word *franc* [denoting a standard of value] is the name of a thing which does not exist' (ibid.: 188), he is telling us both that value as a substance does not exist and that money itself, as a standard, is lacking any proper value. But if we abstract from any intrinsic value of money, we are left with numbers only: the *numéraire* in its purest form.

Unfortunately, Walras does not provide any satisfactory solution to the problem of integrating pure numbers with produced output. Have the attempts of his followers been more fruitful? Let us briefly consider Debreu's emblematic point of view on this question. In his *Theory of Value*, Debreu maintains that commodities, whether simple economic goods such as wheat or complex goods such as trucks, may be expressed by (non-negative) real numbers. 'A quantity of wheat can be any real number .... A quantity of well-defined trucks is an integer' (Debreu 1959: 30). On the same page, he sometimes associates real numbers with a particular dimension of goods such as surface ('A quantity of land with specified condition, location, and date is expressed by a real number of acres'), mass or capacity ('Mineral deposits, oil fields, ... are defined by a complete description of their content, their location, and, as always, their availability date. Their quantity is expressed by a real number of tons, barrels, ...'). The real kernel of Debreu's analysis here is whether or not it is legitimate to move from the numerical expression of a dimension to the expression of goods by way of pure numbers. 'The *quantity* of a certain kind of wheat is expressed by a number of bushels which can satisfactorily be assumed to be any (non-negative) real number' (ibid.: 30). Attractive as it might at first seem, this assumption is far from being acceptable from a logical point of view. While identical trucks may be counted by numbers, there is no way of transforming any of them in a pure number simply 'by assumption'. This is as true for real goods as it is for services. Here again, Debreu takes it for granted that pure numbers can replace dimensional magnitudes. With respect to labour, for example, he claims that 'the *quantity* of a specified type of labor is expressed by the time worked (a real number)' (ibid.: 31). Now, whereas it is possible to express the quantity of a specified type of labour in hours, minutes and seconds, it is logically impossible to express a quantity of time by a real number alone. Two hours are no more equal to the number two than a dozen of (identical) trucks are equal to the number twelve. Debreu seems to be aware of this difficulty as, immediately after the passage quoted above, he states that 'with each commodity, say the hth one, is associated a real number, *its price*, p_h' (ibid.: 32). The French economist does not explain how prices can be expressed in money terms (in a footnote to the second chapter of his book, he admits that his analysis does not provide any answer to the problem of the integration of money into the theory of value). It is no mystery, however, that he shares the neoclassical point of view as to the possibility of determining relative prices through a general equilibrium system. Yet, our central problem remains essentially unsolved because relative prices do not allow for the association of physical output to real numbers.

If it were possible to associate real goods and numbers simply by arbitrarily choosing a commodity as *numéraire*, the system of relative prices could effectively be transformed into a mathematical model of monetary prices. 'Although a commodity conforming to the doctrine of GET [general equilibrium theory] is devoid of any axiological dimension, such as labour-value, it is nevertheless reputed in that school to be a genuine yardstick for measuring prices, under the sole proviso that it be chosen as a *numéraire*' (Schmitt 1996: 112). Yet, as clearly explained by Schmitt, this association is the core of economic analysis, and it would be curious indeed if it could be obtained through a mere mathematical device. Can a telephone, a car, a pencil, a potato or any other real good be transformed into a pure number *by assumption*? 'Let us suppose the price of commodity "a" to be equal to one': this is the way numbers are introduced into GEA. Is it scientifically acceptable? The majority of economists seem to accept this procedure mainly because it allows them to reduce economics to a branch of mathematics. They are convinced that it is only through mathematics that economics can reach the status of an exact science and become trustworthy. Although there can be no doubt about the necessity of transforming goods into pure numbers in order to make them an object of scientific enquiry, it is not true that any procedure of transformation will do. To claim that goods are numbers because we need them to be numbers is scientifically unacceptable. Yet, this is precisely what is implicit in the neoclassical economists' assumption that a commodity can arbitrarily be represented by a number. What must be *explained* is how goods are replaced by numbers, and this is an economic (and not a mathematical) problem. The procedure followed by Walras is not satisfactory as his *numéraire* is still a real good.

Is it possible to transform a system of relative prices into a numerical system by assuming that the price of a good in terms of another good can be considered equal to 1 if the two goods are of the same kind? For example, can it be assumed that the price of a chair in terms of (physically similar) chairs is a pure number? Is the one chair–one chair ratio equal to 1? It is only if the answer to this question is affirmative that the system of general equilibrium is likely to enter the category of scientific theories. Now, if it is certainly true that in mathematics the ratio a/a is equal to 1, the same cannot be said when as numerator and denominator we have two different, albeit physically similar, goods. To be rigorous, the relationship one chair–one chair cannot even be expressed in mathematical terms since it is totally meaningless from a logical point of view. What does it mean to relate one chair to another chair of the same kind, a table to a table, a pig to a pig? Moreover, even if the one chair–one chair ratio made sense, it would not generate 1 because it is formally impossible to divide a chair by another chair and make them disappear. Being two distinct objects, the two chairs cannot be eliminated through a process of mathematical simplification. The passage from the one chair–one chair ratio to 1 is therefore logically unacceptable.

Now, the reader might critically observe that we would have reached a different conclusion if we had considered the ratio between a chair and itself. If, instead of referring a chair to another chair, we relate it to itself, the simplification between numerator and denominator seems to be possible and the ratio reduced to 1. From a mathematical point of view, the relationship a/a may be equal to 1, it is true, but this is so because good a may be taken as a given *numerical* coefficient. Things are entirely different when a is a real good. The relationship between a chair and itself is a strange relationship indeed, and its meaning rather obscure (at least within the boundaries of relative exchange). More important still, there is no logical reason to believe that the one chair–one chair ratio allows for the substitution of our chair with 1. From an economic as well as from a logical point of view, the relationship a/a has no proper significance and cannot be identified with any number whatsoever. Anyway, as every economist knows, this is not even the option chosen in neoclassical analysis. Relative exchange requires the presence of (at least) two different goods, the (absolute) exchange between one good and itself being totally alien to GEA. It is thus definitively confirmed that numbers have no citizenship within the theoretical framework of relative prices.

As Marx saw so clearly, money is a necessary element of the theory of value. So far, however, its numerical nature has not been entirely understood, and it is still somewhat mysterious how numbers can be associated with real goods. 'The value-form, whose fully developed shape is the money-form, is very simple and slight in content. Nevertheless, the human mind has sought in vain for more than 2,000 years to get to the bottom of it' (Marx 1976: 89–90). Classical authors have failed 'to get to the bottom of it' mainly because of their identification of value with a particular substance; neoclassical economists because of their identification of money with a particular commodity. Yet, the elements provided by the analyses of Smith, Ricardo, Marx, Walras, Keynes and some of their distinguished followers converge towards a new conception of money involving the integration of numbers and real goods. Let us try to bring out the key features of this modern approach to money.

Money as a pure numerical form

Money and bank deposits

The primary function of money is that of a unit of account. The meaning conveyed by this expression is clear: money is used to express real goods and services numerically. It immediately follows that money cannot be a commodity (if money were a commodity, it would have to be expressed in monetary terms so that money would have to be conceived as the unit of account of money itself). To avoid any risk of circular reasoning, money must be assimilated to numbers. This means that money is essentially immaterial. One of the main difficulties we are faced with here is to admit of an immaterial entity capable of transforming physically heterogeneous goods and services into homogeneous commodities. The world of monetary economies is real and immaterial at the same time. What distinguishes the physical from the economic world is precisely the fact that, thanks to money, products are numerically accounted for. In the absence of money, products would not be given their economic form, and economics would be deprived of its own object of enquiry. Although entirely immaterial, money is not a pure figment of the imagination. Its real existence is proven by the marks it leaves: pieces of numerical information about current output, its production, its circulation and its final consumption.

Modern monetary analysis vindicates the intuition of the Classics as to the numerical nature of money. A numerical form is indeed immaterial, and does not endorse the idea of money being merely a commodity chosen as general equivalent. At the same time, it also vindicates the neoclassical claim that value is not a substance but a mere relationship between real products and numbers. A full understanding of the true nature of money and of the role it plays as numerical form of value requires a new perception of economic reality. In particular, it is necessary to get rid of the many attempts at providing more or less sophisticated models with no relationship whatsoever with our modern monetary economies. Leaving aside the historical evolution of money, we shall focus on the analysis of bank money, with the explicit intent of showing that in order to transform physical objects into commodities nothing more – and nothing less – is required than a non-dimensional unit of account.

Let us start from the traditional distinction between fiduciary and scriptural money. It is often claimed that fiduciary or fiat money is issued by central banks, while scriptural money results from the activity of commercial banks. As a matter of fact, central money is also of the scriptural kind, even when it is made up of banknotes. Apart from their physical properties (which will be entirely ignored in our investigation), banknotes represent money only insofar as they take the place of an equivalent sum of scriptural money issued by commercial banks. More important still, banknotes are not themselves a form of money, but rather a claim whose object is a bank deposit. It is thus immediately clear that the first analytical point in need of clarification is the necessary distinction between money as such and money in the form of a bank deposit. If we are to understand money in its purest form, we have to start from the *tabula rasa* and analyse the operation leading to its emission. How can banks, whether private or central, issue a positive amount of money? The question allows no easy answer. Let us proceed cautiously, step by step. A first consideration refers to the logical possibility of creating a positive amount of money. If money were immediately assimilated to a net asset, we would have to dismiss any such possibility. No one has ever seriously maintained that banks have the metaphysical privilege of creating a net asset from scratch. What is often claimed instead is that banks may create a monetary asset in exchange for a real one deposited by the public. 'The bank deposits – i.e. the debts of the bank to the public – are always covered by the assets people have offered to the bank in exchange for deposit claims against the bank' (Sayers 1958: 12). The annoying implication of this claim is that money creation seems to derive from an exchange whose terms cannot be logically determined. Unless we assume that the real assets deposited by the public already have a monetary value (which obviously begs the question since money creation cannot be explained by referring to a process that requires the pre-existence of money), we would have no logical way of establishing any objective relationship between real and monetary deposits. Contrary to what is commonly believed, the creation of money must be explained independently of any real deposit by the public. It is only on condition that it does not require any real deposit that the emission of money is a true creation. Hence, money creation is that particular event in which the credit entered in favour of the public is balanced by an equivalent debt of the same sort entered against the public. If money can be created neither as a net asset nor as a monetary asset matching a real one, it follows that money as such can only be conceived as a numerical form of value.

Now, even considered as a numerical entity, money can be positively created only if it is instantaneously destroyed. Let us consider the emission of 100 units of money by a bank whatsoever, B_w. By issuing 100 units of money, B_w spontaneously acknowledges its debt towards its client, C. Now, if the amount entered on the liabilities side of the balance sheet of B_w to the benefit of C were not immediately balanced by an equivalent entry on the assets side to the detriment of the same agent C, the sum created by B_w would define a positive credit of C. Through a cost-free book-keeping entry, B_w would have created a positive deposit of C and a negative deposit of some other client, say A, which would not reciprocally cancel out. The spontaneous acknowledgement of debt issued by B_w would thus define the creation of a net deposit to the benefit of C. But, how is it possible to maintain that net deposits (positive and negative) are created out of nothing? The problem exists whether or not we explicitly define money as a net asset. Banks' double-entry book-keeping is such that, even if we think of money as a pure numerical form, we cannot avoid the instantaneous balancing of its creation by an equivalent destruction. Hence, the emission of money as such is a twofold operation implying simultaneously a creation and a destruction of the same object, the bank's acknowledgement of debt.

At first sight, the expression 'negative deposit' might sound strange, of course. Someone might even be tempted to claim that there are no such things as negative deposits since a bank deposit can only be positive (or void, but in this case we would use the expression 'lack of deposits'). Yet, on second thought, this critique appears to be irrelevant to the reality of banks' double-entry book-keeping.

The distinction between negative and positive bank deposits is not a distinction between negative and positive assets deposited within the banking system but rather between the monetary form in which real goods are 'deposited' and the income arising from their association with money. According to the principles of double-entry book-keeping, liabilities must be exactly matched by assets, the balance defining the perfect equilibrium between what is entered on the two sides. Rather trivially, we might therefore be tempted to maintain that the distinction between positive and negative bank deposits derives from the fact that, if what is entered on the liabilities side of banks' balance sheets is a positive deposit by savers, what is entered on the assets side is necessarily a negative deposit by borrowers. In reality, the distinction is much more fundamental than it appears. Positive and negative deposits do not result from the different perspectives of savers – who are the banks' creditors – and borrowers – who are indebted to the banks – but from the very nature of bank money, which is simultaneously an asset and a liability. Modern book-keeping has been made possible by the discovery that zero is the first number in the series of integers, and that for each positive number there is a correspondent negative number of the opposite sign. Bearing this in mind, we should easily see that bank deposits are simultaneously positive and negative because money is issued as an asset-liability. Any lingering doubts concerning this might be due to the habit of thinking of both money and money income as assets positively deposited with the banking system. Now, if it is true that money income is a positive bank deposit, it is also true that it is so because a stock of real goods is entered on the banks' assets side, where it 'fills up' the negative deposit of debtors. If no production takes place, the negative deposit is not covered, and it is logically impossible to define a net, positive asset. It thus becomes essential to understand both the negative and positive nature of bank money, and the need to integrate numbers with produced output. It is from this integration that positive deposits arise and define a net macroeconomic wealth. The positive deposit defined by the income entered on the liabilities side of banks' balance sheets must therefore be related to a negative deposit on the assets side *and* to the real object (output) that fills it up. If we take the example of the payment of wages, the double-entry recorded by banks may be represented as shown in Figure 1.1.

With real goods and services filling up the negative deposit (debt) of firms, it is immediately clear that the income making up the wage-earner's positive deposit is net and has current output as its real object. This representation shows also the meaning of Schmitt's absolute exchange, namely that income results from the 'metamorphosis' of current output, which disappears momentarily into the negative deposit to reappear as a positive, monetary bank deposit. The meaning and the role of the distinction between positive and negative bank deposits emerge from the modern concept of bank money and are thus central to a rigorous theory of monetary economics.

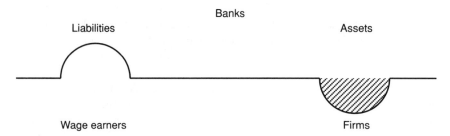

Figure 1.1 Wage payment and bank deposits.

Money and double-entry book-keeping

Double-entry book-keeping is the technical instrument through which banks issue money. The fact that the same amount is entered on both sides of the banks' balance sheets shows how positive and negative numbers concur in the emission of bank money. Highly significant in the field of mathematics, the discovery of negative numbers is at the origin of a substantial progress in economics. It is thanks to negative numbers, in fact, that money can effectively be introduced as a pure numerical form. It is true that this form is instantaneously destroyed because it results from the simultaneous entry of positive and negative numbers. Yet, an instant is all that is needed in order to associate the numerical form with its real content. Likewise, an instant is exactly the lifespan required for the existence of money. Apparently surprising, this last statement becomes significant as soon as it is observed that the presence of money is necessary only when payments actually take place. Hence, since payments are instantaneous events, money itself has an instantaneous lifetime. It thus appears that money as such is essentially a *flow*. Each time a payment is carried out, banks issue money in an instantaneous and circular flow whose result is simultaneously positive and negative. It is only in these instants that money actually exists. To look for money as for a real object would be gravely erroneous for the twofold reason that money is an immaterial entity whose existence is limited to the time required for payments to occur: an instant.

Let us go back to our distinction between money and deposits. Before any payment is actually carried out, banks can simply manifest their capacity to issue money. They do so by opening lines of credit to their clients. A line of credit is the result of a bank's commitment to carry out payments on behalf of its clients. The bank acknowledges owing a given sum to its clients, who acknowledge owing an equivalent amount to the bank. Credit and debit being referred to the same economic agents, they cancel out. Thus, if the opening of a line of credit were entered in the bank's balance sheet, it would give rise to a double-entry of the type shown in Figure 1.2.

The result of this double-entry is clearly zero. Yet, the information conveyed by this particular double-entry is positive. It tells us that banks (in our example bank B) have the faculty to carry out payments on behalf of their clients by issuing their spontaneous acknowledgement of debt.

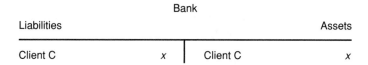

	Bank	
Liabilities		Assets
Client C	x	Client C	x

Figure 1.2 The double-entry of a line of credit.

Money comes into being when a payment actually takes place. When a client of B activates his line of credit asking B to pay his economic correspondent, it is money that performs the operation through its instantaneous flow from the payer to the payee. More precisely still, money is simultaneously issued by B, lent to the payer, transferred to the payee and given back to B, where it is immediately destroyed. Thus, in each payment money describes an instantaneous circular flow from B to B. Considered as a numerical vehicle, money does not survive its emission. Once the payment has taken place, money disappears, leaving behind a numerical information about the economic results of its instantaneous use. It is here that deposits take over from money as such. Monetary payments entail the dissociation of positive from negative numbers, and the formation of positive and negative deposits (Figure 1.3).

As beneficiary of the payment carried out by B on behalf of its client C, A owns a positive deposit of *x* which is balanced but not cancelled out by the debt of C. Now, the question here is to determine what is the object of these entries. Could it be money? Obviously not, because money is a flow and not a stock and because, monetary flows being instantaneous, money is not deposited in real time. Moreover, it would be absurd to claim that money, an immaterial and numerical entity, is itself the object of a positive bank deposit. In fact, bank deposits relate to money income and not to money as such, which is necessarily valueless. What is deposited with banks is not an empty numerical form, but the physical output that is given this form. Once they are given their form of value, commodities become the objects of bank deposits.

Unlike in Latin, where a terminological distinction is made between *nummus* and *pecunia*, in the English language the word money is used indifferently to mean money as such and money income. Analysis shows that this distinction is not merely a terminological one. The two objects defined by money as such and by money income are substantially different, albeit closely interrelated. Money as such is a flow, a numerical vehicle present in every payment; money income (which, as we shall see later on, is instantaneously transformed into capital) is a stock defining physical output monetarily. As a numerical form, money is issued

	Bank	
Liabilities		Assets
A	x	Client C	x

Figure 1.3 The double-entry of a payment.

by banks; as a positive amount of income, it is the result of production. In order for bank deposits to have a real content, it is necessary to associate money with current output. Money must become the form of value of produced goods and services.

The problem is the same as the one faced by the Classics and the Neoclassics: physical products must be associated with numbers. The solution is that suggested by Keynes: physical products acquire their numerical form (and are transformed into commodities) through the payment of wages. Thus, modern monetary analysis corroborates the claim that human labour is the unique source of macroeconomic value, as well as the claim that value is not a substance but a relationship between output and its numerical form. Wages are paid through an instantaneous flow of money. Banks issue the amount of money required by firms, pay it out to wage-earners and get it back from them all in one. Through this (instantaneous and circular) emission of bank money, output is given its numerical form and becomes the very object of the negative and positive deposits generated by the payment of wages. Wages having being paid by banks on their behalf, firms are the owners of a negative deposit in which physical output is (momentarily) stocked, whereas wage-earners have a right on a positive deposit whose object is this same real output, albeit in its monetary form.

As shown in Figure 1.1, the money income deposited on the liabilities side of the banks' balance sheets and owned by wage-earners is the monetary definition of the real product contained in the negative deposit resulting from the debt incurred by firms. Because of the payment of wages carried out by banks on their behalf, firms are entered on the assets side of banks' balance sheets. They owe to banks the amount of wages paid for the production of physical output, which is thus the very object of their debt.

If labour were a commodity (a real input), its payment would require the expenditure of a pre-existing income, whose origin would remain totally undetermined. Being a factor of production, its payment is of a particular nature since it leads to the formation of a new positive income resulting from the association of money with current output. The creation of value is thus an instantaneous event of twofold significance. From a real point of view, it consists in giving matter and energy a new utility-form, whereas from an economic point of view it amounts to the integration of physical output into its monetary form. Hence, labour is the source of an economic value that is expressed numerically by money wages. Value is not a material dimension of produced output, but defines, numerically, its social relationship with human labour. Through the payment of wages, physically heterogeneous products are transformed into economic goods and services of which money represents the form of value. Carried out by a monetary flow, this payment ends up with the formation of a new bank deposit so that the flow of money has a direct consequence on the stock of money income. Both money and income are implied in the payment of wages, but at different levels. Money as a purely numerical form is needed to carry out the transaction, while money income is the result of the payment.

Money, value and absolute prices

Money's value

The non-dimensional nature of money having been established, it remains to be explained how it is endowed with a positive value. In order for payments to be effective, money must be transformed into a sum of income defining a positive purchasing power. 'Money as such, *i.e.* so long as it fulfils the functions of money, is of significance in the economic world only as an intermediary. It is its purchasing power over commodities that determines its utility and marginal utility, and it is not determined by them' (Wicksell 1965: 29). How is this purchasing power determined and how is it measured? Let us refer to Desai's observations on the matter. In one of his selected essays, we are told that 'Jevons, and following him, Edgeworth, developed the theory of index numbers to make more precise the notion of value of money. To this theory, Irving Fisher and Keynes made many significant contributions' (Desai 1995: 295). The problem seems therefore that of establishing whether or not the value of money can be *determined* by referring to the level of prices. As Desai explicitly puts it, price indices (either wholesale or retail prices) are used to *measure* real money balances. Does this mean that the value of money must be determined – through a process still to be explained but which does not refer to price indices – before being measured by the level of prices? Is it possible to determine value without simultaneously measuring it? Certainly not since, logically, the determination of value implies its measurement, and vice versa. However, this is not a proof that value can be determined and measured using the concept of index numbers. Although it is true that value is measured by numbers, it must still be shown that money can acquire a positive purchasing power simply by relating it to the price level.

How are current prices determined? Desai does not ask this question, perhaps because he takes it for granted that, being numerically known to everybody, current prices are to be considered as given. This is not, however, quite satisfactory. It is true, of course, that if prices can be known to us as numerical entities this also means that they have been determined. The point is that their determination must be explained: the existence of current prices results from their determination but does not account for it. Desai's analysis rests on the following assumptions:

1   Money has a positive value measured by referring its quantity to the level of prices.
2   The level of current prices is given.

Yet, neither assumption can be taken for granted. In particular, a theory aiming to explain the value of money cannot assume as its starting point that money is naturally endowed with a positive purchasing power. Analogously, the level of current prices cannot be considered as pertaining to the category of axiomatic entities. It is right to say that the determination of the value of money entails that of current prices, but this does not imply a one-way correlation between the two.

In fact, their determination is simultaneous. As soon as prices are known, so is the value of money. Under these conditions, it would be a mistake to assume that the value of money depends on prices. Their simultaneous determination does not allow a causal relationship to be established between the two concepts, which appear to be two aspects of the same reality. Since money's value and prices are co-determined, it is inconsistent to consider either of them as given in order to measure the other.

Desai's true interest seems to lie in the variation of the value of money. His analysis is concerned mainly with 'the reproductive measure of purchasing power' (Desai 1995: 301), which he relates to 'the expected requirements to reproduce last year's standard of living' (ibid.: 301). His critical assessment of price indices and of their use as indices of variation in purchasing power is a sign of his concern with the need for a better standard to account for the value of money and its variations in time. Yet, his frequency-related indices of purchasing power do not seem to be up to this task. Although they may be used successfully to determine variations in the cost of living, they tell us nothing about variations in the value of money. The point is that, while an increase in macroeconomic prices defines an equivalent variation in the numerical expression of value, the impact of an increase in microeconomic prices (i.e. those with which price indices are concerned) is confined to a new distribution of income.

The value of money and (macroeconomic) prices are determined simultaneously. This seems to be true for classical, neoclassical and modern economists alike. A major difference exists, however, as to the way prices are determined. Whereas within the classical framework prices are absolute and determined by production, in GEA prices are relative and determined through exchange. Now, the attempt to determine prices through relative exchange is seriously jeopardised by the logical impossibility of considering money as a real good. It is obvious that, if prices are relative, money must be conceived of as a commodity. But, if money is a commodity, what is its price? Can a commodity be, simultaneously, the numerical expression of prices and a real good whose price must be expressed in terms of money? Consider the relative exchange between commodity money m and a real good a. If, for example, 10 units of m are exchanged against 1 unit of a, it can equally well be said that 10 units of m are the price of 1 unit of a, or that 1 unit of a is the price of 10 units of m. Thus, m is no more the standard of good a than a the standard of m. Yet, in order for money prices to be univocally determined, it is necessary to have only 1 unit of measure. The problem can be solved neither by choosing one of the two commodities as a reference nor by arbitrarily assuming that it can be taken to be equal to a mere number. Relative exchange can only occur between real terms, a necessary condition which allows neither for the determination of a unique unit of measure nor for the association of numbers with real goods and services.

Moreover, as shown by Schmitt, an economy built on relative exchanges does not admit to any monetary creation. This is so because of the logical requirements of double-entry book-keeping. When a bank carries out a payment on behalf of one of its clients, 'the object of the payment must be deposited with the bank at the very instant the payment takes place' (Schmitt 1998: 13; our translation). Now, in a system of relative exchanges the object of the payment is immediately in the hands of the payee. Since the terms of every relative exchange are real goods, 'it is impossible for the object of a relative exchange to exist twice simultaneously, once as the property of one of the agents, and once as a bank deposit' (ibid.: 13; our translation). The logical impossibility of money to be created within a regime of relative exchanges is therefore the result of the impossibility of banks to get as a deposit the counterpart of their payment. This means that, if exchanges took place according to the principles of GEA, banks would be unable to carry them out, and, as (bank) money is created only when payments occur, this necessarily entails that relative exchanges are inconsistent with the existence of money.

Money and absolute prices

Things are entirely different when prices are immediately expressed in money terms. In this case, prices are no longer relative but are absolute, and they are determined through the association of money and output. Since money is, first of all, a form of value, it can have no proper value *per se*. Hence, when money provides for the social expression of commodities, it would be a mistake to multiply value by two, i.e. to add the value of money to that of the real product. In reality, only one value exists. As soon as goods are socially determined, money takes their place; this is the result obtained through the payment of wages. The exchange between output and money wages is not an exchange between two equivalent and distinct objects, but between one object and its monetary form. It is through this *absolute exchange* that money replaces physical output, which is thus defined by a sum of money income deposited with the banking system. Money as such is present only in the very instant that the payment of wages occurs. Being a flow, money cannot be held by wage-earners, who are simultaneously credited and debited in money terms. In a sense, it is even possible to say that wage-earners are bound (by the laws of double-entry book-keeping) to spend it as soon as their wages are paid to them. Now, by spending their money wages, wage-earners purchase their own real product in its monetary form: they become the holders of a bank deposit whose object is the output deposited on the assets side of banks' balance sheets. Wages are paid through an instantaneous flow of money that allows for the absolute exchange of current output, which is thus transformed into a sum of money income. Unlike what happens in GEA, where transactions pertain to the category of relative exchanges, the payment of wages defines the exchange between an object and itself. Wage-earners are at the origin of this absolute exchange, through which physical objects are given their monetary form and transformed into commodities. When they get paid, wage-earners sell their current output only to purchase it, at the same instant, in its monetary form. Real goods and services are, in fact, the very object of the bank deposit that wage-earners purchase through the flow of money defining the payment of wages. Being simultaneously credited, for their sale of current output, and debited, for their purchase of this same output in its monetary form, wage-earners are thus the intermediary through which absolute exchange takes place. As a result, commodities are produced as a sum of money income, wages being the product itself and not its monetary counterpart.

Another result of the absolute exchange occurring between money and output is the determination of *absolute prices*. Whereas money prices remain intrinsically alien to neoclassical analysis, they are at the core of modern monetary macroeconomics. It is through the integration of money and current output that prices are determined; integration being itself a direct consequence of the absolute exchange defined by the payment of wages. Once it is established that money is a numerical form of value and that physically heterogeneous goods are transformed into commodities when they are given this form, a deeper understanding of the concepts of value and price is within our reach. It is enough to show that human (social) labour is necessarily expressed in wage units to realise that wages are the monetary definition of current output. Then, it is relatively easy to conclude that, given the dialectical identity between value and its form, product and money wages are so closely interrelated as to define the terms of an identity. When output is given its monetary form, it is literally transformed into wages, which become its own definition. Value is nothing other than this particular relationship between the product and its numerical form. For example, if 100 wage units are paid to the wage-earners producing a table, the value of this table is given by the relationship (of identity) established between the table and the 100 units of money wages. From a macroeconomic point of view we would say that the production of the table has added a new value (or a new income) of 100 units to the measure of national output. To be exact, therefore, money's value is not defined by the purchasing power of wages over current output, but by the identity that production establishes between these two terms. The 100 units of income formed through the payment of wages are the very definition of the table: they *are* the table.

Now, as prices are the monetary expression of produced goods and services, it follows immediately that they are essentially identical to values. The integration between money and products takes place through the payment of wages, which determines values and prices alike. At this stage of the analysis, we are therefore led to the conclusion, already reached by the Classics, that value and prices are always necessarily equal. This conclusion is not as surprising as it might first appear if we bear in mind that it applies at the macroeconomic level. Whereas microeconomically prices may vary with respect to values, macroeconomically these two magnitudes are necessarily equal because they are both determined by the absolute exchange between money and output. Thus, modern monetary analysis confirms the intuition of the Classics as to the relationship between value and prices, but vindicates also the neoclassical claim that value and prices are a mere relationship. Determined through an absolute exchange, value and prices are themselves absolute, yet none of them defines a particular dimension of produced output. They result from an exchange (as claimed by the Neoclassics), but, given the particular nature of this exchange, they are absolute (as maintained by the Classics).

The logical (macroeconomic) identity of value and prices is a direct consequence of the integration between money and products. Each time that wage-earners are paid, they are the beneficiaries of a flow of money that is instantaneously spent for the purchase of a bank deposit. We already know that, current output being the object of these bank deposits, the expenditure of wage-earners defines their purchase of real goods and services (in their monetary form). This means that wage-earners are the first purchasers of the product of their own activity. No wonder, then, that this transaction occurs in compliance with the identity of prices and value. To maintain that, within the same operation, wage-earners sell and purchase their product against two different amounts of money would be nonsense. A unique flow of money is implied in the payment of wages, so that a unique sum is paid to wage-earners (for the sale of their product) and spent by them (for the purchase of the same product) at the same instant. If we define as value the relationship established between money and output by the payment of its costs of production, and as prices the relationship established when output is purchased, we immediately conclude that their identity is the necessary result of the payment of money wages. It is because of the particular nature of bank money that real output is given its numerical form through an absolute exchange. And it is because of this particular relationship existing between money and output that value and prices are identical. The clear perception of this reality is not self-evident at all. As observed by Keynes, the difficulty in escaping from the old ideas 'which ramify into every corner of our minds' (Keynes 1973a: xxiii) is a major obstacle towards our understanding of monetary macroeconomics. The tenets of the traditional conception of money as a valuable item (commodity or net asset) are very difficult to eradicate, and the true nature of bank money is far from being obvious. Yet, it is only through a renewed conceptual effort to free economic analysis from a mechanistic view of reality that we shall eventually be able to provide a satisfactory explanation of it. Let us go a step further in our attempt to clarify the notion of money by analysing its relationship with exchange in greater detail.

2   Money and exchange

Money and relative exchange

Money as a medium of exchange

Traditional GEA is worked out in real terms, (relative) prices being determined through the direct exchange of goods and services taking place on the commodity market. In a Walrasian pure exchange general equilibrium model, all trade takes place simultaneously, and there is no obvious need for the use of money. It is widely recognised, however, that several obstacles hamper the smooth functioning of the mechanism that should allow for the determination of prices. In his book on *Money and the Mechanism of Exchange*, Jevons had already pointed out the quandary due to the necessary double coincidence of wants. 'The first difficulty of barter is to find two persons whose disposable possessions mutually suit each other's wants. There may be many people wanting, and many possessing those things wanted; but to allow an act of barter, there must be a double coincidence which will rarely happen' (Jevons 1875: 3). Today, most neoclassical economists agree that, besides Jevons's double coincidence of wants (known also as the condition of monotone excess demand diminution), bilateral trade requires the respect of price consistency (or quid pro quo condition, or budget balance constraint), and the reduction to nil of all excess demands and supplies in the course of trade (excess demand fulfilment). Having observed that 'it is generally possible to find trades fulfilling any two of the three restrictions but not generally all three' (Starr 1989: 129), Starr locates the origin of the difficulties of direct relative exchange in an overdetermination in the demand for commodities that are used both as means of exchange and as consumption goods.

> In a bilateral trade model there are then two reasons to trade goods; (*i*) to arrange for them eventually to go to the agent demanding them, and (*ii*) as means of payment to fulfil the *quid pro quo* requirement. The difficulty of barter is that the combination of (*i*) and (*ii*) may overdetermine the demand for goods, so that for relatively simple (informationally decentralised) trading processes, it may not be possible to fulfil both.
>
> (ibid.: 43)

According to modern neoclassical economists, it is possible to prove the existence of a centralised trading procedure achieving an equilibrium allocation within an Arrow–Debreu Walrasian model. Ostroy and Starr, for example, split up the complex of excess demands and supplies 'into a finite number of elementary configurations chains, so that each agent in the chain has an excess demand for one good, excess supply of another and, for each good, supply equals demand across the chain' (Ostroy and Starr 1989: 146). Yet, as they explicitly admit, this procedure is neither satisfactory nor fully acceptable since the 'decomposition is both complex and arbitrary' (ibid.: 158). According to both authors, the choice of a single commodity as a medium of exchange is required to achieve equilibrium allocation without resorting to this complex centralised procedure. Besides eliminating the overdetermination in the demand for goods resulting from the budget balance constraint, the use of a single commodity-money would thus allow decentralisation of the trading process. 'The informational requirements of barter imply the need for a central co-ordination of trade; *the function of a common medium of exchange is to allow decentralisation of the trading process*' (Starr 1989: 150).

In his paper 'The informational efficiency of monetary exchange', Ostroy distinguishes general from individual equilibrium and maintains that, in a decentralised system, the process of going from one to the other is made possible by the use of money. In the Arrow–Debreu model of general equilibrium, the sum of individual excess demands is zero for each commodity. According to Ostroy, this Walrasian equilibrium of prices must be consistent with another equilibrium in which all individual excess demands are zero for each commodity. Always according to Ostroy, the need for money results from the impossibility of barter to satisfy the properties of trading sequences (technical, informational and behavioural feasibility) in a reasonable period of time. As other neoclassical authors have since pointed out, he underlines the fact that 'exchange is a do-it-yourself affair. Individuals will not exchange with "the market"; they will exchange with each other' (Ostroy 1989: 115). This implies that, in the real world, equilibrium cannot be reached in a centralised way, through the intervention of Walras's auctioneer.

The introduction of money is seen as a necessary requirement 'to overcome the great organisational complexity of non-monetary trade' (Ostroy and Starr 1989: 146) and to avoid overdetermination in the demand for goods. Now, the problem we are confronted with is how money can effectively be integrated into general equilibrium models. As claimed by Starr, the attempt to solve this problem by considering money as an argument in the household utility function is no real solution since it 'would transparently and uselessly assume the conclusion of the enquiry' (Starr 1989: 4). To avoid the vicious circularity implied in this procedure, several neoclassical economists have decided to follow Hicks's suggestion to 'consider money as a device for overcoming "frictions" in the smooth functioning' (ibid.: 4) assumed by the traditional Arrow–Debreu Walrasian model. Their idea is that, although there is no role for money in a model where transactions occur simultaneously, it is still possible to introduce the need for a medium of exchange by 'modelling the process of trade in a fashion that adds some difficulty, structure, and complexity' (ibid.: 5). If their attempt should be successful, the role for money as a medium of exchange would arise endogenously from the Arrow–Debreu model. In a similar way, an impediment to the use of future markets would contrast the assumption that 'all trade takes place simultaneously at a single initial date, and make it possible for money to play the role of a store of value' (ibid.: 6).

At this point of the analysis, it is all important to observe that money is almost unanimously considered by these authors as being a real good. The question to be settled is therefore whether the introduction of a 'monetary commodity' can transform the direct exchange between real goods and services into a succession of sales and purchases. While Starr and his fellow economists are right in maintaining that money is needed to avoid the overdeterminacy of barter, is he also right in claiming that this result can be obtained by using a commodity-money? 'Introduction of a monetary commodity (of sufficient value, held sufficiently widely) provides an extra degree of freedom so that the system is no longer overdetermined' (ibid.: 43). The use of money is of primary importance not because of the too great organisational complexity of barter, but to explain the real world of production and exchange. Contrary to what neoclassical economists claim, however, this aim cannot be achieved by choosing a commodity as a medium of exchange. The problem is not that of 'deciding what good to use in setting up accounts' (Ostroy and Starr 1989: 146). More specifically, it is not true that the choice of a commodity-money allows for the determination of a consistent system of monetary prices.

The fundamental extraneousness of money to GEA has already been stressed by such a leading neoclassical economist as Hicks. In his *Value and Capital*, he points out that, given $n - 1$ commodities and a financial and a monetary market, the number of independent equations of the general equilibrium system is equal to n, since one of the $n + 1$ equations of supply and demand can easily be eliminated. The point is that 'it does not matter in the least which equation we choose to eliminate' (Hicks 1978: 158). This means that 'if we decide to eliminate the money equation, then we can think of prices and interest being determined on the markets for goods and services, and the market for loans; the money equation becomes completely otiose, having nothing to tell us' (ibid.: 158). It is true that any other equation could be chosen for elimination instead of the money equation, yet this does not substantially alter the problem. On the contrary, as observed by Hicks himself, the fact that the equation to be eliminated could always be that of the auxiliary standard commodity chosen to express relative prices shows that 'the whole system of relative prices can be worked out in "real" terms' (ibid.: 159). The result is the world famous dichotomy between real and monetary sectors, which so deeply affects the neoclassical approach to theoretical economics: 'The (relative) values of commodities and the value of money become entirely separate questions, even entirely separate subjects; they can be, and have been, handed over to separate specialists to study and even to teach' (ibid.: 159). Here, we reach the core of the problem. In Hicks's analysis, we are told both that 'it is impossible to determine relative prices except in terms of some standard' (ibid.:

158–9) and that relative prices can be worked out in real terms when 'the equation chosen for elimination is that of an auxiliary standard' (ibid.: 159). We get the impression, thus, that Hicks hesitates between considering his standard as a purely numerical form of value (a *numéraire*) or a merely auxiliary commodity. Of course, had he chosen the monetary concept of the standard, he would have immediately noticed that relative prices are subjected to the determination of monetary prices. Having accepted the axiom that relative prices can be determined independently of money, he is forced to identify his standard of value with a real good. But, at this point, it becomes irrelevant to distinguish between the elimination of the equation relating to the auxiliary standard commodity and that of any other real equation. Then, why does Hicks link the neoclassical dichotomy with the possibility of eliminating the equation of the auxiliary standard? Again, we are led to think that the role played by the standard of value is far more important than that played by a commodity chosen merely as reference or as 'a representative consumption good' (ibid.: 159). Hicks is trapped between the intuitive need to introduce money as a standard of value and the acceptance of the neoclassical paradigm of relative prices. If the standard is not a real good, then the passage from real to monetary prices is no longer a matter of optional equations. Monetary prices cannot be simply calculated by expressing relative prices in some auxiliary standard and by assuming arbitrarily that the price of the standard itself is equal to 1 unit of money. The introduction of a true monetary standard requires money to enter each transaction in such an intimate way as to make it impossible to get rid of it by way of a mathematical trick.

Hicks's hesitation is a serious warning against the risks deriving from the lack of a true standard of value. The failure of classical economists to find a satisfactory standard led neoclassical writers to look for a simple numerical unit. Yet, they seem to have been too keen to deliver economic theory from incorporated labour to pay adequate attention to the problem of money. Their attempt to transform the standard of value in a simple *numéraire* appears simultaneously too drastic and too superficial to lead to a useful result. It is too drastic because it leaves no room for money to play any essential role, and too superficial because by identifying the standard of value with a real good it embraces a materialistic conception of the standard worse than the one it was supposed to supersede.

The consequence of conceiving of money as a real good is that of submitting it to Walras's Law. Instead of being deeply integrated in the world of real goods, money is merely added to it in such a superficial way that it is always possible to eliminate it from the general equilibrium system. A system in which money is introduced as a commodity playing the role of a medium of exchange and in which 'exchange occurs as a sequence of *simultaneous* bilateral trades' (Ostroy 1989: 116) is not fundamentally different from the traditional model of general equilibrium. In both cases, exchange takes place between commodities, and prices are supposed to be determined, simultaneously, at the equilibrium point of supply and demand. This is confirmed by a close observation of the analytical procedure followed by Starr in his attempt to show how a monetary economy can be derived from GEA. From the start, he considers 'a model of two closely related economies'

(Starr 1989: 133), one of which 'is a traditional pure exchange barter economy' whereas the other 'is an identical economy except that an additional commodity is introduced. This N + 1st good is thought to behave like "money" ' (ibid.: 133). According to Starr himself, the two models are essentially identical, and this is because money is introduced as an additional commodity. If a further confirmation of the fundamental similarity of the two models were needed, we could refer to Starr's assumption that equilibrium of a monetary economy can be determined taking 'a price vector p determined as an equilibrium for the barter economy and attaching an arbitrary price of money p^m so that $p^M = (p, p^m)$' (ibid.: 133). Last but not least, we could mention Starr's declared intention 'to perform a bit of a sleight of hand that has unfortunately fallen into disrepute of late, the trick of converting a barter economy to a monetary economy by the introduction of an N + 1st good' (ibid.: 138). Things could not be clearer. According to Starr, Ostroy and many other neoclassical authors, money is a specialised commodity and a monetary economy is a barter economy to which this specialised commodity is added.

The fact that, if the role of money is played by a 'specialised monetary commodity', monetary exchange is not substantially different from barter is hardly in keeping with the recent neoclassical endeavours to prove the need to use a commodity-money in order to achieve competitive equilibrium in a decentralised way. In particular, it is not correct to claim that through the use of commodity-money the requirement of the double coincidence of wants can be avoided successfully because 'monetary exchange requires only single coincidence' (Starr 1989: 167). While it is true that if money is a commodity it has a value of its own and it may be accepted as a real counterpart in any exchange, it is also true that any other commodity may equally well be accepted instead, the only difference being related to their physical characteristics. In this case, however, barter would not be superseded by monetary exchange, the physical qualities of the commodity chosen as a medium of exchange being irrelevant to this task. On the other hand, if it is claimed that money has a (relative) value that can be determined only through its exchange with other commodities, it is immediately evident that Jevons's double coincidence principle cannot be disposed of. Let us consider, for example, the exchange between commodity a and money (commodity m). Relative price determination requires demand for a to be equal to supply of a, or demand for m to be equal to supply of m. Since the demand for a is defined by the supply of m, and the supply of a by the demand for m, it is obvious that the exchange between a and m can take place only if the owner of a wants to purchase the same quantity of m that its owner is prepared to offer, and vice versa (double coincidence of wants). No matter how we analyse the problem, the conclusion is always the same: Jevons's requirement can be avoided only by transforming barter into monetary exchange through the use of non-commodity money, a pure numerical form of bank origin.

Money as a store of value

Another important role that money seems required to play is to serve as a store of value, or temporary abode of purchasing power. Let us briefly investigate the main problems related to the effective capacity of money to play this role within a neoclassical framework of analysis.

According to neoclassical monetary economists, 'the Arrow–Debreu Walrasian general equilibrium model positively denies a role for money as a store of value' (Starr 1989: 177). The reason is that all trades are supposed to take place at a single instant. 'There is no need for markets to reopen in the future – all desirable trades have already been managed' (ibid.: 178). Future markets are thus charged to replace money and capital markets. Should future markets prove to be ineffective (and particularly with transaction costs favouring spot over future transactions), a claim could be made for the use of money as a store of value. 'Hence the role of money as a store of value is confirmed in the sequence economy model as an essential element in achieving an efficient allocation over time in the presence of transaction costs' (ibid.: 178).

Unlike traditional GEA, sequence models assume that different budget constraints apply any time markets are reopened and transactions carried out. For example, following the pioneering work of Hahn, Starrett develops a sequence model in which money is introduced as a store of value in order to overcome the allocatable inefficiency arising from differences in spot and future market transaction costs. It is interesting to observe that, in his analysis, Starrett refers to money as to an asset which has the properties of a 'checking balance' or a 'credit card balance' (Starrett 1989: 233), and maintains that 'we can introduce a paper asset without incurring any additional transaction by simply allowing net credit positions at the clearing house' (ibid.: 233). Hahn himself had already defined money as a particular good, which cannot be consumed, can be costlessly stored and has no intrinsic value. Starrett takes up this point of view, and sets out to prove that this use of 'account balance' money would allow equilibrium to exist and always to be efficient. Unfortunately, having gone so far as to consider money as intrinsically worthless and of a banking nature, neither Hahn nor Starrett, nor their followers, has seen the possibility of working out an entirely new theory of monetary economics. Although they maintain, correctly, that money derives its value from exchange, they do not perceive that it is through an *absolute* exchange that money can thus be integrated into the real world. Hence, they remain anchored to neoclassical equilibrium analysis, and are forced to use a complex mathematical setting rich in technical difficulties and limiting and unrealistic assumptions.

In general equilibrium models of monetary economics, the willingness to hold money balances or, more generally, to use money both as a medium of exchange and as a store of value depends on the existence of a positive price of money. Although the choice of the word 'price' is symptomatic of the fact that money is essentially considered to be a commodity, when we refer to fiduciary or scriptural money its use sounds strange. Is it not true that bank money is the unit in which prices are expressed? And if it is so, is it not absurd to claim that money itself has a price? (Not to say that, even if we were to admit of such a possibility, we would be caught in the trap of having to express the price of money in money terms.) Neoclassical economists seem able to avoid this difficulty through the determination of relative prices. Since prices are determined through direct exchange, they claim, the price of money is given by the real goods and services exchanged against it. Simultaneous exchange would thus allow the price of goods to be expressed in terms of money, and the price of money to be expressed in terms of goods. Yet, this is not a satisfactory solution to our problem. If money is to be a desirable medium of exchange and store of value in a system where transactions do not occur simultaneously (future markets being ineffective), it must have a positive price *before* exchange. 'When money's price is zero, it can perform no transaction function' (Starr 1989: 293).

As clearly pointed out by Hahn, the positivity of money's price must be proved and not simply postulated. Analysing Patinkin's model of monetary equilibrium, Hahn observes that money is assumed to have a positive exchange value, and that this assumption amounts to the use of a technical trick. 'Indeed the role of this assumption is simply to enable us to employ a technical trick to ensure that we can use a fixed point theorem and one cannot believe that it has any fundamental significance to the whole problem' (Hahn 1989: 302). Having shown that the difficulties related to the construction of an abstract model of monetary equilibrium 'are fairly formidable and have not yet been faced' (ibid.: 304), Hahn does not hesitate to claim that even realistic monetary models are far from ensuring the existence of an equilibrium. As he argues, the main difficulty is represented by the presence of discontinuities. In particular, when money is used as a means of exchange and store of value, discontinuities are likely to appear. Hence the conclusion that, unless restrictive and unrealistic assumptions are made, the existence of an equilibrium solution may prove impossible. The only way out of this impasse is to abandon GEA and prove that money is invested with a positive value before being exchanged on the commodity market.

Let us consider Tobin's paper on money and economic growth. In this text, money is introduced as an asset 'supplied only by the central government' (Tobin 1965: 676). To avoid any misunderstanding, he specifies that fiduciary or paper money is 'manufactured by the government from thin air' (ibid.: 676). As a result, money is defined as a valueless asset: a partially contradictory definition because an asset can obviously not be valueless. Tobin seems to be aware of this difficulty when he claims that, although wealth consists of real goods only, 'as viewed by the inhabitants of the nation individually, wealth exceeds the tangible capital stock by the size of what we might term the fiduciary issue' (ibid.: 676). The contradiction of considering money as a valueless asset is thus explained by Tobin by opposing the scientific point of view (according to which fiduciary money has no intrinsic value) to that of individual agents (who believe money to have a positive intrinsic value and are thus victims of an illusion). Although it is well established today that money as such is valueless, it is also true that if it were never invested with a positive value it would never be accepted in payments. Tobin's assumption that money can indeed be used as a means of payment 'by reason of its general acceptability in the discharge of public and private transactions' (ibid.: 676) is wrong on two counts. First, it is wrong because, considered as a means of payment, money is a simple intermediary, a numerical medium. In other words, it is not money as such that discharges public and private transactions, but what is carried by money in its ancillary circulation: its real content. Second, it is wrong because, considered as the definition of produced output, money (income) has a positive value that does not derive from general acceptability, but is, instead, the prerequisite for general acceptance. The value of money is the result of neither a phantom intrinsic quality (being a numerical form it can have none) nor a monetary illusion, 'one of the many fallacies of composition which are basic to any economy or any society' (ibid.: 676).

The terms of the problem are clearly established: a realistic monetary theory must explain how bank money acquires a positive value before being used as a means of exchange and as a store of value. Neither Tobin's 'fallacy of composition' nor Starr's reference to taxation is up to the task. If it is true, as Starr maintains, that 'the transaction demand is not sufficient to ensure price positivity' (Starr 1989: 325), how is it possible to claim that 'the demand for fiat money to pay taxes creates sufficient demand for fiat money so that there is a positive price equilibrium' (ibid.: 325)? In fact, if taxes (as well as interests, dividends, rents, etc.) are settled in money, it is both because money intervenes in a vehicular way, as a means of payment, and because money income has a positive value. The problem remains that of explaining how bank money, issued as a simple and valueless IOU, can acquire a positive purchasing power and be accepted to settle transactions and as a store of value. Starr is right in observing that 'if we say that money is accepted because it is accepted, then we must agree that if money were not accepted then it would not be accepted because it would not be accepted' (ibid.: 326). Yet, this applies also to the monetary payment of taxes. To avoid the vicious circle spotted by Starr, it is necessary to push the analysis of bank money a step further along the lines traced in the first chapter. Before doing so, let us spend a few more words on the neoclassical attempt to integrate money into the general equilibrium framework.

General equilibrium models of monetary economics

General equilibrium analysis and money

Is exchange a relation between commodities, between individuals or between money and output? According to traditional general equilibrium (GE) theorists, (relative) exchange is a relation among commodities, goods and services being exchanged directly on the commodity market. According to Ostroy and Starr (1989), on the contrary, exchange is a transaction requiring the intervention of money, which can be better understood if it is perceived as a relation between individuals. In the examples to which they refer, money is a veil (as they themselves recognise; ibid.: 12), a record-keeping device or a book-keeping transaction medium. One of the ideas put forward by Ostroy and Starr is that money can play the role of a medium of exchange only if it is a store of value, i.e. only if it has a positive value equivalent to that of the commodities exchanged with it. The sale of commodity a would thus imply its exchange for a sum of money of the same value (Figure 2.1).

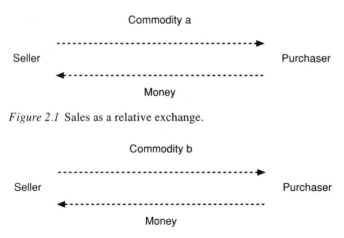

Figure 2.1 Sales as a relative exchange.

Figure 2.2 Purchase as a relative exchange.

By analogy, the purchase of commodity b would imply the transfer of an equivalent sum of money (Figure 2.2).

The initial seller of commodity a becomes the purchaser of commodity b, and the two transactions lead to the relative exchange of commodity a against commodity b. In general, money is seen as a medium of exchange linking a seller with a buyer under a temporal sequence of constraints.

At this stage, two interpretations seem possible. It might be claimed either that money is itself an asset similar to the goods it is exchanged with, or that money is a mere device with no intrinsic value whatsoever. In the first case, exchange between money and current output would pertain to the category of relative exchange, and we would find ourselves within the world of GEA. In the second case, it would be impossible to explain how money might take the place of the real goods it is exchanged with. This is obviously not what Ostroy and Starr have in mind when they define exchange as a relation between individuals. Their idea is that money has a positive value, and that it is precisely because it has such a value that transactions occur between individuals. This is an important suggestion, which has to be pushed to its extreme consequences, one of them being that money can no longer be considered as a commodity. Obviously enough, if money were a commodity, exchange would resume bartering: a relation between commodities. If exchange is a relation concerning individuals, then money must have a positive value without being a commodity. But if money has a positive value, does this not necessarily imply that money must (at least eventually) become a real good? Hence, given that not only goods and services but also financial bonds pertain to the category of real goods, how is it that money *is* and *is not* assimilable to (real) output? This is the challenge that Ostroy and Starr are confronted with. Unfortunately, they do not seem to be fully aware of it. Their analysis takes into account the contributions made by GE theorists such as Debreu and Arrow, in which money has no role to play, and tries to adapt them to a sequence economy with differential transaction costs and spot and future markets. In their attempt, there is no room for a thorough enquiry into the nature of money and the origin of its purchasing power. They simply assume money to exist, and invest it with the role of transferring purchasing power over time. 'Households may transfer purchasing power over time by accumulating and depleting their money balances and by the use of money future contracts (loans)' (Ostroy and Starr 1989: 16). Despite the mathematical formalisation of their model, Ostroy and Starr are not able to propose an adequate theory of monetary economics. Their conception of money as a 'device to record and make public one's trading history' (ibid.: 57) is still too approximate and, although they correctly point out the necessity to go beyond the (neo)classical dichotomy, their analysis does not provide the necessary elements to do so.

A new monetary macroeconomic theory requires a deeper understanding of the nature of money. To assume that money may be introduced into GEA 'as a zeroth commodity for which the household has no direct utility' (ibid.: 22) is to beg the question. What is and where does this zeroth commodity come from? In order to incorporate money into their model, Ostroy and Starr 'assume that there is a positive endowment of spot money' (ibid.: 23), taking it for granted that money can be considered as an initial endowment of the system. However, this is precisely what cannot be taken as a given parameter. Money is at the core of any modern economic system, and is therefore the first concept that economic theorists need to explain.

Can money be introduced in a pure exchange economy?

Ostroy and Starr start from a general equilibrium trading plan and show that money may be introduced as a zeroth commodity if it is accepted as a pure medium of exchange by traders. Yet, their initial assumption is far from self-evident. How is it that traders accept money as a medium of exchange? Is it not true that their acceptance of money rests on it being endowed with a positive purchasing power? And if it is so, where does this purchasing power come from? As soon as this question is asked it becomes clear that, to be accepted as a medium of exchange, money must become what the Classics used to call a general equivalent. Unless it is axiomatically considered to be an asset, money must derive its value from its exchange against real goods. The problem is therefore that of determining which kind of exchange can invest money with a positive value.

Apart from the obvious consideration that modern money is no commodity at all, it is worth analysing the cash-in-advance condition for money to be used as a medium of exchange. In particular, we have to verify whether it is correct that 'if a model is to express money's role as a medium of exchange, it cannot allow expenditure to be financed by contemporaneous income' (Kohn 1981: 192). According to this quotation, purchases and sales cannot occur simultaneously. In order to purchase a given commodity, the purchaser must previously sell another (exchange it for a sum of money). Hence, money splits barter (a relative exchange between commodities) into a net sale and a net purchase. But is this really so? When a commodity is sold, is it not true that a monetary deposit is simultaneously purchased by the seller? Now, the point is that even if the sale of a commodity defines the purchase of a monetary deposit and, reciprocally, the purchase of a commodity defines the sale of a monetary deposit, each transaction is considered as a half of the exchange between commodities occurring in the world of relative exchange. Money is conceived of as a medium of exchange in the exact sense that its use can divide (relative) exchange into two non-simultaneous transactions. If an agent A sells his commodity a against an equivalent sum of money, his purchase of a financial claim is not considered as the purchase of a real asset, but as the momentary transformation of a into a kind of intermediate good: the *medium* of exchange. Once again, the heart of the matter is the nature of money and of its relationship with output. Whereas the cash-in-advance constraint rests on the assumption that money is a store of value able to compete with interest-bearing assets when transaction costs are positive, modern monetary analysis shows that money income is the very definition of current output (and not its equivalent counterpart), so that the exchange between money and real goods pertains to the category of absolute exchanges.

Before addressing a fundamental critique to GEA, let us very briefly consider the attempt to overcome the main shortcomings of Walrasian general equilibrium by resorting to overlapping generations models of monetary economics.

Overlapping generations models

To deal with the 'frictions' of traditional GEA, some neoclassical economists have been working on a series of overlapping generations (OLG) models derived from Samuelson's three-period version of 1958. Assuming that fiat money is intrinsically useless (i.e. produced, transferred and stored at zero costs) and that it does not pay interest, they have tried to set up models in which each generation of individuals, old and young, live for two periods only, so that, by spending in its second lifestage what it has saved in the first, the older generation is the source of a positive demand for labour which has to be satisfied by the younger generation. The aim of these models is to investigate the equilibrium value of money in the stationary states of the economy (where expectations are supposed to be rationally determined). As money is assumed to have a positive value only if the individuals are prepared to accept it in exchange for real goods at any time in the future, overlapping generations models are said to have an infinite horizon because otherwise individuals' rational expectations would drive the value of money to zero in each period of time. So, they rest on the stringent assumption that the current value of money depends on its expected future value: if money is expected to be valueless at some time in the future, its present value will necessarily be zero. 'Individuals with foresight drive the price of money to zero in each period, i.e., the "general price level" in equilibrium must be infinite. The natural way to permit money to be a proper store of value is to go beyond the finite-horizon model' (Balasko and Shell 1981: 113).

As recognised by the defenders of OLG models, the dependence of current on expected future values can be a serious cause of trouble, leading to what is known as bootstrap or bubble paths. The recourse to the rational expectations hypothesis

– an assumption which is rather artificial – is far from being a satisfactory procedure for bringing these models closer to reality. If it is true that '[t]he indeterminacy and instability of monetary equilibria in OLG models lead to the monetary equilibria in these models being designated as *tenuous*' (Handa 2000: 634), how is it still possible to consider these models as a reliable representation of the real monetary world? It should be clear that if monetary equilibria are indeterminate, the whole system is void, and money's heuristic value can only be nil.

There are other reasons to reject overlapping generations models. Besides the fact that they base their analysis on a very limited (and erroneous) conception of bank money, the supporters of this approach introduce a whole series of ludicrous premises to account for the complex working of our monetary economies. For example, to account for a growing money supply and a growing population, they assume that in each period a lump sum of money is gratuitously introduced into the economy for the benefit of the older generation. The absurdity of this assumption appears with even greater clarity as soon as one recalls that money balances are considered to be a capital good. How are we to believe that capital goods are created at zero cost and gratuitously introduced into the economic system? An attempt to justify this weird assumption has been made by referring to *seigniorage*. In the past, seigniorage was the difference between the cost of bullion and the face value of coins, which was claimed as a right of or due to the sovereign. Today, some economists still believe in seigniorage and consider it as a fee or tax paid to the government for coining or printing money. In the case under examination, seigniorage would consist of a lump sum of money created by the central bank and transferred to the private sector. If this were the case, no one doubts that it would amount to an inflationary increase of the money supply. The creation of purely nominal money cannot give rise to a new income and may therefore lead neither to a positive transfer of income nor to a purchase of real goods by the government. A nominal amount of money is a zero amount of income. The attempt to increase income through seigniorage is thus bound to lead to an inflation rise. Fortunately for our own sake, central banks are perfectly aware of this danger and behave accordingly (at least in the most advanced economies). But the supporters of the overlapping generations approach do not confine themselves to resuming the anachronistic concept of seigniorage, they do much better, going as far as to assume that '*the government uses its seigniorage to buy commodities and destroys them* – or gives them away as a unilateral gift to foreigners' (Handa 2000: 650). No wonder that Tobin has no hesitation in claiming that this approach 'should not be taken seriously as an explanation of the existence of money in human society' (Tobin 1980: 83).

The introduction of bonds in OLG models is another example of creative fallacy. For bonds to perform the role of stores of value, it is assumed that they are directly exchanged against real goods at zero transaction costs. As everyone has certainly experienced in his everyday life, computers, cars, tables, chairs, potatoes and carrots are currently taken to the financial markets to be directly exchanged against bonds. But this is only part of the whole story. Not only is it assumed that bonds and real goods are exchanged through barter, but also that, in order for money to be still on demand despite the presence of interest-bearing bonds, the central bank has to pay the same rate of interest on its deposits. Hence, we are asked to swallow the idea that our monetary economies are based on a system in which money is created by the central bank, transferred to the public (in exchange for commodities that are at once destroyed or given away as a unilateral gift to foreigners) and immediately transferred back to the central bank with the commitment to pay a positive interest on the deposit. A question arises spontaneously: where does interest come from? The answer is another interesting piece of 'realistic' thinking: central banks inject money into the economy by purchasing real goods, and interests are paid out of the gross rate of return earned on their storage. One is left wondering whether it is more absurd to claim that central banks are allowed to purchase by simply getting indebted, i.e. without spending any positive income, or that interests are a direct emanation of real goods. Why should stored commodities yield a positive rate of return? Does it mean that the rate of return is equal to the rate of growth of the commodity in storage? Perhaps it means that the commodity's value increases by way of a mysterious process of spontaneous generation, or that its price increases simply because of it being stored? Inflation notwithstanding, is it not true that prices tend instead to decline (in which case, we would have a negative rate of return and interest would remain totally unexplained)?

The assumptions contained in these models are so restrictive and unrealistic that there is no point in analysing them any further. Let us simply observe that modern money cannot be reduced to its banknote form, and that its value cannot be explained by general (and endless) social acceptance. It is a fact that in our modern economies money is issued by commercial banks, and that banknotes are merely a claim (the most liquid kind of claim) on money deposits and must not be identified with money itself. As shown by simple observation, banknotes are a decreasing part of what is (improperly) called the quantity of money, and it is perfectly sound to imagine a world in which they are entirely substituted by credit and debit cards. It would be absurd to claim that, in such a world, economies would not be monetary. Likewise, it is absurd to believe that the value of money is the result of a social agreement. Yet, as claimed by Handa, 'it is characteristic of all monetary models – whether OLG, MIUF [money-in-the-utility-function] or others – that fiat money will have value in exchange only if others are willing to accept it in exchange for commodities' (Handa 2000: 627). At this point, it is perhaps worthwhile investigating the reasons for this widespread belief. How is it that useless and unconvertible money can nonetheless be considered to be an asset? How is it possible for a simple acknowledgement of debt spontaneously issued by the central bank to be transformed into an equivalent counterpart of real goods? The answer given by neoclassical economists is that, although money is essentially nothing but a veil, it can be assimilated with an asset so long as it mediates the exchange between real goods. Relative exchanges are all that matters in GEA, and monetary neoclassical models do not dispute the validity of this axiom. They merely recognise the existence of rigidities and frictions, and try to account for them by introducing money in a more or less functional way. Fundamentally, however, all these attempts rest on the assumption that money is exchanged against real goods according to a numerical proportion determined by a system of relative prices. The problem is, therefore, that of establishing whether or not such a system can account for the determination of money prices when money is introduced as a *numéraire* issued by banks (or by the central bank). This question has been discussed at length by Schmitt (1996), who proposes different proofs of the logical indeterminacy of relative and money prices within the theoretical framework of GEA. We shall not enter into the details of his analysis, nor shall we reiterate the arguments that have been put forward previously (Cencini 1982). The formal proof of the logical inconsistency of GEA is of the utmost importance and deserves all the attention that we can give it. In the present work, however, it is sufficient to observe that the analysis of modern bank money does not support at all the assumptions made by the GE models of monetary economics.

A fundamental critique to general equilibrium models of monetary economics

As pointed out by Bliss (1975: 19), an equilibrium can exist if 'the set of possible actions varies *continuously* with prices'. The assumption of continuity is essential since 'if supplies or demands exhibit discontinuities' the existence of an equilibrium 'may prove to be impossible' (ibid.: 19). Now, continuity supposes the existence of convexity, which, in its turn, supposes that households have quasi-concave preferences. This is the case 'if the set of all consumptions that are at least as good in its preference ordering as a specific consumption is a convex set' (ibid.: 21). But how can this set be determined? Even if it were possible to construe it for a given individual, the problem would admit of no solution at a global level. As every economist knows, utilities cannot be measured. Being logically impossible to find either a cardinal or an ordinal measure of utility, preferences can never be either numerically determined or even ordered in a significant way. Given this state of affairs, is it still feasible and does it make sense to try to work out a general equilibrium model of monetary economics based on relative exchanges? Moreover, what is the point of doing so when it is openly recognised that 'the equilibrium model does not explain why equilibrium obtains and it could not by its nature do so' (ibid.: 31)? Distinguishing the problem of the mathematical determination of a model from that of its logical and economic significance, Bliss claims that 'the narrower the conditions within which we confine our investigations the easier it is to exhibit relations which will determine the values concerned and the less, in a basic and causal sense, we will have explained the values that will obtain' (ibid.: 31). Is this not a distressing conclusion? Does it not clearly indicate that the understanding of economics does not pass through GE modelling? Furthermore, if we add, with Bliss, that 'even from the particular mathematical point of view no determinate equilibrium solution has yet been obtained for the atemporal model' (ibid.: 31), how can we still maintain that GEA is much more than a sophisticated exercise of little empirical interest?

The few preceding remarks are enough to justify the rejection of the GEA paradigm on logical grounds. However, it might be interesting to provide the reader with some further critical elements derived directly from the neoclassical analysis of monetary economics. Let us do so, remembering that even in its monetary version GEA remains anchored to the concept of relative prices.

As money is a simple *means* of exchange, its use does not modify the relationship directly determined between real goods. Hence, if we assume that Walras's Law applies in a world of relative exchanges, we have to admit that it holds also when these exchanges are mediated by the use of money. Let us consider, side by side, the cases in which two commodities, a and b, owned by two different agents, A and B, are exchanged directly, one against the other, or indirectly, through the mediation of money acting as a *medium* of exchange. In the first case, Walras's Law establishes that:

1   Supply of commodity a = Demand for commodity b.
2   Supply of commodity b = Demand for commodity a.

And the relative price of commodity a in terms of commodity b (or, conversely, the relative price of b in terms of a) is determined by one of the following equations:

3   Demand for commodity a = Supply of commodity a.
4   Demand for commodity b = Supply of commodity b.

Thanks to Walras's Law, relative prices can be determined, the number of independent equations (one in our example) being equal to that of the unknowns. At least this would indeed be the case if it could be proved that 1 and 2 hold good not only at equilibrium but also during the whole period of adjustment during which equilibrium is supposed to be determined. Let us momentarily put aside this problem and consider how equations 1–4 are transformed when money is introduced in order to split barter into a succession of sales and purchases. The first two equations now become:

1*   Sales by A = Purchases by A.
2*   Sales by B = Purchases by B.

Equations 1* and 2* express the fact that money enters exchange as a pure intermediary. In order for money to play the role of a mere intermediary, sales and purchases must be equal for every economic agent operating on the commodity market. In other words, every agent must spend the exact amount he earns. Equations 1* and 2* imply that A accepts a given amount of money in exchange for a given amount of his commodity, a, because he can alienate it against an amount of commodity b which maximises the satisfaction he derives from exchange, and, conversely, that B is willing to accept the same amount of money in exchange for his commodity because the amount of commodity a he can purchase from A is the exact amount maximising his satisfaction. In a monetary system, equations 3 and 4 of relative exchange become:

3*   Purchases by B = Sales by A.
4*   Purchases by A = Sales by B.

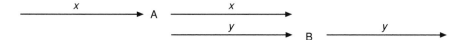

Figure 2.3 Sales and purchases in indirect exchange.

It is easy to note that the equations representing Walras's Law and the system of price determination in a model of direct exchange take the form of those of indirect exchange when commodities are substituted with their owners. We are thus led to think that equations 1–4 are fundamentally equal to equations 1*–4*. If this is correct, it follows that, even within indirect exchange, what holds good at equilibrium is valid also during the search for equilibrium, in particular Walras's Law establishing the necessary equality of sales and purchases of both A and B. But if 1* and 2* are always verified, is it still possible for 3* or 4* to determine a unique set of equilibrium prices? Is it not true that prices defined at equilibrium are necessarily equal to those defined during the phase of adjustment, which thus becomes totally meaningless?

This conclusion is confirmed by a short reflection on the meaning of equations 1*–4*. According to the assumptions made in 1* and 2*, sales by A are equal to A's purchases, and purchases by B are equal to B's sales. Let us call x the amount of money earned (and spent) by A, and y that spent (and earned) by B (Figure 2.3).

Now, indirect exchange occurs between A and B alone. This implies that, at equilibrium, A's purchases are B's sales and, correspondingly, that A's sales are B's purchases. The question is to establish whether or not these relationships are verified also before equilibrium. If Walras's Law did not hold outside equilibrium, there would be no reason to ask this question: 1*, 2*, 3* and 4* would define four independent equations, and the system of GEA would be hopelessly overdetermined. Since Walras's Law is supposed to be valid even during the search for equilibrium, the number of independent equations is reduced to one, and the system is liable to admit to a unique solution. At least this is what we are told by neoclassical economists. In reality, things do not work out this way. As soon as Walras's Law is implemented, it transforms the whole system, making it impossible to distinguish the phase of adjustment from that of equilibrium. Since A can only purchase from B (and B from A) and since, because of Walras's Law, A and B spend necessarily the whole amount they earn, it is logically impossible to find any difference between x and y. If we are to respect the assumptions of GEA, x and y must define the same amount of money. This being the case, it is obvious that 3* and 4* can no longer be considered as 'conditions of equilibrium'. Instead of being determined through a process of adjustment, prices are given from the start; they are imposed on the system by the monetary implications of Walras's Law.

Not surprisingly, the same disruptive result is reached even when Walras's Law is stated in its traditional version, the sum of demands being equal to the sum of supplies. In a monetary context, this takes the form of the following equalities:

5   Sum of sales = Sum of purchases.

In our example of a two-agent two-good economy, equality 5 becomes:

5*   Sales of A + Sales of B = Purchases of B + Purchases of A.

    The statements which must be simultaneously satisfied at equilibrium are those equalising the sales and purchases of A and B, i.e. statements 3* and 4*. Thus, our problem is that of reducing this system of two statements to only one independent statement. This is done by GEA through Walras's Law. Equality 5 implies, in fact, that the price that satisfies statement 3* also necessarily satisfies statement 4* and vice versa. Hence, only one of these two equations can be considered as independent. However, as in the previous case, the acceptance of Walras's Law even outside equilibrium has the annoying consequence of depriving our independent equation of any heuristic value. It should be clear, in fact, that if the sum of sales is always necessarily equal to the sum of purchases, statements 3* and 4* are also always satisfied, whatever the prices chosen by A or B. Since A can only purchase from B and B from A, and given the necessary validity of equality 5, it follows that what is sold by A is entirely purchased by B and the other way around. Statements 1*–4* amount thus to mere tautologies and the system of GEA falls into a complete indeterminacy, with every price proposed to A (or B) being an equilibrium price.

    Let us suppose the monetary price of commodity a to be arbitrarily fixed at 1 unit of money. If the price of commodity b proposed to A is of 2 units of money, he will decide to sell the proportion of his initial endowment of commodity a that will most satisfactorily be substituted with a given quantity of commodity b. For example, he might decide to sell 10 units of commodity a in order to purchase 5 units of commodity b. The price proposed to A would thus define an equilibrium price as it would simultaneously satisfy all the equations of the system. Yet, inexorably the same conclusion applies for any other price proposed to A. There are infinite prices that, giving rise to a possible exchange between commodities a and b, must be considered as equivalent solutions to the system of general equilibrium. For each of them, A has a combination which would maximise his satisfaction and that, satisfying statements 1*–4*, would define an equilibrium price. The same result applies, of course, if the process is analysed from B's point of view. For each price proposed to B, there is a combination that maximises his utility and that may be seen as a possible equilibrium price. Now, unless we adopt Walras's Law, there is no reason to believe that a unique equilibrium price can indeed be determined. Equations 1*–4* will have to be simultaneously satisfied both for A and for B and the entire system would be hopelessly overdetermined. A drastic reduction in the number of independent equations is possible only if we call upon Walras's Law. Yet, this means that we have to assume that prices are actually imposed on the market. It is only in this case, in fact, that it may be claimed that 1* and 2* are always necessarily verified for both A and B. In other words, Walras's Law is the very definition of relative exchange and not the condition for a process of adjustment to occur before exchange actually takes place. Neoclassical theory is thus confronted with a dismaying choice: either to claim that Walras's Law applies at equilibrium only, in which case the *determination* of equilibrium remains totally unexplained (the system of GEA being overdetermined), or to maintain that this law is valid also during the search for equilibrium, in which case every price proposed to the market is as good a solution as any.

As an example of the way that neoclassical economists develop their monetary analysis, let us refer to the paper by Grandmont and Younès published in 1972 by *The Review of Economic Studies*. The two authors choose to develop a model of monetary equilibrium ostensibly to examine the validity of the quantity theory and of the neoclassical dichotomy. Among their basic hypotheses, we find the assumptions that 'money has no "direct utility" but serves as the only means to store wealth' (Grandmont and Younès 1972: 356), that money is an asset used 'as an exchange intermediary' (ibid.: 357) and that 'money is institutionally the necessary counterpart of any transaction' (ibid.: 357). These hypotheses are perfectly in line with the neoclassical point of view according to which money is an asset which can be used as a medium of exchange because it is accepted as a counterpart of real goods and services. Grandmont and Younès go as far as to claim that money is their necessary counterpart, although only at the institutional level. Now, if money could indeed be considered as an asset given in exchange for produced output, economists would be bound to conclude that total wealth is given by the sum of money and output. Neoclassics are only too aware of this risk to be caught in the trap. Issued by the banking system, money cannot have a value of its own (it has no 'direct utility'). Yet, it must be defined as an asset as, otherwise, it could not be given in exchange for a positive amount of goods and services. As so clearly stated by Grandmont and Younès, 'demand for goods must be backed by effective money purchasing power' (ibid.: 357). Although no one would dispute the validity of this claim, the concept of money's purchasing power is not explained by every economist in the same way. The Neoclassics, in particular, seem to believe that money can have a positive purchasing power only if it is an asset or a commodity. Their analytical framework being confined within the limits of relative exchange, they cannot conceive that money's purchasing power might derive from its identification (resulting from an *absolute* exchange) with current output. Hence, they are forced to assume that money can be issued as an asset and, at the same time, that real variables are alone the determining factors of general equilibrium. If the (neo)classical dichotomy did not hold good, neoclassical economists would have to explain how, although money is an asset, its value has not to be added to that of real goods. This is a difficult task since bank money cannot be assimilated to any particular commodity. The only possibility open to them seems therefore that of assuming that money is fundamentally a *veil*. 'This theory claims that, when looking for stationary equilibria, one can determine separately relative equilibrium prices and equilibrium consumption by studying the real sector alone, ignoring monetary factors' (ibid.: 356). But, if money is a veil, how can it have a positive purchasing power? Grandmont and Younès correctly consider purchasing

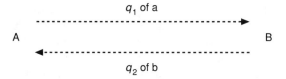

Figure 2.4 Relative exchange between real goods.

power to be 'an essential feature of monetary economics' (ibid.: 357), yet they do not seem able to explain where it does come from and what its nature really is.

As is well known, the quantity theory of money has been elaborated in three alternative models: the transactions, income and cash-balances models respectively. Now, all these versions of the theory rest on the assumption that money is endowed with a positive purchasing power, so that it can split barter into a succession of sales and purchases and plays the role of a temporary store of value. As so clearly stated by Friedman:

> [f]or the act of purchase to be separated from the act of sale, there must be something that everybody will accept in exchange as 'general purchasing power' – this aspect of money is emphasized in the transaction approach. But also there must be something that can serve as a temporary abode of purchasing power in the interim between sale and purchase. This aspect of money is emphasized in the cash-balance approach.
>
> (Friedman 1987: 6)

We are thus confronted with the following dialectical puzzle: how can money be considered a simple veil and serve nevertheless as a temporary abode of purchasing power? According to the homogeneity postulate, money should be neutral. Yet, it should also define a positive value. In neoclassical terms, it would be defined as a veil and as an asset simultaneously. Is this asking too much of general equilibrium monetary economics? Apparently not, since monetarists have never stopped claiming that, although money is actively present in every transaction, economic relationships are essentially determined by real variables only. Relative exchanges remain the keystone of the neoclassical approach even in its monetarist formulation. General agreement, however, is not always a sign of implicit consistency. Let us consider a relative exchange between different quantities of two real goods, a and b, carried out by two economic agents, A and B (Figure 2.4).

Agent A gives up the quantity q_1 of commodity a in exchange for the quantity q_2 of the commodity given up by his economic correspondent B. If barter is to be replaced by sales and purchases, money must be introduced as an intermediary in the direct exchange between commodities a and b. The initial transaction is thus split into two distinct transactions: (1) the sale and purchase by A and (2) the purchase and sale by B (Figure 2.5).

As stressed by Friedman, in order to be accepted in exchange for commodity a, money must represent a positive purchasing power. Yet, nothing is said about its origin and nature. The only possibility consistent with the neoclassical

Figure 2.5 Exchange through the intermediation of money.

framework of analysis is to assume that it is through exchange that the purchasing power of money is revealed. The sale by A becomes a relative exchange between the quantity q_1 of commodity a, and the quantity x_1 of an asset called money. The relative price of money is given by the exchange ratio between money and commodity a, and defines its purchasing power in terms of this very commodity. Analogously, the exchange between the quantity q_2 of b and the amount x_2 of money is supposed to determine the relative price of money in terms of commodity b. Now, sale and purchase being two distinct transactions, there are no reasons for x_1 to be equal to x_2. Each relative price is autonomously determined by the supply of and the demand for the two terms of every exchange. The equality between the quantity of money given in exchange by A and B is a condition for money to be a veil. Yet, nothing allows us to believe that the amount of money accepted by A in exchange for his commodity is necessarily equal to the amount he is prepared to give in exchange for the quantity q_2 of commodity b. Thus, if we want to persist in determining prices through exchange, along the lines of GEA, we have to add another independent equation to our system, which becomes overdeterminate. The equations linking the supply of and the demand for money to the supply of and the demand for each commodity are not enough to guarantee the equality of sale and purchase because x_1 will normally be different from x_2. To satisfy the neoclassical homogeneity postulate, we have to introduce a very restrictive constraint (i.e. $x_1 = x_2$), which jeopardises the entire system.

The reader will notice the absurdity of the neoclassical attempt to reconcile two fundamentally distinct conceptions of money. On the one hand, money has to be considered as an asset since it must enter a relation of exchange with real goods and has to be subjected to the forces of supply and demand. On the other hand, it is considered as a simple veil since, according to the neoclassical dichotomy, only real factors enter the determination of (relative) prices. Unfortunately for the promoters of the neoclassical paradigm, these two definitions of money cannot apply simultaneously to the same process. In reality, neoclassical economists must choose one of the following alternatives: either (1) they claim that money is an asset, in which case every transaction (sale and purchase) is independent of the other and determines two independent relative prices, or (2) they maintain that money is only a veil with no value at all, in which case it becomes impossible to explain why traders should accept it in exchange for their commodities. Neoclassical authors are trapped between the two horns of a dilemma for which they are unable to find a satisfactory solution, largely because they have misunderstood the nature of bank money.

Money and absolute exchange

From relative to absolute exchanges

In a recent paper on Keynes's monetary theory and modern banking, Rogers and Rymes argue against Fama's claim that 'an accounting system works through book-keeping entries, debits and credits, which do not require any physical medium or the concept of money' (Fama 1980: 39). They refuse to accept both the fact that in a modern monetary system money is no longer a physical medium of exchange and that in a cashless payment system the concept of money becomes redundant. 'Reflection will confirm that even if a medium of exchange is not required in a world with a sophisticated electronic accounting system, it does not follow that the *concept* of money is thereby redundant or that media of exchange no longer exist' (Rogers and Rymes 1997: 306). Now, if we can certainly agree with them that it is a serious mistake to confuse the concept of money with its physical manifestation, we must reject their idea that money is a tangible thing. 'Even if money evolves to the stage where cash is replaced by a sophisticated accounting system, money as a tangible thing still exists' (ibid.: 306). In a cashless system, the concept of money is as essential as in any other (more or less sophisticated) monetary system. Yet, this does not at all imply that money must be a 'tangible thing'. Whereas a system of book entries is tangible, money is not. By claiming the contrary, Rogers and Rymes are doing precisely what they reproach Fama with: they confuse money with the physical support used to represent it. Money is merely a numerical form, a dimensionless vehicle whose task is to provide information through the intermediation of banks' book entries. As money is immaterial, it is impossible to identify it with a tangible medium of exchange. This is the core of modern monetary analysis. If this fact is not fully understood, if we insist, anachronistically, on considering money as a material entity, as a physical medium of exchange, we cannot avoid falling into the trap of the neoclassical paradigm.

In *A Treatise on Money*, Keynes argues against the supposed neutrality of money upheld by neoclassical analysis. He claims that, since relative prices are influenced by changes in the distribution of available purchasing power, and since 'a change in the quantity of money generally involves a changed distribution of purchasing power, ... relative prices can be affected, not only by a change on the side of things, but also by a change on the side of money' (Keynes 1971: 82). An interesting point that emerges from this critique is the radically different conception of money adopted by Keynes and by the Neoclassics. The homogeneity postulate holds good only if money is a mere unit of account introduced to express numerically a relationship already fully determined in real terms through relative exchange. This is precisely the meaning conveyed by the definition of money as a 'veil'. Let us suppose the terms of a relative exchange to be given, say, x units of commodity a for y units of commodity b, and the monetary price of 1 unit of commodity a to be equal to 1. Hence, the price of x units of commodity a is equal to the number x which, as x a is equivalent to y b, is also the numerical expression of the price of *y* units of commodity b. According to this theoretical framework, a change in the numerical expression of commodity a is of no consequence over relative prices because the relationship between commodities a and b is always determined by relative exchange alone. A variation in the quantity of money would simply amount to a proportional change of the numerical expression of commodities a and b, but it would not modify the initial ratio of *x* a for *y* b. By contrast, Keynes's conception of money is more complex as it includes that of purchasing power. Money is no longer a number arbitrarily chosen and related to real goods only once their ratio of exchange has already been determined. Issued by banks, money is associated with real goods via the process of production, and its purchasing power derives directly from this association. The numerical expression of real goods becomes their monetary definition, and corresponds to their costs of production (in wage units). Real goods are the very object of money's purchasing power, whereas money is the numerical form of current output. This is, in terms of the modern monetary approach to macroeconomics, the message implicit in Keynes's argument.

Far from being a simple veil, money becomes the expression of the (numerical) economic value of goods determined through production, i.e. through an *absolute* exchange between money itself and current output. Money's purchasing power results from this absolute exchange. Hence, if the quantity of money were pathologically increased – as a consequence of an inflationary process – money's purchasing power would proportionally decrease without modifying relative prices (which, in this analytical framework, are not directly determined by but are derived from absolute prices). Clearly, this first result does not confirm Keynes's claim that 'monetary changes do not affect all prices in the same way, in the same degree, or at the same time' (ibid.: 83–4). Yet, it is enough to carry the analysis a step further to verify the correctness of his point of view. Because of the inflationary increase in prices, wage-earners will in fact ask for an increase in nominal wages, a request that firms are bound to accept or reject differently, leading to different variations in absolute prices and, as a direct consequence, in relative prices.

Keynes's analysis could not be more antithetical to that of the Neoclassics. His object of enquiry is a monetary world of production, whereas theirs is a hypothetical world of direct exchange. His money is bank money, whereas theirs is a collection of numbers arbitrarily introduced once the ratio of relative exchange has already been determined, or a commodity chosen among the set of real goods. His prices are absolute money prices, whereas theirs are relative ones. Now, since it has been logically proved that relative prices cannot be determined through direct exchange, it is along the path traced by Keynes that we must pursue our research of the founding elements of monetary economics.

Let us say it once again. Since money does not pertain to the category of real goods, the exchange between money and current output cannot be a relative exchange. If exchanges took place between real goods already produced and available on the commodity market as the initial endowment of traders, they would be relative. In this hypothetical world, money would have no citizenship, the terms of every relative exchange being real necessarily. Of course, it could be claimed that in this case money itself would have to be conceived of as a real good or as an asset. But it should be evident that by doing so we would abandon any hope of explaining the workings of a true monetary system, the exchange between money and output being reduced to barter. Hence, in order to explain how a numerical entity such as bank money can be exchanged against current output, we have to move from relative to absolute exchange. Even within the context of absolute exchanges it remains true that real goods can be exchanged against real goods only: a numerical form cannot be the object of an exchange. Yet, contrary to what happens in the neoclassical setting, exchange does not occur between two different goods, but between a real good and itself.

A difficulty arises as to how money can be associated with physical output. Does this absolute exchange occur between already produced output on one side and a given amount of money on the other side? Obviously not, as it is precisely through an absolute exchange that output is *formed*, i.e. that it is given its numerical form. Furthermore, as we have noted before, no relative exchange can take place between real goods and numbers. But if money and goods cannot be exchanged for one another, are we not forced to conclude that they cannot be exchanged at all? If we limit our analysis to the commodity market, the answer is yes. If the association between money and output has not taken place already, it is hopeless to look for it on the commodity market. However, this is not the right place to look for the *first* absolute exchange between money and output. Since it is through an absolute exchange that physical products are given their numerical form and are transformed into goods, it is at the level of production that this exchange occurs. Before turning our attention to production in order to understand how current output is changed into money and which kind of relationship exists between bank money and credit, let us try to show how – in conformity with the monetary version of Walras's Law – bank money allows for the logical identity between the purchases and sales of each single economic agent.

The necessary equality of sales and purchases

As the reader will remember, by analysing the monetary models of GEA we have emphasised the fact that Walras's Law takes the form of the necessary equality between sales and purchases of each individual agent, and that it holds good at equilibrium only. Once we abandon the neoclassical paradigm of relative exchanges, the very notion of equilibrium has to be reconsidered. Absolute exchanges do not pertain to the world of relative exchanges and cannot be assimilated to them. In particular, macroeconomic prices are not determined through a process of adjustment leading to the equalisation of supply and demand. In this context, Walras's Law acquires a new *raison d'être*. It no longer is a characteristic of equilibrium, but the definition of a current and necessary state of affairs of monetary macroeconomics. The passage from relative to absolute exchanges marks the transition from conditions of equilibrium to identities, the new Walras's Law being one of them.

The following quotation shows how money is usually conceived of as an asset or a temporary abode of purchasing power allowing the gap between sales and purchases to be bridged.

> The transaction theory traditionally has treated the demand for money as arising from the problem of finding the least costly combination of money and bond holdings with which to bridge time gaps between purchases and sales.
>
> (Clower and Howitt 1978: 461)

Money and bonds are thus considered as alternative assets that are held in competition with other real goods as stores of purchasing power. What has to be made clear in this context is that what is referred to as 'money' is in reality a bearer bond, a highly liquid security which bears no interest and can easily be transferred from an economic agent to another. The word 'money', as used by Clower and Howitt, does not refer either to money as such, which is merely a valueless numerical form, or to money income, which is necessarily deposited with the banking system. As a bearer bond whose object is a bank deposit, Clower's and Howitt's money is not substantially different from other categories of bonds. Thus conceived, money defines a claim over an equivalent part of produced output. In this sense, it might even be correct to identify it with a commodity, but not with a particular commodity opposed to the set of real goods and services: to hold bonds means to hold output in its financial form. Because money income is deposited with the banks, traders can never really hold it. Their bonds (banknotes, current or deposit account certificates) are not a temporary abode of purchasing power (which banks lend at the very instant it is formed with them), but a title over a given amount of money income.

Another important consequence of the fact that traders cannot hold money or money income but only bonds is that no gap can ever exist between purchases and sales, which are necessarily simultaneous and equivalent for each single trader. This will certainly sound strange to the reader used to analysing monetary transactions from a microeconomic point of view. However, if money were a commodity, the simultaneity of purchases and sales would immediately result. Monetary exchanges would pertain to the category of relative exchanges, and it would always be true that when a trader exchanges money against another commodity he acts simultaneously as a seller (of the commodity-money) and as a purchaser (of the other commodity). If the reader resists the necessary coincidence of sales and purchases, it is because it is widely believed that money can split barter into two non-concomitant transactions. Yet, this belief is fundamentally disproved both by neoclassical analysis (which does not allow for half-exchanges) and by modern monetary analysis. Once it is recognised that money is not a commodity, but a numerical form issued by the banking system, it is compulsory to admit that its circular emission leads to the simultaneous credit and debit of each agent concerned in monetary transactions. Since money flows back instantaneously to its point of emission, it is impossible for any economic agent to be credited without being immediately debited for the same amount.

Let us consider two economic agents, A and B, one of whom is a seller and the other a purchaser. What monetary analysis shows is that both A and B are simultaneously purchasers and sellers. Let us start with A, the seller of commodity a. If A is directly paid by B, he receives a bond in exchange for commodity a, and thus becomes the owner of another commodity (for example, of the commodity b produced by B) in its financial form. As the seller of commodity a, A is thus simultaneously the purchaser of commodity b. If the payment of A is made by a bank on behalf of B, the result is the same. At the very instant that A is credited, he is also debited as the deposit of a money income (which is immediately lent by the bank) defines the purchase of equivalent financial claims. As the reader will have noticed, the introduction of money does break barter, but it does not allow for the existence of net sales and net purchases since transactions occurring on the commodity or on the labour market concern also necessarily the financial market. In our example, the object of the financial claim purchased by A is a sum of money income deposited with the banking system so that his sale of commodity a on the commodity market is immediately balanced by his purchase of bonds on the financial market.

As far as B is concerned, the analysis runs along the same lines. To finance his purchase, B must either earn or borrow a positive income. Hence, his purchase on the commodity market is always balanced by an equivalent sale on the labour or on the financial market. The necessity of financing a purchase through an equivalent sale is confirmed twice: first, when B obtains a positive income by selling his activity on the labour market or by selling a financial security to his bank, and, second, when he transfers his income to A. Let us suppose that B borrows from his bank the amount of income required for his purchase of commodity a. In this case, B receives a bank deposit in exchange for a claim over his future income. He sells a claim to his bank and, simultaneously, purchases a right over a bank deposit: he is, at the same moment, a seller and a purchaser on the financial market. Likewise, when the order he gives to his bank to transfer his income to A in exchange for commodity a is carried out, he becomes a purchaser on the commodity market and a seller on the financial market.

As Kohn reminds us, to account for an explicit role for money, some economists have introduced the concept of the finance constraint on expenditure. In his defence of this concept, Kohn shows that the finance constraint holds even when money is not assumed to be the only asset available, when credit is introduced 'and when the time structure is generalized to allow overlapping income periods of differing lengths' (Kohn 1981: 177). Now, when borrowing is taken into account, Kohn is led to admit that the finance constraint is verified at the aggregate level only. 'Borrowing by households may alleviate the household constraint, but not the aggregate finance constraint' (ibid.: 184). Yet, analysing the borrowing case, Kohn notices that household borrowing corresponds to the sale of securities, a fact which stands for the respect of the finance constraint by each single household. If he does not reach this conclusion, it is mainly because his analysis is not based on an entirely dematerialised concept of money. The finance constraint is thus more like a theoretical 'device' (ibid.: 177) than a true law of monetary macroeconomics. In order to transform the finance constraint into a law, it is necessary to start from the modern concept of bank money.

Mainstream economists still believe that money can be a medium of exchange only if it is given the chance to exist as general equivalent during a finite period of time. This is so because monetary exchanges are not considered to be fundamentally different from relative exchanges. The introduction of credit money in traditional models seems to allow for a radical change, it is true, yet promises are not fulfilled entirely because money is identified with an asset of a positive value. The passage from commodity to credit money is an important analytical advance if it is followed to its extreme consequences: the total dematerialisation of money. What Kohn and his fellow economists are not aware of is that money can be a valueless numerical form and purchasing power can still be positive. What is missing from their analysis is the distinction between money proper and money income. As for money proper, its existence in time is strictly limited to the very moment that payments take place. Its function as a means of exchange consists precisely in allowing for the existence of monetary payments, and is entirely fulfilled in the space of an instant. Things are different when money income is taken into consideration. This time it would be absurd to maintain that, like money proper, income is destroyed at the very instant that it is created. However, contrary to Kohn's claim, expenditures are in fact financed by contemporaneous income. As is clearly shown by banks' double-entry book-keeping, income is lent as soon as it is deposited. If we take the payment of wages as an example, we observe that firms finance their payment by borrowing from banks the income earned and deposited by their wage-earners. As a result, income generated by current production is immediately spent to finance current output.

Let us consider the relationships among money, produced output and exchange from a modern point of view. As we know, money proper is a numerical form issued by banks through their spontaneous acknowledging of a debt. The first exchange that we are confronted with is between money and output, as it occurs on the factors market. If real goods had a positive and measurable value independent of their exchange with money, and if money also had a positive and measurable value regardless of this exchange, money and current output would confront each other on the commodity market. Since money is not created as an asset and since in the absence of money physical goods are a mere heap of heterogeneous objects, this is not the case. Moreover, precisely because money and output define one another, their first exchange cannot be of a relative kind. Money is not given in exchange for real goods in the same way as commodity a is given in exchange for commodity b. The exchange between money and current output is an instantaneous process which brings them together, transforming one into the other and vice versa. Thus, money and real goods become the two aspects of one and the same entity. Real goods are changed into money, and money becomes the numerical form of real goods; this is the meaning of the absolute exchange taking place on the factors market.

It is through the payment of the macroeconomic costs of production that output is assimilated to money, and money proper transformed into money income. At the very instant that production costs are paid, money is created and destroyed by banks in a circular flow that leads to the formation of a positive income. Let us consider the payment of wages. As a means of payment, money exists only when payments actually take place. This does not require more than an instant so that money proper has a zero duration in time, a result perfectly in line with its non-dimensional nature and with the rules of double-entry. As a consequence of this payment, a positive amount of income is formed that defines current output in its monetary form. Through this absolute exchange, produced goods and services are changed into money; they are given a numerical form which transforms them into economic entities. By the same process, money is given a real content that transforms it into income. Thus, wages define a positive purchasing power resulting from their association with current output. Money's value is not simply postulated, as it is by the Neoclassics, but effectively determined through the identity that the payment of wages establishes between money and output. It follows, then, that the value of money is neither a particular substance that money is naturally endowed with nor a quality bestowed upon it by some sort of social agreement. As a matter of fact, money has no proper value: it is through the payment of the costs of production that money is momentarily invested with a positive purchasing power. Its value results from its assimilation to current output, and it is bound to disappear as soon as real goods shed their numerical form to recover their physical one.

A question might be raised as to whether the payment of production costs defines a purchase of current output and, if so, who purchases what and how. Let us again refer to the payment of wages. Wages are paid by banks on behalf of firms. Does this mean that firms purchase the product of their wage-earners? If the question refers to the *final* purchase of current output, the answer is no. Unless firms spend a positive amount of money income that they own – which is not the case here – they cannot become the final owners of the product. Yet, it is true that firms spend a money income at the very instant that they pay their wage-earners. The fact is that when wages are paid they define an income in the form of a bank deposit which, because of double-entry book-keeping, is immediately lent to firms. Hence, firms indeed purchase current output, but they do so by spending a money income received as a loan from their wage-earners, who are the true purchasers of current output on the financial market. The result of the entire process is that wage-earners sell their physical product to firms and purchase this very product in the form of a bank deposit. Through the intermediation of money, real goods are thus exchanged against themselves. Walras's intuition that real goods are exchanged against real goods and that purchases and sales of each economic agent are always necessarily equal finds here a new and definitive formulation. It is fundamentally true, in fact, that real goods are the terms of every exchange, but of an absolute and not of a relative kind. If money were a commodity, its exchange with output would define a relative exchange, and monetary transactions would amount to barter. As money is a simple numerical form, barter is definitively disposed of, and exchange becomes absolute. Real goods are still exchanged against real goods, but in the exact sense that current output is transformed (literally changed) into current output, albeit in a monetary form. As a result of this exchange, output is created as a sum of money; monetary economics becomes a reality and the way is wide open to a new interpretation of production, distribution and capital accumulation.

3   Money, credit and banks

Money and credit

As an introduction to the arguments that we shall develop in this chapter, let us refer to the analyses proposed by Johnson (1969) in his article 'Inside money, outside money, income, wealth and welfare in monetary theory', and by Morishima (1992) in his book on *Capital and Credit*.

Johnson's views on monetary theory are emblematic of the efforts to incorporate money into neoclassical analysis by referring to 'the welfare or real income effect consisting in the consumer's supply obtained on holdings of money' (Johnson 1969: 35). Criticising Gurley and Shaw's distinction between inside and outside money, Johnson tries to show how money can be introduced into barter economy in static equilibrium through 'the invention of a new form of capital equipment yielding no observable flow of output but instead a return in the form of a utility yield' (ibid.: 32). Where the utility yield on money balances comes from remains a mystery. To claim that people behave 'as if they derived satisfaction from their money stocks' (ibid.: 32) is obviously no more than a *petitio principii* of no heuristic value. The further assumption that 'a return should be imputed to the wealth embodied in the commodity money stock, equal to the return on wealth used in production' (ibid.: 33), is no better, and it is at least curious to claim that the substitution of credit for commodity-money adds to the wealth of the community (the resources previously embodied in the commodity-money) and to its real income (imputing an alternative opportunity cost return to holdings of money). While the wealth effect that Johnson refers to here is of very little significance (as it might, at most, occur once), the real income effect is given the status of a steady increase in social welfare. Johnson maintains, in fact, that, when competition leads to the transfer of the increase in wealth to money holders (through the payment of interest on bank deposits), real social income is increased further because of 'the superior value of intra-marginal units of consumption' (ibid.: 37). A note in which Johnson criticises Pesek and Saving for failing to distinguish between two notions of purchasing power helps to understand his idea of social income. In this note, he claims that money can have no purchasing power 'over the income streams yielded by other assets' (ibid.: 37), and yet can have a positive purchasing power over commodities. Hence, the social welfare effect of money must be related to the services it can supply thanks to its purchasing power over produced output.

Now, although it is certain that the use of bank money is crucial for the very existence of an economic system, the increase in social welfare deriving from it cannot be measured in real terms. Moreover, since money is essentially the form of produced output, the analysis proposed by Johnson must be modified drastically. Instead of taking barter as a point of departure, it is necessary to start from the creation of money, otherwise, without a uniform unit of value, output would remain a heap of disparate physical objects. Thanks to money, products can be given their numerical form and transformed into commodities. This implies that, being the form of the real product, money cannot add any proper value to it. Although money has a social function, its creation does not increase either wealth or income. In reality, money is a condition for an economic system to exist at all. The social gain derived from the presence of money is thus much greater than suggested by Johnson. It is not confined to an increase in real income with respect to barter, but it extends to the entire economic system. Johnson is right in claiming that efficiency is improved by the introduction of credit money and financial intermediation and that 'the growth of banking and other intermediary institutions may exercise a more important determining influence on the proportion of output saved and invested in the accumulation of material capital than that of monetary policy as analyzed in these [growth] models' (ibid.: 40). Unfortunately, his analysis is still influenced by a material conception of money (money being considered either a consumer capital good or a form of producers' capital), and he never goes as far as defining money as the general numerical form of the whole output.

Let us switch now to Morishima. Referring to Schumpeter's work, Morishima (1992) claims that, contrary to mainstream analysis, a monetary theory of the firm is needed in order to account for production and innovations. Like Schumpeter in his *Theory of Economic Development* (Schumpeter 1955; first published in 1912), he maintains that production can be started only if entrepreneurs are previously given a certain amount of purchasing power or, in Schumpeter's own words, if they previously get indebted with banks. Now, this approach hardly explains how entrepreneurs can obtain the purchasing power they need *before* production takes place. Morishima's obvious suggestion is that purchasing power may be raised by firms by issuing new shares and by selling them to the public. Yet, this answer seems to beg the question because it takes for granted what must in fact be proved: the existence of purchasing power. To buy shares, individuals must spend their income; the real problem is to explain where this income comes from, and whether or not it is possible to suppose that a given amount of purchasing power may exist independently of production.

Morishima develops his analysis on the assumption that banks lend money by granting credit to firms. Does this mean that money income exists before it is lent to firms? Is this what happens in the real world? This is probably what Morishima has in mind as he supposes that banks start buying bonds issued by firms. However, like the purchase of any other real good, the purchase of bonds requires a positive expenditure of income. Whether banks are believed to own a positive amount of purchasing power since the beginning of their activity, or whether it is merely assumed that they can create it through lending, the crucial question remains that of referring to the logical possibility of money income to exist irrespective of production. Morishima assumes that this is in fact the case: 'The firms f for which funds are advanced in this way will use this newly created purchasing power to buy physical capital goods, raw material, etc., A^0_i, and factors of production, L_i' (Morishima 1992: 161). The Japanese economist could not be more explicit: the purchasing power is *created* by banks and lent to firms. 'To carry out an investment plan an entrepreneur needs credit which enables him to obtain purchasing power' (ibid.: 164). No one will deny that banks play an important role in the economic process and, in particular, that they are asked to provide credit to firms. What has to be clarified, however, is the exact nature of this credit. Although it is true that banks lend income to firms, this does not necessarily imply that the purchasing power thus lent is created by banks. In fact, it is exactly the opposite that happens in the real world: banks lend an income, which they do not create.

When Morishima recalls Walras's and Schumpeter's claim that productive services can be transferred between firms through credit operations, he is simply providing an explanation of the mechanism allowing investment to be distributed among firms. What remains entirely unexplained is the origin of the money income being thus invested. Despite his explicit attempt 'to provide the theoretical, monetary foundation to the general equilibrium system' (ibid.: 141), Morishima is trapped in the same vicious circle as his predecessors as he fails to understand the particular nature of money. Although he repeatedly insists on the fundamental role played by bankers, he does not seem to be aware of the essential immaterial nature of bank money, and goes on considering it as a stock of assets (purchasing power) available for the financing of production. Even when he refers to the possibility of banks financing production through credit expansion, he does not provide a satisfactory account of the way in which money can be integrated into his system.

Yet, the idea that purchasing power is created when banks buy bonds newly issued by firms deserves careful examination. Let us consider the payment of wages carried out by banks on behalf of firms (Figure 3.1).

Is it not true that firms (F) benefit from a credit and that this credit is granted by banks through their purchase of bonds issued by F? The very fact that firms are entered on the assets side of the banks' balance sheets means that they are the sellers of bonds, which define their debt towards the banking system. It is because wages are paid to wage-earners on their behalf that firms get indebted to banks, i.e. that banks own a claim against firms. Now, what is the object of this claim?

Bank			
Liabilities			Assets
Workers	x	Firms	x

Figure 3.1 The accounting payment of wages.

The answer is univocal: the current output produced by wage-earners. The entry in Figure 3.1 tells us, in fact, that wage-earners own a claim on a bank deposit whose object (income) is immediately lent to firms and spent by them for the purchase of current output. It is precisely because firms purchase current output on credit that produced goods and services are the object of their debt to banks. Current output is not only the object of the debt incurred by firms but also that of the deposit owned by wage-earners. It is double-entry book-keeping that leads to this duplication, current output being simultaneously present on the assets and the liabilities sides of the balance sheets of banks. Purchasing power is thus the obvious result of the association between money and output defined by the payment of wages. In this sense, purchasing power is created simultaneously with the purchase of bonds newly issued by firms. It is important to note that purchasing power is thus defined by the income lent to firms, but is not generated by this loan. Although it is a transaction taking place at the very instant that wages are paid, the purchase of bonds does not generate income. Bank credit is a fundamental part of money and income creation, of course. Without the monetary and financial intermediation of banks, output would never be given its numerical form and physical products would never be transformed into economic goods. On the other hand, however, without production the intermediation of banks would be void and meaningless. It is through the close association of firms and banks – both taken in their function of intermediation – that money and current output are integrated, and income (or purchasing power) created.

The widespread belief that money is issued as an asset is at the origin of the claim that purchasing power can be newly created by banks through their purchase of bonds issued by firms 'for raising the funds in order to carry out the investment programme *i*' (Morishima 1992: 161). In reality, the purchase of bonds requires the expenditure of a positive amount of income, which either pre-exists in the form of capital or is created simultaneously with the credit granted by banks. In the first case, the purchase of bonds would be carried out on behalf of savers, and would define a transfer of income from them to firms and not the creation of a new purchasing power. In the second, a new income is indeed created, but this does not allow us to conclude that the creation is the banks'. Let us start from a situation in which no production has yet occurred, and suppose that a firm F asks bank B for a credit of *x* units of money in exchange for an equivalent amount of bonds. Because of double-entry book-keeping and given the flow nature of bank money, what F obtains from B is a payment that the bank carries out on its behalf. No real goods having been produced yet, the payment can only refer to the process that will give rise to F's output. In other words, the payment is necessarily that of the costs of production incurred by F. Hence, F deposits with B its future physical output – in the financial form of bonds – and B pays F's costs of production. What should be clear here is that what is lent to firms is not a positive amount of money, but the income generated from production. From a monetary point of view, firm F benefits from a payment, which the bank carries out on its behalf, whereas from a financial point of view it is credited (and instantaneously debited) with the purchasing power created by production. As a result of this first payment, F is financially indebted to B and the owner of a stock of real goods of equivalent value, the income lent to it by B being immediately invested in the formation of the new stock.

Finally, the bonds sold by F are purchased by the beneficiaries of the payment carried out by B, and these beneficiaries lend to F the income earned through their productive activity. In their function as pure intermediaries, banks do not create the income they lend to firms. What they do create is the payment as such; the flow allowing for the debit of F and the credit of the factors of production. Income is the result of this payment, and it is because of production that it defines a positive purchasing power.

As long as the distinction between money and money income is not fully understood, the relationship between money and credit is bound to remain blurred. It is very important to realise that money as such is a simple numerical form, which is present in every payment as a flow and not as an asset. When Morishima assumes 'a general economy in which money may circulate in the markets and be deposited with a bank' (ibid.: 141), he is hopelessly losing contact with reality. Money would circulate in the markets only if it were a real object. Modern bank money, however, is entirely immaterial. Hence, money 'circulates' only within every payment carried out by banks. Since payments are triangular transactions in which money flows back instantaneously to its point of emission, the circulation of money has nothing to do with that of a real object whatsoever. Instead of saying that money circulates – albeit instantaneously – it would be better to say, then, that money is the circulation itself: it is a flow (Figure 3.2).

The circularity of money may be better perceived if we refer to double-entry book-keeping. When a payment takes place, the payer is debited and the payee credited. This means that, at the same instant, the bank carrying out the payment cancels (literally destroys) the deposit of the payer and enters (literally creates) a new deposit to the benefit of the payee. No deposit or material money is spatially transferred from one economic agent to the other. There is no proper circulation from one to the other. Now, payments are instantaneous events that, through the destruction and creation of bank deposits, allow for the settlement of real transactions. This is so not because a positive amount of money is given in exchange for an equivalent amount of goods but because the payee is entitled to a bank

Bank

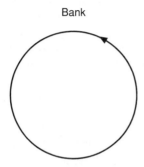

Figure 3.2 Money as a flow.

deposit whose object is a positive amount of money income. To claim that it is through the circulation of money that a bank deposit is transferred from the payer to the payee is twice mistaken as neither money nor deposits circulate. A better alternative would be to say that, through the instantaneous flow defining money, information is passed that leads to the simultaneous destruction of a deposit and creation of another, equivalent, deposit.

As for the real object of payments, it is evident that it cannot result from an act of creation *ex nihilo*. The bank deposit earned by the payee has a positive value only if it defines a positive purchasing power, a condition which is fulfilled only if money income results from the association of money with current output. The credit that banks grant to firms is thus strictly related to production. It is also certain, however, that without the monetary intermediation of banks no income would be created, and no credit ever granted to firms. To explain credit, it is necessary, therefore, to explain both the monetary and financial intermediation carried out by banks. Let us do so by starting from the creation of money.

Money and banks

From Smith to Schmitt

In his *Theory of Economic Development*, Schumpeter (1955: 98) maintains that 'the creation of money by the banks establishing claims against themselves, which is described by Adam Smith, and indeed by still earlier authors in a way quite free from popular errors, has become a commonplace to-day'. Is this really the case? Are we sure that the creation of money is an event that has been understood and described correctly at least since Smith's publication of *The Wealth of Nations*?

In his most famous book, the Scottish economist claims that if 'a particular banker lends among his customers his own promissory notes ... those notes serve all the purposes of money' (Smith 1974: 389). According to Smith, the promissory notes issued by bankers can play the role of money since they represent the gold and silver held as a 'provision for answering occasional demands' (ibid.: 389). The creation of bank money is thus seen as an operation by which gold and silver are given the more convenient form of a promissory note. To the extent that bank money is anchored to these precious metals, Smith's analysis could no longer be used today. Convertibility and legal definition in terms of gold and silver having been abandoned definitively, there is no point in explaining the creation of money as a process by which banks transform their real reserves into promissory notes. It seems impossible, therefore, to agree with Schumpeter as to the obvious and generalised acceptance of Smith's description. Further investigation is required in order to achieve a correct understanding of money creation. Now, there are at least two arguments in Smith's analysis that can lead us in the right direction. The first is his claim that banks can issue their promissory notes far beyond the amount of their reserves of gold and silver. Referring to the activity of a particular banker, Smith claims in fact that 'though he has generally in circulation, therefore, notes to the extent of a hundred thousand pounds, twenty thousand pounds in gold and silver may, frequently, be a sufficient provision' (ibid.: 389). Unlike Ricardo, Smith is not opposed to the possibility of banks creating money beyond the boundaries of perfect convertibility. On the contrary, he believes that the use of bank money can increase riches by saving on the use of gold and silver. 'If different operations of the same kind should, at the same time, be carried on by many different banks and bankers, the whole circulation may thus be conducted with a fifth part of the gold and silver which would otherwise have been requisite' (ibid.: 389). But if we consider the amount of money issued without a real counterpart in terms of gold and silver, how are we to determine its value? It is here that Smith's second argument can put us on the right track towards a new conception of bank money. In the second chapter of Book II, we are told that 'the great wheel of circulation [money] is altogether different from the goods which are circulated by means of it. The revenue of the society consists altogether in those goods, and not in the wheel which circulates them' (ibid.: 385). As repeatedly stated by Smith, money's worth is defined by current output. 'The whole revenue of all of them taken together is evidently not equal to both the money and the consumable goods; but only to one or other of those two values, and to the latter more properly than to the former' (ibid.: 387). The indication that we derive from Smith's analysis is, therefore, that money is a valueless means of circulation issued by banks as their acknowledgement of debt and invested with a positive value only insofar as it is associated with current output.

Another important contribution towards a modern theory of bank money is due to Keynes. It may be interesting to observe that in the *Treatise*, conforming to consolidated analysis, he starts by considering two categories of money – bank money and State money (money proper) – but soon decides to concentrate on bank money: 'the tendency is towards a preponderant importance for bank money … and towards State money occupying a definitely subsidiary position' (Keynes 1971: 27). Chapters 2 and 3 of his 1930 book are devoted to bank money entirely, and it is around this concept that the whole of his analysis develops. Now, Keynes defines bank money both as a spontaneous acknowledgement of debt and as a deposit. He claims also that a bank may create a claim against itself, either adding to its investments or 'in return for his [the borrower] promise of subsequent reimbursement; i.e. it may make loans or advances' (ibid.: 21). Thus, the creation of bank money is immediately perceived by Keynes as the creation of bank deposits and related to the operation of credit. This is undoubtedly correct if the aim of the analysis is to explain the formation of money income. Yet, since the lack of a rigorous distinction between money as such and money income – i.e. between money and credit – may be the source of serious misunderstandings and preclude the possibility of a correct understanding of the laws of monetary macroeconomics, it is wise to spend a few more words showing the logical difference between these two concepts. Although it is true that the creation of money is always related to the creation, the transfer or the destruction of a bank deposit, it is possible to separate them analytically. Let us do this, and concentrate in this section on the emission of money as such.

As noted by Keynes, 'only the bank itself can authorise the creation of a deposit in its books entitling the customer to draw cash or to transfer his claim to the order of someone else' (ibid.: 21). The crucial idea here is that by issuing money the bank authorises the beneficiary of the emission to transfer his claim to someone else. If we consider money in itself, and abstract from production, the object of the promise issued by the bank is the possibility of transferring its acknowledgement of debt. The role of banks acting as monetary intermediaries is to carry out payments on behalf of their clients, and they do so through the circular emission of their acknowledgement of debt. When Keynes speaks of overdraft facilities, he refers explicitly to the possibility of banks issuing their acknowledgement of debt in exchange for a simple promise of reimbursement. Now, what banks themselves promise to their clients is to carry out payments. Since payments are instantaneous events in which – financially – banks debit the payer and credit the payee, the creation of bank money appears to be functional to these events. This means that payments take place thanks to the intermediation of money, which is thus simultaneously created and destroyed in each of them. It is double-entry book-keeping that requires a perfect and instantaneous balance between creation and destruction. If payments could be carried out by commodity-money, there would be no place for creation and destruction. But there would be no place for monetary transactions either. Things being what they are, and Keynes was not fooled by deceptive appearance to the contrary, money is issued by banks as an instantaneous flow. When a bank pays C on behalf of A, the transaction is made possible by an instantaneous flow through which a deposit is destroyed on A and another equivalent deposit is created on C (Figure 3.3).

Money itself being present only at the very instant that the payment occurs, it would be vain to look for it outside the payment. In more practical terms, we would say that when overdraft facilities are granted to A the bank simply promises him to carry out payments up to a given amount of money units, and that at the moment a payment is carried out the promise is fulfilled through the emission of a monetary flow. As rightly pointed out by Keynes, unused overdrafts do not 'appear anywhere at all in a bank's statement of its assets and liabilities' (ibid.: 37). This is so because, as a promise of payment, bank money is essentially an asset and a liability for the bank and its client at once, for each owes a debit to the

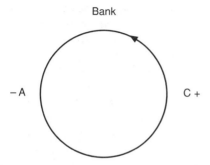

Figure 3.3 Money flow and bank deposits.

other and each is the other's creditor. 'Properly speaking, unused overdraft facilities – since they represent a liability of the bank – ought, in the same way as acceptances, to appear on both sides of the account' (ibid.: 37). It is only when the bank pays C that money is created (and destroyed); the result of this instantaneous flow being the formation of a bank deposit whose object is simultaneously a money income and the promise of the bank to carry out a payment in the future.

The object of C's credit is double. He owns a right on a bank deposit and is at the same time entitled to ask the bank to issue a payment on his behalf. While the existence of the bank deposit has to be related to that of money income, the promise of the bank to issue a monetary flow is only the result of its capacity to act as a monetary intermediary. Whereas money income implies that the bank is a financial intermediary and requires the intervention of production in order to be accounted for, money as such defines an asset-liability that can be issued by the bank every time that one of its clients asks it to carry out a payment. Hence, whereas money is concerned with the vehicular or circular character of transactions, money income is their necessary real content. Money as such carries out payments; money income finances them.

Following the analysis of overdraft facilities worked out by Keynes, Rueff has no hesitation in claiming that the counterpart of the acknowledgement of debt spontaneously issued by the bank is the acknowledgement of debt of its client. 'Il est essentiel de bien comprendre que le titre ne constitue là qu'une garantie accessoire et que la contre-partie de l'avance ce n'est en aucune façon le titre déposé, mais la créance de la banque sur le titulaire du compte' (Rueff 1979: 226). It is only with the work of Schmitt, however, that a rigorous definition of bank money is achieved. As early as 1966, he claimed that bank money is a flow implying a positive and a negative creation. 'Instead of transferring a stock of money income (an operation which they carry out as financial intermediaries), banks issue simultaneously a negative money (debt entered on their liabilities side) and a positive money (debt entered on their assets side)' (Schmitt 1966: 235; our translation). The idea of bank money being a flow is present in all of his work, the distinction between flows and stocks being of paramount importance for the understanding of his approach to monetary economics. While money as such is a flow, bank deposits are stocks. Money exists only at the very instant that payments are carried out; deposits exist between payments. The object of money – of the acknowledgement of debt issued by banks – is a payment (a flow), whereas the object of each payment is part of the output financially deposited with the banks (a stock).

Now, Schmitt's point of view is not shared by the majority of economists, who still think of money as an asset. Let us refer, for example, to Patinkin's analysis. According to the author of *Money, Interest and Prices* (Patinkin 1965), the establishment of banks can be described in two different ways that stem from the same point of departure: the 'production' (this is Patinkin's term) of government fiat money. He then assumes that the private sector can increase its assets thanks to the fiat money injected by the government. 'Though there may be differences of interpretation there can be no doubt that money in this case should be considered as a net asset of the private sector' (Patinkin 1972: 169–70). On this basis, banks may be established either by letting the government forgo part of its monopoly on the 'production' of money authorising certain individuals of the private sector to issue paper money or by allowing the creation of a fully competitive banking industry. Patinkin's arguments are clearly expounded and corroborated by a numerical example running through a series of book-entries concerning the balance sheets of government, non-financial private sector and banking sector. Yet, his analysis is seriously flawed, from both an empirical and a theoretical point of view. Let us consider his assumption that fiat money is issued as an asset first. It is important to note that, although it is declared by the government to be legal tender, fiat money is not convertible into any standard species. Unlike that of gold or of any other commodity, the 'production' of fiat money is cost free, and its result can only be an 'object' with no proper value. How is it possible, then, to consider fiat money as an asset? The absurdity of this claim should be evident to anyone who is well aware of the fact that money is properly 'issued' and not 'produced', its physical form (paper or electrical impulse) being entirely irrelevant to its nature. The absurdity becomes even more patent when fiat money is entered as a net asset on the balance sheet of the private sector. Yet, Patinkin seems to be aware of this danger only when he assumes that the government can grant the private sector the right to issue paper money. In this case, he claims, the right to issue money should be restricted, 'for otherwise individuals would ... issue an infinite quantity of money which would be valueless in terms of purchasing power over commodities' (ibid.: 170). But how is it possible to reconcile the claim that money is an asset with the claim that the more money is created the lesser its value? Obviously, what Patinkin has in mind is the possibility of relating money to output. How this relationship may be established, however, remains a mystery. Moreover, even if he were able to explain it, it would be wrong to claim that an infinite quantity of money is valueless, unless output were equal to zero. Had Patinkin followed this line of thought, he would have reached the conclusion that, in the absence of produced output, money can only have a zero value. Issued by the government before production has taken place, fiat money is necessarily valueless and, therefore, may in no way be considered as an asset.

Marked by this initial flaw, Patinkin's analysis does not provide a satisfactory explanation of commercial banks' initial book-entries. What Patinkin calls the right to produce paper money can no more be considered an asset than money itself, and it is absurd to believe that a government may grant a private institution the supernatural power of issuing net wealth out of nothing. Patinkin's analysis seems to improve and get closer to facts and logic when he considers the activity that commercial banks develop when they start issuing their own money. In his example, he claims that 'the increase in bank assets must have been accompanied by an equal increase in liabilities' (ibid.: 178), so that, additional assets having been acquired in exchange for bank money, 'the increased bank liabilities must equal the amount of bank money issued' (ibid.: 179). Let us reproduce the balance sheet of banks that is proposed by Patinkin (Table 3.1).

On the assets side, we find $10,000 of fiat money issued by the government,

Table 3.1 Balance sheet of banking sector

Assets		Liabilities	
Reserves (government fiat money)	$10,000	Bank money	$300,000
Debt of non-financial private sector	$285,000		
Plant, equipment and other assets	$10,000	*Net worth*	
		Common stocks	$5,000
Total	$305,000		$305,000

half of which is derived from the non-financial private sector in exchange for banks' common stocks and the other half is obtained in exchange for an equal amount of newly issued bank money. Plant, equipment and other assets are also acquired in exchange for an equivalent amount of bank money, whereas the debt of the private sector is the difference between the total money issued and the monetary and real assets obtained from it. Accordingly, on the liabilities side are entered the bank money and the common stocks transferred to the private sector. The interesting thing here is that for $285,000 out of $300,000 the monetary liabilities of banks are perfectly matched by equivalent monetary assets. Unfortunately, instead of working out the implications of this significant correspondence, Patinkin maintains that 'it is not necessarily bank money *per se* (whatever that may mean) which is a liability; instead, all that has been established by our formal argument is that there must be liabilities equal in value to that of the bank money' (ibid.: 179). Patinkin thus misses the opportunity of discovering the true nature of bank money and remains anchored to a truncated vision of monetary economics. His representation of reality would be correct if money could be issued as an asset. In this case, money could be considered as a real good and exchanged against other assets of the private sector. Yet, contrary to Patinkin's beliefs, bank money cannot be issued already endowed with a positive value.

By defining it as a spontaneous acknowledgement of debt, modern economists recognise that it is indeed a liability; and by observing that money is actually issued at the moment this acknowledgement of debt is lent to the private sector, they implicitly or explicitly admit that, as a matter of fact, bank money is simultaneously a liability and an asset. This result is confirmed by the way in which entries are recorded in the banks' balance sheets. According to the principle of double-entry book-keeping, money cannot be entered on the liabilities or on the assets side alone. By issuing money, banks lend an IOU to the private sector, which they enter on the liabilities side (as a credit of the private sector) and on the assets side (as a debit of this same sector). Patinkin respects this logical requirement up to $285,000. For the remaining $15,000, he balances the bank money entered on the liabilities side with real and financial assets of equal value entered on the assets side. He thus fails to respect the principle of double-entry book-keeping which, when money creation is concerned, requires liabilities to be balanced by assets referring to the same agent. The necessary equality of debits and credits of every single economic agent is one of the fundamental laws of monetary macroeconomics. First formulated by Schmitt in his *Théorie unitaire de la monnaie, nationale et internationale* (Schmitt 1975), this law can only be properly understood once money has been perceived as a simple numerical form, a necessary but immaterial intermediary of every transaction. In the following chapters, we shall see how this law applies at every level of complexity. For the time being, let us simply note that if money can be issued without resorting to miracles it is because banks comply with it each time they agree to lend to the public their own IOUs.

Patinkin claims that fiat paper money 'does not involve the payment of either interest or principal, and hence does not represent any future burden of "debt servicing". Hence it is a net asset of the private sector' (Patinkin 1972: 146). This is a very curious reasoning indeed. How can one conclude that fiat paper money is a net asset of the private sector from the fact that it is a government non-interest-bearing debt? It is true, as claimed by Patinkin, that, if the payment of interest and principal on government securities is financed through taxation, these securities cannot be considered as a net asset of the private sector. Yet, the non-payment of interest and principal is not enough to transform them, or fiat paper money, into net assets. This would be the case only if the government could increase wealth simply by injecting its acknowledgement of debt into the private sector. The absurdity of such a proposition should be evident to anyone. If this is not so, it is because it is still widely believed that fiat money derives its value from that of the central bank's actual or potential reserves. At least since August 1971, however, it has been an undisputed fact that money is no longer convertible into gold or into any other real asset held as a reserve. In the absence of any official link between currency and reserves, how is it possible to maintain that by issuing money central banks increase the assets held by the private sector?

The analysis becomes clearer if we start from square one. Let us suppose that money has not yet been introduced in a system composed of a central bank and a private sector made up of firms and wage-earners. Although production may already take place as a physical process, its result is still a mass of heterogeneous physical objects (values-in-use) with no proper economic value. Part of this heterogeneous output may even be stocked with the central bank as a reserve. The fact remains that, before the introduction of money, this reserve has no numerical form. Now, let the central bank issue money as its own acknowledgement of debt and lend it to firms. Two arguments lead us to conclude that the money thus issued has no positive value and can therefore not be considered as a net asset of the private sector. The first reason is that the physical objects stored with the central bank have no objective relationship whatsoever with the money issued. Since they have no proper economic value, they cannot guarantee that of the acknowledgement of debt spontaneously incurred by the central bank. The second reason is that the same amount of money cannot have simultaneously two different real values, one derived from its official link with the reserves and one derived from its association with current output. It is certain, in fact, that, through the intermediation of firms and wage-earners, money is associated with current production and becomes one with its physical output. It would be absurd to maintain, thus, that money has a value derived from the reserves of the central bank and equal to its purchasing power over current output. The correct solution lies in the numerical nature of bank money. Being issued as a numerical form, money has no proper value and does not increase, as such, either social or private sector's wealth. As an acknowledgement of debt spontaneously issued by banks, money is not an asset; it is a mere IOU whose object is a monetary flow: the capacity of banks to carry out payments on behalf of their clients. It is at the moment it is paid out to the factors of production that money is invested with a positive value. The net asset held by the private sector comes out of a process of production, and not out of the blue, as if banks were endowed with the supernatural power of creating *ex nihilo*.

Patinkin seems ready to accept this analysis, at least with respect to credit money. 'Hence this money does not represent a net asset of this sector. For to every dollar of deposits thus created and held by some individual in the economy, there corresponds an offsetting debt of some other individual. Thus, in the case of expansion of bank credit to the private sector, the offsetting debt is that of the borrower from the banking system' (ibid.: 146–7). In reality it must be observed that, although credit money is not issued as an asset, its association with current output defines an increase in wealth which is not offset by any corresponding liability. Hence, Patinkin's analysis has to be modified when the expansion of bank credit to the private sector is related to the monetisation of a new production. In this case, the debt incurred by the borrower from the banking system is balanced by new current output and no longer offsets the deposit earned by the factors of production, whose income defines a net asset for the whole system.

A further critique to traditional analysis

In the third section of their paper on the supply of money and the control of nominal income, Papademos and Modigliani (1990: 420) 'examine the determinants of the money supply for the type of monetary system prevailing today', i.e. leaving aside the unrealistic assumptions that money is exogenously determined and directly controlled by the central bank. According to these authors, (fiat) money is a liability 'created by banks, both the central bank and private banks, in payment for the acquisition of government and private financial debt' (ibid.: 421). Hence, money is an acknowledgement of debt issued by banks and lent to the public (government included) in exchange for equivalent financial bonds. Now, what is the value of the money created as an IOU and lent to the public? As observed by Papademos and Modigliani, money 'has no intrinsic value and is produced and maintained at virtually no cost' (ibid.: 421). But if its value is zero, how can money finance the acquisition of financial bonds? This is the crucial question to be answered if we are to lay down the principles of monetary macroeconomics. Papademos and Modigliani try to answer it indirectly, by relating the determination of the money supply to bank liability management.

Since the multiplier approach 'does not provide a theoretical analysis of the process through which banks' behavior influences the supply of bank deposits' (ibid.: 432), it is replaced by a structural approach to the money supply mechanism. Playing down the distinction between banks and non-bank financial intermediaries, Papademos and Modigliani refer money creation to the role assumed by the demand for and supply of money and non-monetary assets in a setting where portfolio adjustments 'are not invariant to the policy actions of the monetary authorities' (ibid.: 432). Instead of analysing the model that they elaborate, let us consider one of the assumptions on which it is based, namely that 'the supply of demand deposits reflects the bank's demand for earning assets' (ibid.: 433) subject to a balance sheet constraint. Two distinct questions seem to be systematically mixed up by Papademos and Modigliani: the initial determination of the money supply by banks, and their management of financial assets and liabilities. Yet, this distinction is fundamental. It must not be forgotten, in fact, that banks play the distinct roles of monetary and financial intermediaries. Furthermore, it must also be remembered that banks have a different economic status according to whether they act as banks proper or as income holders. It is certain that banks are service-producing firms and that, as such, they are not essentially different from other economic agents operating on the labour and on the commodity markets. It is also true, however, that banks have a particular role to play as monetary and financial institutions and that, in these functions, they do not belong to the set of producers and consumers. As money creators, banks are neither firms nor purchasers. By issuing money, they simply provide the economic system with a numerical instrument, a unit of account and a means of payment with no intrinsic value whatsoever.

By claiming that the creation of money can be assimilated to the banks' purchase of earning assets, Papademos and Modigliani seem to be unaware of the fact that any demand is determined by the amount of income available to finance it. Banks' demand for earning assets is positive only if banks are income holders. But this means that the creation both of money and of income must have already been explained before banks exert their demand. If it cannot be assumed that by issuing money banks exert a positive demand on the financial market, it cannot either be claimed that they provide the economy with a positive supply of demand deposits. Since the creation of money is not a metaphysical event, it will not result either in a positive purchase of assets by banks or in a positive increase in the deposits held by the public, unless it is associated with production.

Papademos and Modigliani are on the right track when they consider the creation of money as an exchange between claims, i.e. the liability of banks and the financial debt of the private sector. What they do not seem to realise, however, is that through the process of money creation banks are mere intermediaries between the public and itself. The object of the financial claim deposited with the banks (on their assets side) is also that of the debt incurred by the banks and entered on their liabilities side. They also seem to miss the point that money itself is a flow, so that its creation (and its instantaneous destruction) must coincide with a payment. The exchange between claims must result from a payment which, being carried out by a bank on behalf of its clients, cannot lead to the bank's purchase of earning assets.

The exchange defined by the emission of money is of a particular nature, and requires further investigation. In fact, the emission of money would be meaningless if it were not associated with the financial deposit of produced output. Money creation and bank credit are closely interrelated, as no payment is carried out without a financial intermediation. To understand the relationship between monetary and financial intermediation fully, it is necessary, therefore, to analyse the way in which credit is granted by banks in a system where the function of banks is to transform real into monetary assets. To introduce the argument, let us refer to the classical distinction between endogenous and exogenous money.

According to Desai, money is considered as exogenously determined when price level, interest rate and/or output depend on the stock of money, whereas it is endogenously determined if it is the stock of money that depends on price level, interest rate and/or output. But how do we choose between these alternatives? Desai suggests that 'the best way to consider the issue of exogeneity of money is to specify the type of money economy envisaged – commodity money, paper money, credit money – and look at the variables likely to influence the supply of money and its relation with other variables' (Desai 1987: 136). Yet, it is a fact that our economic systems are based on the use of bank money. Economists are thus not given the choice between equivalent alternatives: they are bound to explain the working of a credit money economy. In this context, what is the criterion that helps us decide whether money is exogenously or endogenously determined? Following Desai, we could say that what matters is the fact that money is created by banks, and as 'banks create inside money and inside money can only be regarded as endogenous' (ibid.: 136) it is endogeneity which characterises a credit money economy. Although partially attenuated by the consideration that narrow (high-powered) money is exogenously determined by monetary authorities, this is Desai's conclusion. Now, on closer examination the whole debate rests on a complete misunderstanding of the nature of money and of its relationship with output. To claim that money is endogenously determined amounts to maintaining that banks create money on demand. This is correct only so long as it is recognised that the demand for money must be linked to present, past or future production. Furthermore, it must also be kept in mind that money as such is a mere numerical form whose existence is strictly instantaneous. The concept of the quantity of money is ill-founded. Only if money were material could we speak of its mass or quantity and of its 'physical' velocity of circulation. Since money is immaterial, no theory derived from physics or from a physical approach will explain its nature and use. The creation of money is a very peculiar process, which does not lead to a positive increase in the quantity of assets produced in a given economy. Money simply gives production its numerical form without adding any positive value to it.

Hence, the traditional concepts of endogenous and exogenous money are both essentially wrong. Bank money is neither exogenously determined as a physical mass 'produced' by the monetary sector nor endogenously issued to match a level of prices, interest rate and output autonomously determined. Present in every payment, money does not survive its instantaneous circulation, yet its presence is absolutely necessary for the determination of prices, interest and output.

One of the most frequent mistakes in monetary economics is to identify money as such with money income. It is income, and not money, which is deposited with the banking system, and it is money, and not income, which is created as a numerical vehicle of payments. Let us consider, for example, the succession of three payments, each of value x, corresponding to the payment of wages, the purchase of consumers' bonds and the purchase of current output. It can easily be observed that each of them implies the presence of money and leads, therefore, to a total creation of $3x$ units of money. Would it be right to conclude, then, that the total money supply is equal to $3x$? Is it not true that the three transactions refer to the same income and do not increase its total amount? In this case, the claim that the money supply is $3x$ simply means that banks have been asked to deal three times with the same income of x. In other cases, the same claim would mean different things. For example, that total income is itself equal to $3x$ (if banks are asked to monetise three new productions of x), or that production is equal to $2x$ and the purchase of bonds equal to x, and so on. Being immaterial and valueless, money can be created n times without increasing or decreasing wealth. Its supply is functional to the needs of economic agents and tells us nothing about the actual amount of income available in the system. At the same time, however, it would be wrong to claim that the supply of money is determined by the level of output. As modern monetary analysis shows, there is no unilateral order of causality between these two variables. Without money, output could not be determined, but without the presence of output the creation of money would be void. Thus, what we have to investigate further is the way in which money is related to income in the process of credit carried out by banks.

Credit and banks

Credit and money creation

In his *Theory of Economic Development*, Schumpeter claims that an economic agent 'can only become an entrepreneur by previously becoming a debtor. ... What he first wants is credit. Before he requires any goods whatever, he requires purchasing power. He is the typical debtor in capitalist society' (Schumpeter 1955: 102). How are we to interpret this claim? Schumpeter himself specifies that credit 'can only consist of credit means of payment created *ad hoc*, which can be backed neither by money in the strict sense nor by products already in existence' (ibid.: 106). The idea conveyed by the Austrian economist is therefore that banks are asked to create a positive amount of purchasing power in favour of entrepreneurs, allowing them to purchase a positive stream of real goods: 'credit is essentially the creation of purchasing power for the purpose of transferring it to the entrepreneur' (ibid.: 107). However, as Schumpeter recognises, such a creation of purchasing power out of nothing defines an inflationary increase in demand. Since 'the purchasing power really represents nothing but existing goods' (ibid.: 108), it is obvious that an increase in purchasing power which is not matched by an increase in real goods and services can only be of a pathological nature. The strange thing is that Schumpeter, although perfectly aware of this implication, maintains that 'there is nothing illogical or mystical in it' (ibid.: 109). In fact, credit-led inflation results from an illogical extension of credit beyond the amount of available income. In this respect, it is relatively unimportant whether credit is allowed for consumption or production purposes. In both cases, a 'false' or 'void' purchasing power is created which is spent for the purchase of already produced goods and services. Moreover, and contrary to what Schumpeter claims, in both cases the plethoric purchasing power created by banks is bound to be destroyed when credits are repaid by borrowers. Schumpeter's idea that when credit is used to buy production goods 'the credit inflation is more than eliminated' (ibid.: 110) (because production enriches the social stream with new goods and services) does not take into account the fact that production increases the amount of purchasing power as well. In his analysis, Schumpeter does not seem to be sufficiently aware of the close relationship existing between money and output. He is thus led to reason as if his dichotomous perception of reality were the true state of affairs in economics. As a result, his theory of inflation and deflation is too mechanistic to provide a deep insight into the realm of monetary macroeconomics.

Let us go back to our main concern. It is of the greatest importance to understand that, contrary to what is often claimed by a number of economists, credit is not created by banks. Schumpeter is right in maintaining that when banks grant a credit they transfer a purchasing power to their clients (borrowers). Yet, he is wrong in believing that this purchasing power is created *ad hoc*, without being backed by any real product. A credit is a transfer, not a creation, of purchasing power. Hence, when granting credit, banks act as financial intermediaries, not as money creators. The beneficiary of a credit obtains part of the income saved by the public and held by banks as a deposit. If banks did not hold any financial deposit on behalf of the public, they could grant no credit. As far as credit is concerned, banks act in conformity with the principle according to which 'deposits make loans'. To claim the contrary would amount to the assumption that banks can create a positive asset out of nothing, a hypothesis which has consistently been rejected by the greatest economists since Adam Smith. As the Scottish economist had clearly perceived, although money as such is indeed created by banks (as a pure numerical form) money income results from its association with production and has its primary source outside the banking system. In other words, through credit, banks lend a positive amount of money income and not a mere acknowledgement of debt with no real object. What distinguishes money from income is the fact that income is a bank deposit with a real object. It is this real object that is lent to the borrower in the form of a claim on the banking system.

In order to develop our understanding of bank credit further, let us refer, critically, to Jaffee and Stiglitz's analysis of credit rationing. In their paper, they observe that 'credit markets deviate from the standard model because the interest rate indicates only what the individual promises to repay, not what he will actually repay' (Jaffee and Stiglitz 1990: 838). This simply amounts to saying that, while in standard markets delivery and payment occur simultaneously, in financial markets credit is exchanged for a promise of repayment in the future. Now, whereas it is certainly true that the beneficiary of a credit obtains today an object different from the one he will give up at redemption, it is not likewise certain that the operation of credit itself does not entail the necessary equality of sales and purchases.

Let us clarify the terms of the problem. Jaffee and Stiglitz seem merely to share the common point of view according to which, on standard markets, a sale is simultaneously a purchase of the same commodity. Nobody would deny the validity of this simple truism. It is evident that the same transaction is seen as a purchase from the buyer's point of view and as a sale from the seller's point of view. What they do not seem to be aware of is that the simultaneity of purchases and sales is always verified not only with respect to the same commodity but also with respect to each agent. This law (see Schmitt 1975) acquires its whole significance when financial markets are also taken into consideration. Although credit markets are in some respects different from commodity markets, it cannot be denied that a single transaction can involve them simultaneously. The final purchase of a commodity, for example, implies the selling of a deposit certificate by the buyer of the real good, who thereby becomes a seller on the financial market *and* a buyer on the commodity market. This is so because income is formed as a bank deposit and may be spent by its owner only if the latter is prepared to part with his entitlement to it. By selling his certificate of deposit, the buyer of the real good gets back the income he had initially saved (or, more precisely, an equivalent amount) and has it transferred to the seller of the commodity. The law of the logical identity of sales and purchases is verified also when transactions occur only on the financial market – the buyer of bonds being simultaneously a seller of deposit certificates – or only on the commodity market, in the exceptional case that the purchaser of real goods and services is simultaneously a seller of real goods and services.

Once this law is taken into account, the claim made by Jaffee and Stiglitz (1990: 838) that 'credit received today by an individual or firm is exchanged for a *promise* of repayment in the future' can be interpreted afresh. In particular, it becomes clear that nobody can obtain a credit without simultaneously selling something equivalent. This is precisely what happens in real life. The individual or firm receiving the credit has to give in exchange (i.e. sell) a promise to repay it on a given expiring date. In other words, the individual or institution granting the credit becomes the purchaser of a financial claim sold by the beneficiary of the credit and whose object is an equivalent future output. By selling his financial claim to the lender, the borrower is thus giving up part of his future income in exchange for a present one. Finally, the purchase of today's output by the borrower is made possible by his actualised sale of tomorrow's output. In this sense, transactions on the credit market imply payments as real as those occurring on other markets. Yet, it is true that the repurchase of the financial claim initially sold by the borrower might fail to take place when due. Jaffee and Stiglitz's analysis has to be considered in this context, which is essentially microeconomic.

As they maintain, in the absence of a credit market, or 'when credit is allocated poorly, poor investment projects are undertaken, and the nation's resources are squandered' (ibid.: 839). At the macrolevel, however, their analysis is not satisfactory. Sharing the traditional view of monetary macroeconomics, they believe that credit has a life of its own, which can affect the working of our real economies. 'Changes in credit allocations are one likely source for the fluctuations which have marked capitalist economies over the past two centuries' (ibid.: 839). Let us try to avoid a possible misunderstanding. It is a fact that, through credit rationing, banks could cause investment activity to fall. What is claimed here is that, once a certain production has taken place, banks are bound to lend the total of available income, so that their activity cannot be the cause of deflation.

Credit may correspond either to the financing of a new production or to the lending of a pre-existing deposit. In the first case, banks lend to firms the very income generated by the new production, whereas in the second case an already existing income is lent to consumers or firms. If banks refused to grant credit of the first kind, production would fall and so would income. Newly created deposits would be smaller and the economy would shrink. If this is the message conveyed by Jaffee and Stiglitz, then we can agree with them. But, if they maintained that expenditures may be affected by credit rationing so that a restriction in bank loans may result in deflation, their theory would not be supported by facts. Because of double-entry book-keeping, deposits entered on the liabilities side of a bank's balance sheet and not borrowed by consumers are necessarily lent to firms, F, entered on the assets side. Being a mere intermediary, a bank cannot avoid lending to F the amount deposited by savers, S.

Let us reason in terms of supply and demand. As claimed by Jaffee and Stiglitz, 'in principle, the amount of credit rationing could be measured as the demand for credit minus the supply of credit' (ibid.: 874). But how are demand for and supply of credit determined? Quite simply, the supply of credit is given by the sum deposited within the banking system. In our numerical example, the supply of credit is measured by 100 units of money income. As for the demand, it should be clear that its determining amount does not correspond to its desired level. The demand for credit must be calculated on an objective basis. It is the need for financial backing of production costs that forms this basis. If we consider the totality of costs incurred in the production (and distribution) of national output (goods and services) we can determine, on objective grounds, the total demand for credit of the economy. This means that, production being the unique source of positive bank deposits, the demand for credit is always necessarily equal to the supply of credit. Again, this does not at all mean that at the microeconomic level demand and supply can never diverge. If behavioural considerations are taken into the picture, credit rationing appears to be a possibility insofar as the demand for credit is determined on a subjective basis. It is always possible, of course, that a producer's demand for credit relative to his projects of investment does not find the necessary backing from the banking system. In this case, the producer will have to modify his initial plans to conform with the overdraft facilities that banks are prepared to offer him. What must be understood clearly is that the difference between the demand for credit of our entrepreneur and the offer of banks is only a virtual magnitude. As long as production is only planned, the demand for credit defines a desired amount, which may well differ from the amount that banks are willing to lend. Demand and supply pass from the desired to the realised level only once production has taken place. At this moment, there can be no difference between them, the demand being necessarily matched by an equivalent supply. The credit required by the entrepreneur in order to cover his costs of production is equal, in fact, to the income generated by these costs and deposited on the liabilities side of banks. What we want to stress here is that in the absence of an objective determination it would be impossible to work out any credit system, let alone one of credit rationing. An objective theory of credit can be derived directly from the analysis of banks' double-entry book-keeping, bearing in mind that the matching of assets and liabilities makes sense only if it is related to a real object financially deposited with the banks and lent to the beneficiary of the credit.

Money supply: an ill-founded concept

As credit is a transfer of bank deposits and not a creation of money, it has nothing to do with the traditional concept of money supply. Although perfectly in line with the logical distinction between money as such and money income, this conclusion is not shared by mainstream economists. According to Brunner and Meltzer, for example, theories of money supply must account for the distinction between a central and a commercial bank's money, the role of credit and the interaction between credit and money markets.

In their paper, they start by considering a model in which it is assumed that 'there are no banks or intermediaries .... There is a government that finances its spending by issuing base money (currency), B, and bonds, S' (Brunner and Meltzer 1990: 362). Let us analyse the consistency and implications of these assumptions. It is immediately apparent that the absence of banks or intermediaries is related to commercial banks and financial institutions, but not to central banks. However, it is well known that, when they act on behalf of governments, central banks belong to the category of commercial banks. The principle is clear: when a bank acts as the Bank of banks, it is a *central bank*; when it acts as the bank of one or more economic agents (purchasers, sellers, producers, investors), it is a *commercial bank*. Brunner and Meltzer assume that there are no banks, but that base money is issued by the central bank. Are they being inconsistent? Obviously not, since when it issues base (central) money, the central bank acts as the Bank of banks and not as the private bank of the government. Yet, Brunner and Meltzer move on to claim that, jointly with the emission of bonds, the emission of base money finances government spending. Hence, the central bank is supposed to issue money to the benefit of an economic agent among others, a transaction that relies on the capacity of the bank to issue money as an asset.

Brunner and Meltzer are not so naïve as to claim that the money issued to finance government spending is created *ex nihilo*. They suppose, instead, that money is issued by the central bank as a counterpart of 'gold, foreign exchange and special drawing rights' (ibid.: 362). Several questions could be raised at this stage regarding the relationships among gold, foreign exchange, special drawing rights and national money. Let us assume that they can be answered satisfactorily and let us stick to our main concern. The problem that has still to be faced is whether the base money issued by the central bank is an asset or not. The answer is positive if the emission of central money corresponds to the monetisation of the country's external gain due to its commercial surplus. Is this the situation that Brunner and Meltzer refer to? We cannot discard this possibility entirely; yet it is clearly not the simplest starting point of a theory that aims at explaining the money supply. Furthermore, another consideration seems to corroborate a less generous interpretation of Brunner and Meltzer's analysis. In their text, we can read the following sentence: 'The central bank acquires government debt by purchases in the open market, i.e. by exchanging base money for government securities' (ibid.: 362). Having correctly discarded the direct purchase of government debt by the central bank, Brunner and Meltzer admit its indirect purchase through open market transactions. This implies that, having previously been bought by the public, government securities can be repurchased by the central bank. If this is carried out through the emission of base money, the transaction increases pathologically the supply of money. If government securities were repurchased using an amount of income (derived from government holdings), the public would simply get back what it had initially transferred to the central bank and there would be no inflationary increase in the money supply.

Let us try to imagine how the economic system could work according to the model initially considered by Brunner and Meltzer. To avoid inflation, the government would have to finance its spending by selling bonds. But how could the public purchase government securities given the absence of non-central money, banks and financial intermediaries? The aim of the whole story being that of working out a satisfactory model of a monetary economy, it cannot be assumed that government bonds are exchanged directly against real goods and services. Government bonds have to be sold, but who can purchase them? How can their monetary and relative prices be determined if the monetary price of output is not? As previously observed, if the government were to finance its spending by issuing base money, there would be an inflationary increase in demand, unless (but this is not the case considered by Brunner and Meltzer) base money were derived from the monetisation of an external gain of the country.

The inflationary character that the credit to the government would have if it were financed through a monetary emission patently shows that it is a serious mistake to identify credit with money creation. The concept of money supply is inappropriate, therefore, from a double point of view. On one hand, it cannot denote the result of a simple creation of nominal money because, being a flow, money does not survive its instantaneous use as a means of payment. Being destroyed as soon as the payment for which it has been created has taken place (i.e. in an instant), money cannot be the object of any supply by banks. On the other hand, money cannot be the object of the credit granted by banks either since this object is necessarily real (a stock, and not a flow). It is only if the money supply is conceived of as representing the stock of money income that this concept can become meaningful. This means, however, that it would have to be reinterpreted entirely, namely with respect to the possibility of its being quantitatively determined by the monetary authorities. Income is the result of production, and there is nothing miraculous to it (as would be the case if banks created it).

The purchase of government bonds is a credit operation and, as such, it needs to be financed out of a positive income. This is also the case, of course, if banks (or the central bank) finance it in advance. In so far as they allow the present expenditure of a future income – which, having already been spent, will be destroyed as soon as it is formed – advances are perfectly legitimate. In any case, whether advanced or not, it is always an income that is the object of credit. It is a source of dangerous confusion, therefore, to claim that the money supply is determined through the central bank's purchase of government bonds.

Furthermore, even if we accepted the idea that purchases of government securities are financed by issuing central money, the model would still be unable to account for the monetary price of produced output. The monetary price of real goods being unknown before the quantity of money has been determined, how can the government fix the price of its bonds? The problem could be solved by reversing the order of causality (the monetary price of goods being determined by that of government bonds) only if the (relative) price of real goods could be determined autonomously. This not being so (see Chapter 2), we are bound to conclude that Brunner and Meltzer's analysis fails to provide an explanation of the way in which money can be integrated with current output, thus leaving prices entirely undetermined.

The old-fashioned (and wrong) concept of money supply is a result of the dichotomic representation of the world propounded by the quantity theory of money. Now, one of the ideas endorsed by this theory is that the price of money must be positive in order for the price level to be finite. The problem arises because of the inverse relationship established between the price of money and the absolute price level. On the assumption that money and output are two distinct masses, or stocks whose equilibrium determines the price level, this reciprocal relationship is unavoidable. A consequence of this peculiar conception of bank money is that it becomes part of the net wealth of the economy. The wealth effect becomes thus the 'necessary condition for the determinateness of the absolute price level' (Marty 1969: 106). In his review article, Marty (1969) rejects most of the propositions advanced by Pesek and Saving (1967). He also rejects Gurley and Shaw's (1960) distinction between inside and outside money as items which are and are not part of net wealth on the grounds that 'all types of money are part of net wealth' (Marty 1969: 109). His own point of view is that, although all types of money are part of net wealth, there are 'monetary arrangements under which alternative rates of growth of the nominal stock of money produce a wealth effect' (ibid.: 109), and others under which no wealth effects are produced. Although Marty rigorously points out that Pesek and Saving's use of the expression 'the price of money' is sometimes confusing, he does not seem to be able to propose a unique and unequivocal definition of this concept. In his text, the price of money is thus identified with the reciprocal of the general price level, with the opportunity cost of holding money or with the purchasing power of money over commodities. His effort to avoid confusion among these definitions is laudable, yet a correct analysis of monetary economics cannot be built on three alternative concepts of money.

Another idea that has been only imperfectly developed is that of bank money being part of net wealth. The terms fiat money, cash, demand deposits and time deposits are all considered as possible synonyms for bank money, the only criteria of demarcation being generically indicated as an empirical one. 'The question of what items can be called money is an empirical one and cannot be settled by the a priori theoretical arguments advanced by the authors [Pesek and Saving]' (ibid.: 110). In reality, the question raised by Marty is of a fundamental theoretical significance and can be settled only by recurring to both empirical observation and theoretical elaboration. A thorough observation of bank deposits shows that they are initially formed through the monetisation of output. If money were an asset created by and deposited with the banking system, income could not be the result of current production, and the very concept of monetary emission would be rather mysterious. Empirical observation, however, is sufficient to dismiss any remaining doubts: in our monetary systems, gold is entirely demonetised, and no other real good has been substituted for it. Analysing banks' double-entry book-keeping we notice that money as such defines simultaneously a positive and a negative deposit of the same amount and of the same agent. Banks issue money as a spontaneous acknowledgement of debt, which they lend to the economy. Money in itself is, at the same time, an asset and a liability. It is thus clear that money can have no positive value at all and is, therefore, not a part of net wealth.

The reasoning changes when, instead of considering money as such, we analyse bank deposits. In this case, we can correctly speak of net wealth because bank deposits are formed through the association of money and current output. What is deposited is income, and not money, which, flowing back to its point of emission, is instantaneously destroyed. Entering its numerical form, current output is transformed into income, which, deposited with the banking system, defines the total net wealth newly produced.

This result should not surprise the reader well acquainted with the problem of the real balance effect. As was pointed out by Kalecki back in 1944, an increase in the real value of the stock of money generated by a price decline could lead to an increase in the real value of possessions 'only to the extent to which money is backed by gold' (Kalecki, in Patinkin 1972: 169). Patinkin confirms this drastic limitation of the real balance effect on gold or government fiat money, even though he admits to a possible wealth effect produced by bank money 'if because of restricted entry the banking sector enjoys monopoly profits' (Patinkin 1972: 190). Now, modern monetary analysis provides a deeper understanding both of the nature of money and of the way it is issued by the banking system. The time has come to do away definitively with the asset conception of money and with its metaphysical implications. Once this is done, Patinkin's analysis can be amended and pushed to its ultimate consequence: money is at the origin of no real balance effect since, money being a flow, 'the difference between the value of the stock of money and the present value of the costs of maintaining that stock constant' (ibid.: 190) is always zero. Do things change when we move from money to income? Unlike money, income is a stock deposited with banks and having output as its proper object. Does this mean that bank deposits may be subject to a real balance effect? Not at all. The close relationship existing between income and output (the two being one and the same object) does not allow for any such effect. Once the dichotomic conception of the quantity theory of money is rejected, the absolute price level is no longer the reciprocal of the value of money. The entire theory of prices has to be reformulated in order to account for the valueless nature of bank money, the identity between money income and output, and the existence of a degree of freedom between prices and value compatible with their necessary macroeconomic identity.

Monetary and financial intermediations

Although they are two fundamentally different operations, money creation and credit are very closely interrelated, neither of them occurring without the other. Each monetary transaction implies both an emission of money and a transfer of income. Banks are thus asked to act simultaneously as monetary and financial intermediaries. This is obviously the case when they lend to consumers part of the current income saved by the public. Let us consider the example of a consumer, C, borrowing from his bank the income deposits of a client, S (saver). The loan entitles the borrower to a bank deposit in exchange for a financial claim, which has his future income as its object. The purchase of the borrower's financial debt is a monetary transaction and, as such, it requires the bank to intervene as a monetary intermediary. Through the creation of a money flow, the bank carries out the transaction between S and C. As a result of this instantaneous payment (purchase of the financial bond issued by C), the borrower obtains the income saved by S, i.e. a financial claim whose object is the output (financially) deposited on the assets side of the bank's balance sheet. Since the credit granted to C is backed by the income saved by S, and since income has necessarily a real object, it is easy to distinguish the financial from the monetary aspects of the transaction. It is perhaps slightly more difficult to appreciate fully that the credit implies the simultaneous destruction and creation of a bank deposit rather than its transfer from S to C. As pointed out by Schmitt and confirmed by double-entry book-keeping, S's bank deposit is destroyed and instantaneously replaced by another, equivalent, bank deposit created to the benefit of C. Of course, S is not at all penalised by the credit granted to C by the bank. His loss of a current bank deposit is compensated by the right he owns over an equivalent (or greater, if interests are taken into account) sum of future bank deposits.

The analysis we have sketched here does not essentially differ when no bank deposits are available before credit is granted. Let us verify this in the case where credit is related to production instead of consumption. Even though there is no pre-existing income out of which the credit can be financed, it remains true that no credit can be granted unless the bank has a positive deposit at its disposal. These two statements can be reconciled perfectly well as soon as the payment of the costs of production is taken into consideration. When a bank pays the factors of production (labour) on behalf of a firm, F, a new bank deposit is formed, whose object is the output financially entered (as a debt of F) on the assets side of the bank. The credit granted by the bank to F is therefore financed by the income earned by the factors of production and deposited on the liabilities side of the bank. This time, the distinction between monetary and financial intermediation is even clearer than in the case of the credit being granted to consumers. The transaction requiring the creation of money is the payment of the factors of production, whereas the financial intermediation of the bank is required in order to lend to F the income generated by production.

Present in every payment, money disappears (i.e. it is literally destroyed) as soon as the payment has taken place. What remains is an entry in the book-keeping of banks, an entry that defines an equivalent part of current output and that may be related to a creation, to a transfer or to a destruction of income. Like money, income is not material. Yet, since it results from the monetisation of production, it has a real content made up of physical output. Hence, whereas money, as a numerical form with no intrinsic value, is created at zero costs, income has a positive cost corresponding to the costs of production of current output. In practice, the creation of money is always related to income and, therefore, to output. As we have seen, this is so when money is used to pay the costs of production: the creation of money coincides with that of current income and with the emission of current output (which is instantaneously created, 'emitted' as an economic entity). This is also the case when money is used in the purchase of current output. The use of money allows the final expenditure of income (which is thus definitively destroyed), and the retransformation of current output into physical goods and services. Finally, this is again the case when income is transferred to firms (either through the purchase of bonds or through profits). Money intervenes as a numerical vehicle, and income is transformed into capital-time (to be subsequently retransformed into income and distributed as dividend and interest or converted into fixed capital).

Modern monetary macroeconomics must be founded on the correct distinction between money and credit. It should be clearly understood that banks cannot create credit but merely lend what is deposited with them, the creation being limited to nominal money or, more precisely, to the flow of payments. When it acts as a monetary intermediary, the bank creates the numerical form of transactions. What the bank cannot create is their real object, which can only be obtained through the intervention of the real world of production. The analysis of credit must therefore be completed by that of production. Before turning our attention to this subject, let us end the present chapter by an emblematic quotation from Schmitt's book on monetary sovereignty:

In popular representation as well as in many scientific texts, 'money' and 'credit' often get mixed up. ... True credit has an object that may be monetary or real. Now, even when it is the object of credit, money is created neither by the borrower nor by the lender. A loan implies the transfer of already existing income while the borrower merely replaces the lender as the owner of an income that is neither created nor destroyed in the process. ... Thus the analysis must be based on the incontrovertible fact that, while creating currency, banks lend a *zero* sum.

(Schmitt 1984a: 46–7; our translation)

4   Money and production

Is production merely a physical process of transformation, or can it also be viewed as a process of creation? If it were a process of physical transformation, would it still be possible to determine its result economically? And would there be a place for the definition of a net product? If we chose, instead, to express production in terms of value, would it be legitimate to consider output as the result of the implementation in (continuous or discontinuous) time of land, capital and labour? These are some of the questions we need to answer if we are to provide a satisfactory theory of production. Once again, our analysis will have to develop consistently with the nature of bank money, and with the laws governing the logical workings of a monetary system. To clarify the terms of the problem, we take up the distinction between 'circular process' and 'one-way process' theories of production, and we confront the theories pertaining to these two categories with the modern conception of production as a process of creation.

Production as a circular flow

Quesnay

The first example of production analysed (at least partially) as a circular process is the *Tableau économique* worked out by Quesnay. A medical surgeon, Quesnay was to become the leading member of a school known as *l'école physiocratique*, which propounded the idea that agriculture is the only truly productive activity since it is only thanks to the intervention of God that a net product can be derived from a process of physical transformation. Of the three classes into which society is divided by Quesnay, only the class of land labourers is productive; the class of craftsmen being defined as 'sterile' and the aristocracy (King, landlords and beneficiaries of tithes) being entirely supported by the other two. What Quesnay attempts to prove is that production is both a circular process through which the initial conditions are constantly reproduced and a process of creation, Nature being the source of a positive increase in physical output. Now, while it seems possible to argue for the circularity of production (at least from a physical point of view), the idea that God takes part in the process, allowing for the creation of new physical units of output, is clearly metaphysical. As shown by the laws of thermodynamics and by Einstein's theory of the equivalence between matter and energy, in the world of physics it is impossible to find an output greater than its corresponding input. Once fertility, sun heat, rain, astral influences and all the other conceivable factors are taken into account along with seeds and labour, the result of production can only be physically equivalent (in terms of matter and energy) to what has been put into it. Hence, from a physical point of view, agricultural production, from seeds to crops, is not essentially different from that of handicraft, from raw materials to manufactured goods. It is true, of course, that the work of artisans gives a new form to raw materials, yet the form is immaterial and can therefore not be the object of a real value. We seem thus to be led to the unavoidable conclusion that no net product can be accounted for within the context of Quesnay's *Tableau économique*.

Yet, the analysis can be pushed further. The *Tableau économique* is reproduced in Figure 4.1. The amounts quoted in brackets are the initial endowments of each class; M is manufactured goods, F is foodstuff and RM is raw materials. Farmers sell foodstuff to landlords and craftsmen for an amount of 2 milliards – which they transfer to landlords as tithes – and exchange 1 milliard of raw materials for 1 milliard of manufactured goods with the artisans. Having transformed raw materials into manufactured goods, craftsmen sell them to landlords – for 1 milliard – and to farmers for another milliard (the exact amount spent for the purchase of raw materials).

Let us consider the exchanges among landlords, craftsmen and farmers relating to the production of manufactured goods only. One interesting feature of Quesnay's representation is the fact that craftsmen sell their products for 2 milliards even though the materials that constitute them are worth only 1 milliard (Figure 4.2).

From a physical point of view, it is unrealistic to maintain that the manufactured goods sold by craftsmen are greater than the raw materials from which they have

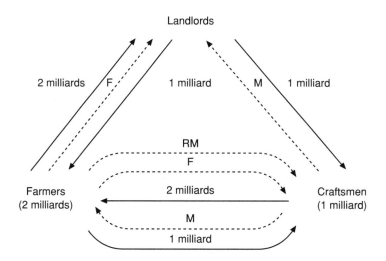

Figure 4.1 Quesnay's *Tableau économique*.

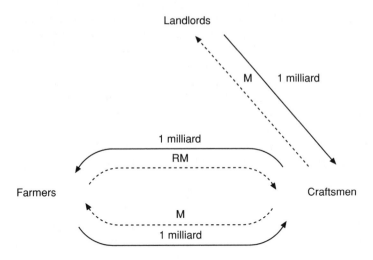

Figure 4.2 The production of manufactured goods.

been derived. The difference between the craftsmen's sale of manufactured goods and their purchase of raw materials can therefore be attributed only to the value added by their activity. We cannot help concluding that Quesnay's analysis is implicitly based on a labour theory of value. This conclusion is hardly acceptable, of course, since it would amount to saying that workers, whether craftsmen or farmers, are the true source of economic value. Instead of being sterile, the class of artisans would be as productive as that of farmers, God being a metaphysical entity and not a factor of production. Hence, it is not surprising that, according to a widespread belief, Quesnay's *Tableau* may be reinterpreted by means of input–output analysis. The condition for doing so is to accept the idea that, together with raw materials, foodstuff is part of the input necessary for the production of manufactured goods.

The concept introduced here is that of *productive consumption*, in which labour is considered both as an output (the activity of craftsmen being the result of their consumption of foodstuff) and as an input (the activity leading also to the production of manufactured goods). Now, much as we would like it to be the case, it would be hard to maintain that consumption pertains to the category of production. The consumption of foodstuff by manufacturers can only take place once its production process has been completed. Production and consumption are two distinct processes, and the result of consumption is the destruction of foodstuff and not the creation of manufactured goods. We would thus be wrong if we claimed that part of the initial input is consumed during the process of production and replaced by a new value created by labour. In fact, it would be very strange indeed to maintain – in line with the traditional interpretation of Quesnay's *Tableau économique* – that a positive value is generated through consumption. If foodstuff is partially consumed by craftsmen, it is destroyed, and it is not reasonable to believe that its value can survive its physical destruction. The creation of value is not a process through which value replaces matter and energy.

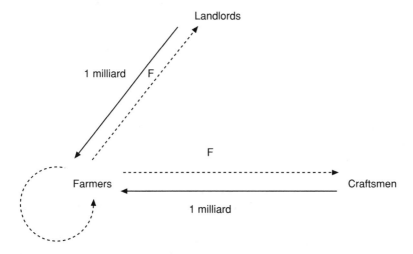

Figure 4.3 Productive consumption and value creation.

Interestingly, the concept of productive consumption introduced to explain how craftsmen may produce a final output worth 2 milliards is also implicitly used to justify the value attributed to the consumption goods (foodstuff) sold by farmers (Figure 4.3).

It is certain, in fact, that farmers act both as producers and as consumers of consumption goods. Their working activity is necessary, for example, to account for the transformation of seeds into vegetables, part of which enters their own consumption. If, as supposed by Quesnay, the value of foodstuff is globally equal to 2 milliards, and if farmers consume part of their products for their own subsistence, the remaining foodstuff sold to landlords and craftsmen is worth 2 milliards only if their consumption can be assimilated to a production of value. Hence, if we dismiss as metaphysical the hypothesis that value is generated by the consumption of physical input, we are confronted with the fact that both farmers and craftsmen are at the origin of positive value. This conclusion is strengthened by the observation that the value added by labour exceeds that of the foodstuff produced by Nature and consumed by farmers. Given Quesnay's numerical example, it is reasonable to assume that, farmers' initial endowment being of 2 milliards, this is the value attributed to the work of Nature. Now, once farmers' own consumption (equal to 1 milliard) has been taken into account, it appears that the value of the foodstuff sold to landlords and craftsmen – as well as that consumed by farmers – is composed as follows:

1/3 × 2 milliards (value produced by Nature) + 1/3 × 1 milliard (value added by labour) = 1 milliard

In sum, landlords and craftsmen obtain foodstuff whose value is the product of Nature for 2/3 of 2 milliards and the product of labour for 2/3 of 1 milliard. It thus follows that farmers' self-consumption destroys a product of Nature worth 1/3 of

2 milliards while their working activity creates a value of 1 milliard. Hence, if productive consumption were an acceptable assumption, we might explain at most an increase in value of 1/3 of 2 milliards. Even if it made sense to maintain that physical consumption generates value, we would have to admit that the difference between 1 milliard and 1/3 of 2 milliards may be accounted for only if labour is recognised as a genuine source of value.

Now, as labour does not add anything physical (matter or energy) to current output, it can be argued that production is a peculiar human activity and not a mere process of physical transformation. As a consequence, it is also possible to maintain that, always from an economic point of view, the entire output is a net product. The physical equivalence between input and output does not explain any net product so that, if human labour did not enter the process, production would be reduced to a circular repetition, leaving the product totally unexplained. This means that, in economic terms, produced output has to be seen as the result of an act of creation. Of course, this is not to say that human activity may be the source of a physical creation of matter or energy. As we have already repeatedly observed, from a physical point of view production is nothing more than a process of transformation. Considered from this particular point of view, labour itself is energy. As such, it enters the physical process of transformation and plays no original role in the determination of the product. But labour is not merely a physical activity through which energy is transformed into matter or matter into energy. Thanks to human labour, the process of transformation acquires its full significance, matter and energy being given a *new utility-form*. Men create by conceiving a new form and imposing it on matter and energy. It is as a result of this process that the product appears to be net. '[P]roduire signifie couler une matière ou une énergie dans une forme-utilité préconçue, une sorte de moule, imaginé par l'homme' (Guitton 1984: 15).

Even if largely incomplete and partially contradictory, Quesnay's analysis has the merit of allowing labour to play a significant role in the production process. The circular vision of this process, traditionally attributed to Quesnay, is, in reality, limited to its physical aspect and does not give the monetary aspect of the circuit the attention it deserves. Is this to say that the analysis of production developed in terms of input–output relationships will lead nowhere unless it is substantially modified to account for the particular role played by labour? Let us try to answer this question by referring to the works of the most serious and famous supporters of input–output analysis.

From Leontief to Pasinetti

The starting point of Leontief's analysis of the input–output relationship is national accounting. In particular, he refers to the receipts and expenditures account relative to interindustrial sales and purchases, i.e. to goods and services that flow into and out of firms as inputs and outputs of their process of production. Evaluating outputs by the receipts that firms obtain from selling their products, and inputs by the expenditures that they have to face for the purchase of the goods and services entering production, Leontief sets up a table of interindustrial relationships based on the principle that 'each revenue item (as defined above) of an enterprise or household must reappear as an outlay item in the account of some other enterprise or household' (Leontief 1951: 12). As it is assumed that output is sold entirely to firms (or individuals), it is obvious that what is entered as output (income or revenue) by each enterprise appears also as input (expenditures or outlays) of the others, columns simply mirroring rows. As is easily verified, the table of interindustrial transactions is already fully complete once its rows have been written down, no further analysis being required for the determination of columns (Table 4.1).

We have reproduced Leontief's first table here with the precise intent of showing that no formal critique can be addressed to it as long as it is used to represent the distribution of income and expenditures among industries. To this extent, Table 4.1 is perfectly consistent with the principle of the necessary equality of sales and purchases, which is verified both at a global (sum of rows and columns) and at an 'individual' (sum of rows and columns for each single agent) level. Unfortunately, this is a point that has not been sufficiently investigated by Leontief and his followers. Leontief was not even aware of the fact that the equality of expenditures and income is necessarily true at both levels. He actually maintained that although 'the credit and the debit side of the account for each particular enterprise or household will not necessarily balance, the total expenditures of all the firms and households must, for obvious reasons, equal the sum total of their combined revenues' (ibid.: 14). Had he realised that, independently of their distribution among

Table 4.1 Accounting scheme for description of interindustrial transactions

Distribution of outlays (input)	Distribution of output (revenue)					
	1	2	3	4	5	Total
1	–	v_{21}	v_{31}	v_{41}	v_{51}	$\sum_{i=1}^{i=5} v_{i1}$
2	v_{12}	–	v_{32}	v_{42}	v_{52}	$\sum_{i=1}^{i=5} v_{i2}$
3	v_{13}	v_{23}	–	v_{43}	v_{53}	$\sum_{i=1}^{i=5} v_{i3}$
4	v_{14}	v_{24}	v_{34}	–	v_{54}	$\sum_{i=1}^{i=5} v_{i4}$
5	v_{15}	v_{25}	v_{35}	v_{45}	–	$\sum_{i=1}^{i=5} v_{i5}$
Total	$\sum_{k=1}^{k=5} v_{1k}$	$\sum_{k=1}^{k=5} v_{2k}$	$\sum_{k=1}^{k=5} v_{3k}$	$\sum_{k=1}^{k=5} v_{4k}$	$\sum_{k=1}^{k=5} v_{5k}$	S

Note
v, revenue (output); i, the different firms considered as purchasers; k, the different firms considered as sellers; S, the grand total of all transactions.

firms or households, sales and purchases are the terms of an identity, he would have developed his theory along different lines, leaving aside any attempt to build it on the principles of neoclassical analysis. This is all the more disappointing in that his own initial analysis of national accounting has nothing to do with the framework of relative prices. Let us now contemplate his fourth table, which is reproduced here as Table 4.2.

If we consider this as a representation of the relationship existing between income distribution and income expenditures, and not as an input–output table, and if we do away with double counting (as suggested by Leontief), we observe that the total income earned by households is spent for the purchase of goods and services produced by firms. In fact, '[t]he value added in business is equal in its magnitude to v_{bh} (i.e., the services contributed to business by households), and this is equal, under static conditions, to the value of goods and services supplied by business to households (v_{hb})' (ibid.: 18). According to this analysis, the income earned by households defines the production of firms, whose output is entirely net. 'The item v_{hb} ($= v_{bh}$) is defined as the net product of industry. ... On such a net basis national income is v_{hb}, which equals the value added, v_{bh}' (ibid.: 18). Two interesting suggestions are thus conveyed by Leontief's table on the interrelations between business and household accounts (Table 4.2). The first is that the total income is necessarily spent for the purchase of final output; the second that national income is generated by the work done by households. If the Russian economist had been aware of these two suggestions, his analysis would have emphasised the particular role played by human labour in the economic process of production. Likewise, it would have stressed the role played by money, and led to a monetary concept of production, output and labour.

The missing element in Leontief's table is the financial market. It is only when this market is introduced that the law of the identity between sales and purchases asserts itself. To understand it fully, we need to have a clear perception of the nature of bank money and of its relationship with physical output. From this point of view, Leontief's analysis lacks consistency. He starts by evaluating inputs and outputs in monetary terms (i.e. as results from his first tables, in terms of expenditures and income), then chooses as theoretical referent the neoclassical framework of general equilibrium and comes up with three systems of equations

Table 4.2 Interrelations between business and household accounts

Distribution of outlays (input)	Distribution of output (revenue)		
	H (households)	B (business)	Total
H (households)	v_{hh}	v_{bh}	$v_{hh} + v_{bh}$
B (business)	v_{hb}	v_{bb}	$v_{hb} + v_{bb}$
Total	$v_{hh} + v_{hb}$	$v_{bh} + v_{bb}$	S

Note

v, revenue (output); h, household; b, business; S, the grand total of all transactions.

Table 4.3 Flows of commodities in physical terms

	w		i		t		
w	240	+	90	+	120	=	450
i	12	+	6	+	3	=	21
t	18	+	12	+	30	=	60
	↓		↓		↓		
	450 (w)		21 (i)		60 (t)		

Note
w, wheat; i, iron; t, turkey.

where goods and services are expressed in physical units. In the first system, derived from the input–output table, equations 'describe the fact that the total output of each industry (measured in physical terms) equals the sum total of the amounts of its products consumed by all other industries' (ibid.: 35). The second system introduces relative prices, while the third 'describes the technical relation between the physical output of an industry and the input of all the different cost elements absorbed in production. In short, it describes the industrial production function' (ibid.: 36). Obviously, Leontief does not realise that the monetary and the neoclassical are worlds apart, and that, by abandoning the first to marry the second, he denies his analysis any chance of describing the reality of economics.

Let us go through the main shortcomings of input–output analysis by referring to Pasinetti's very clear exposition of 1977. Referring to the numerical example used by Sraffa (1960) in *Production of Commodities by Means of Commodities* (and changing pigs into turkeys), Pasinetti represents the input–output table of an economy producing wheat, iron and turkeys as follows (Table 4.3).

It is important to observe, with Pasinetti, that the commodities of each column are heterogeneous, so that 'the numbers appearing in any column cannot be added', whereas in each row 'there appear physically homogeneous quantities' (Pasinetti 1977: 36). Table 4.3 reproduces Sraffa's self-replacing state, a situation in which the quantities of wheat, iron and turkeys available at the beginning of the process are entirely used up in the production of wheat, iron and turkeys. Inputs are equal to outputs, and production is pictured as a circular flow. Things seem to change when we move from Table 4.3 to Table 4.4.

Although the system represented here is still in a stationary state, a surplus is shown as the product of the final sector. How is this result obtained? Apparently, it is the logical consequence of the fact that commodities 'will serve in part as means of production and in part as consumption goods for those working in each industry' (ibid.: 36). Hence, the formation of a positive surplus is derived from the distinction 'between an economic activity of production and an economic activity of consumption' (ibid.: 36). Now, the fundamental question here is whether or not a net output can be derived from production. Let us first consider production as a physical process of transformation. From this point of view, what is consumed by workers (as a means of subsistence) is transformed into energy and is present

Table 4.4 Flows of commodities and labour services

	w	i	t	Final sector		
w	186	54	30	180	=	450
i	12	6	3	–	=	21
t	9	6	15	30	=	60
Final sector	18	12	30	–	=	60
	↓	↓	↓			
	450	21	60			

Note
w, wheat; i, iron; t, turkey.

as such in the final output. Apart from what is lost in the process (but preserved in the physical macrosystem), it is thus logically impossible for output to be physically greater than input. The passage from Table 4.3 to Table 4.4 shows that if there is substitutability among wheat, iron, turkeys and labour, and if labour can partially replace these inputs as assumed by Pasinetti, production may be viewed either as a flow of commodities or as a flow of commodities and (physical) labour services. Thus conceived, labour is not essentially different from any other physical input, and should be accounted for accordingly. In particular, the column and the row corresponding to the final sector should be modified, the process leading to the reproduction of physical labour as well as to that of wheat, iron and turkeys (Table 4.5).

From a physical viewpoint, there are no reasons for considering labour to be on a different footing from the other three inputs. Hence, the production of wheat, iron, turkeys and labour services implies the consumption of wheat, iron, turkeys and labour. For what reason should physical labour be given a different status and its consumption alone considered as productive? Once it is admitted that 'the output in excess of these industrial requirements (the part of output which is required as input by all the industries) is delivered to the final sector for consumption', and that 'from the final sector, in turn, labor services flow to the various industries for their production needs' (ibid.: 37–8), does it not clearly follow that labour's consumption is as productive as that of any other input?

Table 4.5 Flows of commodities and labour services

	w	i	t	Final sector		
w	186	54	30	180	=	450
i	12	6	3	–	=	21
t	9	6	15	30	=	60
Final sector	168	12	30	–	=	210
	↓	↓	↓	↓		
	450	21	60	210		

Note
w, wheat; i, iron; t, turkey.

A totally different result could be reached if production were conceived of as an economic process, and labour as a very peculiar input, entirely distinct from the set of physical inputs. Before developing this alternative approach, let us mention a major shortcoming of traditional input–output analysis by referring to the work of Sraffa.

In his book, the Italian-born economist represents a three-commodity economy, as shown in Table 4.6. Contrary to what Pasinetti does in his 1977 publication, Sraffa uses the sign '+' among physically heterogeneous goods such as wheat, iron and pigs. Is he allowed to do so? Not in the least, unless he can positively argue to have been able to make them homogeneous. Is this the case? Let us proceed with caution. Sraffa himself does not introduce the '=' sign between the two components of each row immediately, but uses an arrow instead. This shows that he is perfectly aware of the fact that technical methods of production do not allow the writing of equations before their terms are made homogeneous. However, this makes the use of the '+' sign among iron, wheat and pigs even more astonishing. Only the use of the conjunction 'and' would have been consistent with that of the arrow, the mathematical addition of wheat and pigs (iron and wheat, pigs and iron) being a perfect nonsense if these three goods are expressed in purely physical terms. But, is it likely that such a rigorous and meticulous author as Sraffa missed this point? Sraffa himself dispels all doubts immediately. His use of the '+' sign is justified, in fact, by his assumption that wheat, iron and pigs are made homogeneous through the determination of '[t]he exchange-values which ensure replacement all round' (Sraffa 1960: 4). Given the methods of production implicit in Sraffa's numerical example, the system is in a self-replacing state if these exchange values 'are 10 qr. wheat = 1 t. iron = 2 pigs' (ibid.: 4). Thus, if the three commodities are exchanged according to these values, the production of each of them equals its total consumption. Exchanges may not respect these terms, of course. Yet, if they do respect them, the system can circularly renew itself in a process in which total inputs are necessarily equal to total outputs.

The aim of Sraffa's first chapter is to show that his system of technical relationships allows the determination of exchange values 'which if adopted restore the initial position' (ibid.: 4). In this respect, his approach does not seem to differ substantially from that of the Neoclassics. Whether we refer to production (following Sraffa) or to circulation (as initially done by Walras), exchange is taken to be the operation through which (relative) values are determined and real goods made homogeneous. The same critique developed against the neoclassical attempt to determine relative prices therefore applies here. In particular, we can reiterate

Table 4.6 Sraffa's self-replacing state

240 qr. wheat	+	12 t. iron	+	18 pigs	→	450 qr. wheat
90 qr. wheat	+	6 t. iron	+	12 pigs	→	21 t. iron
120 qr. wheat	+	3 t. iron	+	30 pigs	→	60 pigs

Note
qr., quarter (28 lbs); t., tons.

the observation that neither Walras's Law (in GEA) nor the self-replacing state (in Sraffa's theory) can be assumed to hold *before* equilibrium has been reached. Like Walras, Sraffa can make good of his system of equations only if he assumes that '[s]ince in the aggregate of the equations the same quantities occur on both sides, any one of the equations can be inferred from the sum of the others' (ibid.: 5). As he notes, '[t]his formulation presupposes the system's being in a self-replacing state' (ibid.: 5). But if the values allowing for the system being in a self-replacing state have to be determined by the equations of production, how is it possible to eliminate any of them before the self-replacing state has actually been determined? If these values are still unknown, the system is entirely undetermined and no equation can even be written down. In Sraffa's simplified example, the condition for the use of the '+' sign among wheat, iron and pigs is the determination of their exchange values. However, these values have themselves to be determined. To assume them as given would amount to begging the question. Surprising as it may be, this is precisely what is implicitly done by Sraffa when he presumes to be authorised to add wheat to iron and pigs. In reality, this addition presupposes the commensurability of the three commodities, which presupposes the determination of their (relative) values, which presupposes the possibility of adding wheat to iron and pigs. A good example of vicious circularity, this way of reasoning is emblematic of the situation that theorists are trapped into when they try to determine values through direct exchange (whether on the commodity or on the factors market). The main difficulty here is related to the possibility of expressing real goods in a uniform unit of measure. As we have endeavoured to prove in the third chapter of this work, goods cannot be taken to be numbers. Goods can be associated with (or integrated into) numbers, it is true, but this does not mean that numbers are an intrinsic property of real goods. Unfortunately, this is what is assumed by neoclassical analysis as well as by Sraffa's. The tenants of these theories are thus led to develop a hopelessly and viciously circular approach that is doomed to failure.

As far as the analysis of surplus is concerned, Sraffa's point of view is particularly interesting in his unpublished working notes. In those classified as *Item 161*, we can read the following passage:

> [f]inally, if one attempts to take an entirely objective point of view, the very conception of a surplus melts away. For if we take this natural science point of view, we must start by assuming that for every effect there must be sufficient cause, that the causes are identical with their effects, and that there can be nothing in the effect which was not in the causes: in our case, there can be no product for which there has not been an equivalent cost, and all costs (= expenses) must be necessary to produce it.
>
> (Sraffa *Item 161*)

The message conveyed by this quotation is clear: from the natural science point of view, no net surplus can ever exist since the effect (output) cannot exceed its causes (input). And yet there can be little doubt that 'the study of "surplus product" is the true object of economics' (ibid.). How are we to determine net output then? Reference to the expenses that are 'necessary' for producing a given commodity and those that are not is of no help since the concept of 'necessity' is either too wide or too narrow to allow for a rigorous determination of the surplus. The way followed by Sraffa in his main work is also not satisfactory since it amounts to assuming the existence of a physical surplus – in open contradiction to his statement of *Item 161* – and to introducing the rate of profit as an additional unknown in a system whose very existence is based on the determination of the variables, relative values and rate of profit, which it is supposed to determine. Now, Sraffa usefully suggests that 'the surplus may be the effect of outside causes' (ibid.). What these causes might well be is left unexplained by the editor of the *Works and Correspondence of David Ricardo* (Ricardo 1951–5). Moreover, his conception of labour does not help us in our quest for them. Instead of looking at human labour as at an original input, entirely distinct from real goods, he enters it in his system of equations as a physical quantity and expresses wages in real terms. By doing so, he reduces production to a circular process of physical transformation in which commodities are actually produced by means of commodities.

Sraffa's analysis has marked the economic thought of the 1960s. So numerous are the works devoted to it throughout the world that it would be arduous to mention them all. Let us simply observe that his input–output analysis has appealed to Marxists and Keynesians as well as to Neoclassics. Among the leading members of this last group, we would like to mention Hicks, his own version of the circular approach to production giving us the opportunity to reconsider the main points of input–output analysis.

In his 1973 book on *Capital and Time*, Hicks defines production as 'a scheme by which a flow of inputs is converted into a flow of outputs' (Hicks 1973: 14). Let us concentrate our attention on the idea implied in the concept of conversion. Traditionally, the term conversion denotes a change in form, character or function. In Hicks's quotation, it is used as a synonym for transformation and conveys the idea that production is a process by which a stream of inputs is changed into a stream of outputs. Yet, nothing is said about how this transformation actually takes place. To avoid the difficulty of comparing a whole flow of physically heterogeneous outputs with a whole flow of physically heterogeneous inputs, let us simplify the problem by assuming that one single output is obtained from a process of transformation of a single input. If it is proved that our single output can be derived, through conversion, from our single input, then a case could be made for production to be defined and analysed along the lines proposed by Hicks. This seems indeed to be the case as Hicks assumes from the beginning that 'inputs and outputs can be made homogeneous by taking them in value terms' (ibid.: 14), i.e. by measuring them in money prices. But how are these prices determined? This is the fundamental question that needs answering if Hicks's analysis is to be considered more than a simple *petitio principii*. We are all well aware that money prices exist, but this is precisely why it is so important to explain their formation instead of taking it for granted. It is only fair to say that Hicks never avoided the problem. As a matter of fact, his very starting point is the concept of value, and every economist knows how much effort he put into elaborating a revised version of the neoclassical theory of value. However, for the case in point, the neoclassical determination of relative prices is of little help. In the absence of relative exchanges, the relative price of our single input is a figment of one's imagination, and so is the relative price of the single output. Hicks seems to be aware of this difficulty because he introduces a hypothesis that, if accepted, would eliminate the problem at its roots. He assumes, in fact, that 'the prices of inputs and outputs are given (and are the same whatever the date to which they refer)' (ibid.: 14). Now, since it cannot be explained how these prices are determined, this assumption is tantamount to saying that inputs and outputs are essentially one and the same object.

Let us consider our simplified example. If the price of the input is 10 and that of the output is 11, and if these prices are assumed to be constant, then input and output are entered in a fixed relationship. It is thus always possible to pass from one to the other by multiplying or dividing one of the two by a given (and constant) coefficient, c. But if it is always true that output equals $c \cdot$ input, there is no longer any reason to consider input and output as two distinct objects. Hicks's assumption therefore has the double effect of making input and output comparable, and reducing production to a process of self-reproduction. Unfortunately, this cannot be considered as a faithful reproduction of reality. Input–output analysis has the merit to bring to the fore the main difficulties of any economic theory that attempts to explain production as a process of physical transformation. One of these difficulties is due to heterogeneity (of inputs, of outputs and between outputs and inputs), the other to the introduction of labour. In his attempt to explain production, Hicks overcomes these obstacles by assuming that all original inputs and all final outputs are homogeneous, and by calling 'the homogeneous input Labour' (ibid.: 37). He then immediately adds that 'no characteristic of actual labour comes into the argument, except that it is an input into the productive process' (ibid.: 37). What is the message conveyed by this sentence? Literally, it could mean that 'labour' is merely an alternative way of designating input terminologically. Any other term would obviously serve, and the whole exercise would substantially amount to nothing. Of course, it is hard to believe that this is indeed what Hicks is telling us. Alternatively, we could interpret his message as the claim that it is labour 'in general', irrespective of the great diversities existing among the various kinds of physical and intellectual activities of human beings, that must be taken as the only 'original' input. In this case, however, we are faced with a major problem that Hicks seems to have overlooked, namely whether labour may logically be considered as an input at all. According to classical economists, labour is the source of value. Keynes defines it as the sole factor of production. None of them considers labour to be a real good. Now, it is only if labour could be identified with a real good that it would be meaningful to include it in the category of inputs. On the contrary, if labour does not pertain to the set of real goods and services, it is logically impossible to consider it as a physical input. Hicks takes it for granted that labour can be assimilated with a real good. Having chosen relative exchanges as the theoretical framework of his analysis, he believes that he can relate goods (physical output) to labour in order to determine wages as an input–output price ratio – an operation that requires labour and output to be the terms of a relative exchange. But is this a legitimate query? Is it legitimate to take labour for a real good? Not in the least. Labour is a human activity; goods are the result of this activity. Now, as the result itself is not material (labour gives a new *form* to matter and energy but does not create any), the activity cannot be assimilated to a physical quantity. Labour is not a quantity of matter and energy, which may be transformed into another, equivalent quantity called output. From a purely physical point of view, labour is an activity that is energy consuming, but even from this particular point of view it would be wrong to claim that the energy lost is to be found, albeit in another form, in the final output. In economics, labour is not merely perceived as a physical or mental activity, but as an economic activity consisting in creating new utility-forms for matter and energy.

Traditional input–output analysis is unable to account for a process of creation, whether in physical or in economic terms. Physically because it is bound to respect Lavoisier's law of conservation; economically because labour cannot enter a physical input–output relationship. As far as the analysis of labour is concerned, a more promising investigation is suggested by Pasinetti (1993) in *Structural Economic Dynamics*.

By reversing Sraffa's starting point, Pasinetti sets out to develop a pure labour production economy. 'Sraffa started by characterising his economic system as "production of commodities by means of commodities"; we start by characterising it as "production of commodities by means of labour alone" ' (Pasinetti 1993: 16). As claimed on the cover page, Pasinetti's book 'is a theoretical investigation of the influence of human learning on the development through time of a "pure labour" economy'. The same introductory note ends by emphasising that, as a result of this investigation, '[i]nstitutional and social learning, know-how, and the diffusion of knowledge emerge as the decisive factors accounting for the success and failure of industrial societies'. What sounds particularly interesting in Pasinetti's declaration of intentions is the awareness that human labour plays a role in the process of production, which cannot be assimilated to that of physical inputs and capital. Know-how, advance in knowledge and creativity are peculiar to human labour. Thus, if analysed from this point of view, production can be seen as a process of creation and not only as a physical transformation. However, this interpretation remains latent in Pasinetti's analysis of a pure labour economy. He never goes as far as to assume labour as the sole factor of a process in which production is perceived as a creation. In his system, human labour (assumed to be uniform in quality) is a physical quantity entering the process of production as any other physical input. The possibility of maintaining that output altogether is a net surplus is, thus, totally alien to Pasinetti's analysis. And yet it is remarkable that the Italian economist sticks to a model in which income is entirely defined in terms of wages and the natural wage rate 'represents each labourer's equal share into the net national product' (ibid.: 24). Had he developed his analysis further along these lines, he might have contributed to setting up a monetary theory of production.

Pasinetti's crucial choice is that of measuring labour in physical terms. Even if it is not explicitly mentioned in his 1993 book, wages are expressed in real terms, and prices 'turn out to be proportional to labour coefficients: quantities of labour are multiplied by the wage rate' (ibid.: 19). His theory suffers from the same shortcomings as the traditional labour theory elaborated by the Classics. Physical heterogeneity of labour services is a problem that we cannot get rid of simply by wishing it away. Nor can we hope to determine money prices simply by adopting a commodity as *numéraire* and 'closing the price system with the equation: $p_k = 1$' (ibid.: 18). Note that Pasinetti seems aware of this difficulty or, at least, of the difficulty of fulfilling the conditions of price determination when choosing a physical *numéraire*. In his fifth chapter, he refers to the important asymmetry existing 'between monetary regimes in which the numéraire of the price system is physical, and monetary regimes in which the numéraire of the price system is a purely nominal unit of account' (ibid.: 63–4), and he tries to explain 'why industrial economies have through time all gone over from physical to purely nominal numéraires' (ibid.: 76). What is curious in Pasinetti's approach to money is that he considers the monetary *numéraire* to be 'a unit of account made up of a basket of various commodities' (ibid.: 76). He is thus trapped between two incompatible conceptions of money: if the *numéraire* is purely a unit of account it cannot be a commodity or a basket of commodities, and if it is a commodity or a basket of commodities it cannot be a purely numerical unit. Pasinetti does not realise that his choice of expressing wages 'in terms of the monetary unit of account' (ibid.: 76) is logically inconsistent with using a dynamic standard commodity 'as the key standard of reference' (ibid.: 77). His choice of a monetary unit of account does not involve any fundamental revision of his theory, which rests on a dichotomous perception of reality in which monetary magnitudes are thought to be purely nominal and essentially independent of real ones. Hence, while his intuition as to the need for the *numéraire* to be introduced as a numerical form is certainly correct, his analysis is still set up in real terms and does not provide the basis for the construction of a truly monetary theory. As a consequence, Pasinetti's theory of production differs only marginally from those developed by Leontief and Sraffa, and suffers from the same drawbacks. It is only fair to recognise, however, that Pasinetti is one of the few economists to have consistently attempted to develop a labour theory of production after the Classics. His endeavour deserves all the more credit as it emphasises the need for a new approach in which labour is made to play an entirely original role with respect to physical inputs. The definition of the whole product as a net output is related to this conception of labour and to the possibility of moving from its physical measure to its expression in monetary terms.

Production as a one-way process

Based on the concept of (marginal) productivity, this vision of production may be traced back to the works of Jevons, Menger, Marshall, Böhm-Bawerk and Wiser. It is to Walras and Pareto, however, that we owe the explicit formalisation of this approach into what was to become known as the production function. Let us therefore start our analysis from the work of the founding father of general equilibrium theory.

Walras analyses production in the same way as he analyses exchange, trying to determine the equilibrium prices of productive services and 'formulate as exact an idea as possible of the mechanism of free competition in the domain of production' (Walras 1984: 218). Like relative prices of products, prices of productive services are determined by equating their supply and demand, the overall system of exchange and production being in equilibrium when 'the selling prices of products equal the cost of the productive services that enter into them' (ibid.: 224). As clearly stated by Walras, according to the law of the establishment of equilibrium prices in production, for the market to be in equilibrium *'it is necessary and sufficient (1) that the effective demand for each service and each product be equal to its effective supply at these prices; and (2) that the selling price of the products be equal to the cost of the services employed in making them'* (ibid.: 253–4). Without entering further into Walras's analysis, let us observe that the French economist himself was well aware of the difficulties related to the determination of equilibrium in production, particularly if we refer to the process of *tâtonnement* (groping). His own solution, based on the assumption that entrepreneurs, landowners, workers and capitalists use *tickets* (*bons*) to represent the successive quantities of products and services 'which are first determined at random' (ibid.: 242), is hardly satisfactory. In the case of production, the entire process of groping towards equilibrium is even more unrealistic than in the case of pure exchange, the use of tickets being added to the intervention of the auctioneer. However, this is not the main cause of worry by far. The introduction of a new condition of equilibrium – the equality between the price of products and that of productive services – is a source of much greater trouble because it reinforces the logical indeterminacy of relative prices. As claimed by Walras, equilibrium in exchange and production requires prices to result from the simultaneous solution of three sets of equations. The first set is made up of the equations determining equilibrium on the factors market, i.e. 'a state in which the effective demand and offer of productive services are equal and there is a stationary current price in the market for these services' (ibid.: 224). The second set is that of the equations allowing for equilibrium to be realised also on the products market, i.e. for 'a state in which the effective demand and supply of products are also equal and there is a stationary current price in the products market' (ibid.: 224). Finally, the third set, which relates specifically to equilibrium in production, defines the necessary equality between the price of products and the cost of productive services. The whole equilibrium system is thus made up of the following sets of equations:

1 Supply of products = Demand for products.
2 Supply of productive services = Demand for productive services.
3 Price of products = Cost of productive services.

Three sets of equations to determine one set of prices is two too many. Now, even if it were possible to apply Walras's Law during the process of groping after equilibrium – thus reducing the sets of independent equations by one – our system would still be overdetermined. The unknowns being reduced to only one set of relative prices (of products in terms of productive services), the system should also be reduced to one set of independent equations. This not being the case, we are bound to conclude that Walras's system is hopelessly undetermined.

As we shall see in the last section of this chapter, a solution can be found provided we are prepared to follow Walras's intuition as to the possible, instantaneous transformation of productive services into products. However, this would take us far away from the realm of GEA, towards a world in which current output's prices are determined independently of the relationship between output and productive services. Before moving further on this path, let us look into the neoclassical theory of production.

On production functions

Analysed from a neoclassical point of view, production is seen as a one-way process taking place through time and yielding results thanks to the implementation of one or more factors of production. Traditionally, neoclassical analysis considers production as a function of land, labour, capital and time. Thus, in its usual acceptation, a production function is a mathematical representation of the rate of production of a single output in terms of capital and labour (and, when possible, some other primary inputs). As is well known, the possibility of establishing a functional relationship among different inputs depends on that of considering them as homogeneous. The problem is indeed multiple. Capital and labour themselves must be shown to be homogeneous. Thus, it must be shown that capital goods can be aggregated in a single quantity and that complex labour can harmlessly be reduced to the same indistinct category of human labour. None of these operations may be assumed away. Moreover, if it were possible to aggregate capital goods and reduce labour to a single quantity, one would still need to show how capital and labour can be part of the same homogeneous set.

Instrumental goods are physically heterogeneous, so are consumption goods, investment goods, etc. Unless they are made homogeneous through monetisation (which is precisely what production function theories lack), they cannot enter even the simplest of functions. And it should be obvious to everybody that this difficulty cannot be overcome simply 'by assumption'. 'The equipment, of course, is heterogeneous. This has often been thought to be a difficulty, but – as is common practice, a practice that has been followed in this book – I shall assume it away' (Hicks 1973: 178). However much we may admire the work of Hicks, we cannot accept his argument simply on the grounds that it is in line with common practice. Scientific practice requires logical evidence, and rejects 'assuming away' as a substitute for 'explaining'. The heterogeneity problem is the first that our science needs to tackle. Classical as well as neoclassical economists are perfectly aware of this fact, as is shown by the importance they give to the search for a consistent theory of value. Although none of their solutions is entirely satisfactory, they are emblematic of the great efforts spent on explaining what common practice assumes away.

Finally, as observed by Bliss, the problem is not limited to inputs, but extends also to output. 'If the production function is to describe the productive activities of the entire economy, and if that economy can, and typically does, produce more than one kind of final output, then is there not a parallel problem of justifying the representation of Y by a single number?' (Bliss 1975: 170–1). Bliss tries to overcome this difficulty by assuming stationary equilibrium and resorting to the chain-index method. Now, the stationary equilibrium hypothesis is admittedly very restrictive, and the chain-index method can be applied only if other limiting conditions are satisfied. One of these conditions is that aggregation must be a real possibility of the model. 'The chain-index method of aggregation is a natural and theoretically reasonable method when aggregation is possible' (ibid.: 194). By this Bliss means in particular that there is a whole set of special instances to which a theory must conform in order to allow for the aggregation of capital goods (produced means of production). In the case of general aggregation, these instances are so peculiar 'that the theory gives no support to widespread use of the approach' (ibid.: 162). If we are prepared to assume that the relation between capital and output is independent of the composition of final output, that there is no capital accumulation and that the economy consists only of fully integrated production sectors (whose respective aggregate capitals may not be comparable), it seems, on the contrary, that aggregation may come under our theoretical grasp. In reality, it may equally be claimed that, on the whole, Bliss's solution rests on too many restrictive assumptions to be considered as valid evidence that production functions can be used to describe 'the productive activities of the entire economy' (ibid.: 170).

Fundamentally, the freedom to accept Bliss's assumptions is more apparent than real. Logic is compelling. No economic theory of production can ever be built if its factors are bound to remain heterogeneous. Hence, for a theory to be eligible as a means of explaining reality, homogeneity must be proved to be always possible under any circumstances. The more restrictive the hypotheses that are introduced, the less their validity and their chance to be a useful instrument of knowledge. Does this mean that production functions must be definitively set apart?

As Hicks puts it: '[t]he question is this. If production (in some sense) is X, labour (in some sense) is L, capital (in some sense) is K, is there any relation $X = F(L, K)$ which can be expected to hold, even very approximately, in a closed system, under a given technology?' (Hicks 1965: 293). The famous Fellow of Nuffield College answers in the affirmative. He starts by showing that a production function can indeed be formally construed whenever we want to compare stationary equilibrium positions, and goes on to prove that, on some strong assumptions, a production function may be devised even for the period of adjustment between equilibrium stationary states. Let us confine our analysis to the first step of Hicks's logical exercise.

When comparing two stationary equilibria, he assumes that '[p]roduction has been increased by the change in technology; the supply of labour (by assumption) is unchanged; and the supply of capital is unchanged' (ibid.: 297). In order to reconcile the fact that the two stationary states are equilibria of the same economy with the hypothesis of technological change, Hicks maintains that capital has to be expressed in terms of value. He then writes an equation in which the capital–labour ratio is reduced to an expression 'in terms of technological coefficients *for a given technique*' (ibid.: 298). How does he manage to do so? How can he go from values to technical coefficients? The answer is to be found in the way he works out his elementary growth equilibrium model, in particular in the assumption that prices depend on fixed coefficients of production [the quantities of factors 'that are needed *in equilibrium*' (ibid.: 137)]. The feasibility of a production function thus depends on establishing a direct relationship between physical inputs and physical outputs. Let us write down Hicks's price equations:

$$p_1 = qa_1 + wb_1 \qquad\qquad p_2 = qa_2 + wb_2$$

where p_1 is the price of the consumption good, p_2 is the price of the capital good, w is the wage of labour, q is the earnings of the capital good, a_1 (capital) and b_1 (labour) are the production coefficients in consumption good production and a_2 (capital) and b_2 (labour) are the production coefficients in capital good production.

It is immediately clear that price determination depends on the determination of the coefficients of production. At this point, we are back to the various attempts of expressing output in terms of used up inputs. As already pointed out, within this theoretical framework heterogeneity is dealt with by assuming (albeit implicitly) that goods can be reduced to one another because they are merely different expressions of the same reality. Thus, iron and wheat may be considered as homogeneous because they are taken to be fundamentally one and the same good. Despite their physical properties, they are dealt with as if their difference might be expressed by a numerical coefficient, which is tantamount to assuming that they are essentially identical.

Like the majority of his fellow economists, Hicks maintains that 'any bundle of goods can be treated as a single good, as long as the proportions in which the component goods are combined are kept constant' (Hicks 1973: 144). Hence, variations in these proportions define variations in the specification of the single good. But, how can we measure these changes in specification? How can we establish a numerical relationship between two different single goods? The problem has no solution within Hicks's theoretical framework. This is so because each single good is a bundle of heterogeneous goods that can only be described in each of its component parts, without it being possible to express it in a single unit of measure. Every change in specification gives rise to a new single good that cannot even be compared with the others since each of them is made up of different proportions of different (and heterogeneous) component goods. Let us take a very simple example and suppose that good I is made up of 3 t. of iron and 2 t. of wheat, while good II is composed of 2 t. of iron and 3 t. of wheat. What kind of relationship may we establish between good I and good II? Is good I greater or lesser than good II? It should be obvious that in order to answer these questions we have to make iron and wheat homogeneous. If we were able to measure both iron and wheat in a common unit, there would be no difficulty in expressing the relationship between our two single goods. Conversely, if iron and wheat remain heterogeneous, there are no possibilities of evaluating good I in terms of good II or vice versa.

The same problem arises when capital is concerned. Having assumed that labour and product are homogeneous, Hicks claims that, as long as constant proportions are maintained, 'we need make no assumption about the units in which Equipment is measured' (ibid.: 179). Hicks's idea is that if the composition of capital is constant (i.e. if the quantity of each machine varies in the same proportion), 'Equipment is made homogeneous' (ibid.: 179). Here again, the heterogeneity problem is disposed of by assuming that, because of constant proportions in its composition, capital can be transformed into a number. Resting on the hidden assumption that real goods are all essentially identical (iron being a kind of wheat, wheat a kind of pig, and so on), the neoclassical analysis of production is thus seriously flawed, from both an empirical and a logical point of view. Now, this distressing conclusion is corroborated by another critical observation, referring to the functional relationship that is supposed to exist between production and time.

Is production a function of time?

In order to analyse production as a physical process of transformation of inputs into outputs, economists have built a series of models whose capacity to represent reality is proportionally inverse to the number of restrictive assumptions allowing for their mathematical solution. The linear production model is emblematic of this approach. As clearly stated by Bliss, the assumption of constant returns to scale on which it rests is unrealistic, yet indispensable to its existence. 'The assumption of *linearity* is very usual in economic theorising of the abstract kind and economists have become quite accustomed to it. Nonetheless, it is an unrealistic assumption and it is necessary to keep in view at all times the fragility of results that are critically dependent upon it' (Bliss 1975: 199). Another strong assumption introduced in linear production models is that of 'additivity', i.e. 'the absence of external effects and interrelationships between productive activities' (ibid.: 200). Like the constant returns to scale hypothesis, additivity is 'not always a realistic' (ibid.: 200) assumption. A fact, however, which does not prevent its adoption, mainly 'for reasons of convenience' (ibid.: 200). Thus, 'for reasons of convenience', production is reduced to 'a finite set of activities, which are combined together in a simple additive manner, and each of which can be scaled at will so long as the appropriate ratios are conserved' (ibid.: 200). As everybody knows, economic reality is much more complex, too much to be even approximately represented by a model. Then, we are apparently stuck between the two horns of a dilemma: either we refuse to recur to modelling and we limit our analysis to an *ex post facto* description of events, or using models we accept the risk of developing an analysis that has very little to do with economic reality. In fact, the dilemma would be real if production could be investigated only as a physical process, if economics had necessarily to be derived from a whole series of social activities that can be analysed in physical terms only. Now, this is precisely what is taken for granted by the majority of economists. Their choice to use modelling as a theoretical framework for analysis is thus perfectly consistent with their aprioristic conception of economics. Linear production models become, together with other models, the only possible means of reproducing, albeit unsatisfactorily, a reality that is bound to remain beyond the reach of theoretical investigation. What must be clearly understood, however, is that this way of looking at economics is not the only possible one. On the contrary, it can be shown that there is a red thread going through the works of the great economists of the past and leading towards a truly economic conception of economics. The method followed here is to highlight the principal elements of this conception by deriving them from a critical appraisal of the traditional approach to economics. With regard to the analysis of production, this implies a critical appraisal of the assumption concerning its functional relationship with chronological time.

If economic production were a physical process, it might be reasonably considered as a function of time, and it might likewise be legitimate to recur to modelling as a means to represent reality. What has to be established, therefore, is whether or not production can be reduced, economically, to a process of physical transformation, and if it can then be considered as an activity taking place in a time continuum. Earlier in this chapter, we saw that the physical conception of production does not allow for its economic expression since direct exchange (either between outputs or between inputs) does not allow for the determination of prices (or values). What we would like to do here is to show that, from an economic point of view, production is not an activity whose result is determined by its implementation in time.

According to a widely shared belief, output results from the activity exerted by labour with the aid of capital. Whether the production function displays diminishing, constant or increasing returns to labour and capital, it is assumed that production is a function of time. Let us take the example of the case in which output is a function of a fixed (capital) and a variable (labour) factor of production. As represented by Stiglitz (1997), when marginal returns to labour decrease, the slope of the production function becomes flatter as labour increases (Figure 4.4).

Both output and labour are measured in physical quantities (thousands of bushels and thousands of hours worked in Stiglitz's example). This describes how total output changes when the variable factor of production (labour) changes. From Figure 4.4, we can move onto another diagram (Figure 4.5), in which output is related to the flow of time.

The slope of the curve represents the decreasing returns to the continuous implementation of production in time. A given level of production corresponds to each point in time, so that output is itself perceived as a function of time. Hence, for any given period of time $t_0 - t_1$, output is determined by the integral of its level over this period (Figure 4.6).

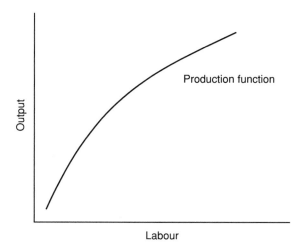

Figure 4.4 Production function with diminishing returns to an input.

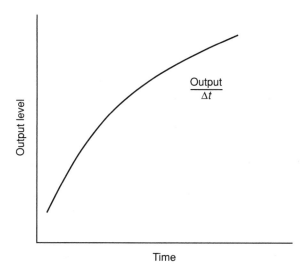

Figure 4.5 Production and the flow of time.

It is significant that the belief that production is an economic activity taking place continuously (or discontinuously) in time is shared by almost every economist, independently of the theoretical approach he is committed to. It is not surprising, therefore, to read in Scazzieri's book *A Theory of Production* that a 'production process may be represented by the vector of "use-times" $\mathbf{T}_j$ .... The elements of $\mathbf{T}_j$ include: the total labour time employed in process j for any given type of skill, the length of time worked by machines of different types, and the length of time for which the various raw materials actually take part in the production process' (Scazzieri 1993: 88–9).

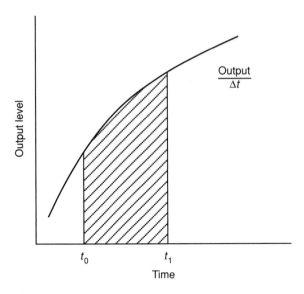

Figure 4.6 Output as a function of time.

Why is it so widely believed that output is a function of time? As we have already observed, one major reason may be the fact that production is mostly considered from a physical point of view. The analogy that is commonly used is that of velocity in classical physics. For example, when production is considered as a constant activity in continuous time, it is claimed that, in the same way as distance is the product of velocity and time, output is obtained by multiplying production by its time of implementation. As observed by Schmitt, however, there is a substantial difference between velocity and production, namely that while instantaneous velocity is positive production tends towards zero when Δt approaches the instant. 'La production s'annule en même temps que le produit, tandis que la vitesse ne s'annule pas quand on fait tendre vers zero le temps de son application' (Schmitt 1984b: 43). In the first chapter of his book, Schmitt proves that the relationship between production (the activity) and product (its result) is an equivalence since the two terms have one and the same measure. 'La production est l'opération et le produit son résultat; mesurés dans la même unité et la même échelle, les deux grandeurs sont nécessairement égales entre elles, une seule et même mesure s'appliquant indifféremment aux deux' (ibid.: 51). It thus follows that the product of Δt is the instantaneous result of an activity that is not multiplied by Δt. In the equation

Product = production · Δt

Δt is necessarily equal to 1.

If, like velocity, production were an action performed continuously in time, its result could only be either zero or infinity. Zero, if we claim that instantaneous production is itself zero; infinity, if we maintain that instantaneous production is positive and finite (as velocity is in the case of a body moving continuously in a given period of time). Here again, the analogy between economics and classical mechanics breaks down. In fact, if instantaneous production is positive, its implementation in continuous time 'can only lead to an infinite output in a finite interval of time, whereas the product of a finite velocity in the same interval of time is a finite displacement' (ibid.: 43; our translation). How is it that a positive velocity applied during an infinity of successive instants of a finite period gives a finite result, whereas a positive production applied continuously in the same time period (made up of an infinity of instants) would give an infinite result? As explained by Schmitt, while a positive and finite displacement is possible only if a positive velocity is sustained during a positive period of time because velocity and displacement are not the terms of an equivalence, production and product define one another, so that, if instantaneous production were positive, its result would also be positive at each instant in time. But, if production does not take place in a time continuum, how can it be positive at all? The answer to this question leads us to the last section of this chapter, in which production is seen as an instantaneous event (an emission) whose result is a newly created output.

Production as a process of creation and exchange

The idea that production is a process of creation is not new in our science. As we have seen, it is possible to find its origin in Quesnay's monetary circuit provided we are prepared to reason in terms of value. This is what Walras does in his critique of the physiocratic doctrine.

> Consequently, since the Physiocrats themselves admit that the labour added by the industrial class to raw materials makes it possible for the raw materials bought for 1 milliard to sell for 3 milliards, surely we have the right to say that this so-called sterile class annually produces and consumes 2 milliards worth of social wealth.
>
> (Walras 1984: 395)

Walras himself considers production as a process leading to an increase in value, even though the values he refers to are those the Classics called values-in-use: 'final products possess a utility for each individual which we may express by a want or utility equation' (ibid.: 237). By introducing the concept of utility, he makes it possible to apprehend production as a process which, by giving a new utility-form to matter and energy, leads to a creation of value. The annoying aspect of this approach, however, is the logical impossibility of measuring utility. We know, in fact, that, being subjectively determined, utilities cannot be expressed either by cardinal or by ordinal numbers. Hence, unless production is identified with a monetary creation – which is not the case for Walras and his followers – utility cannot be retained as a measurable result of production.

Even though Walras's attempt avoids the trap of considering value as a substance (a materialisation of labour time in the tradition of the Classics), it does not provide a satisfactory theory of production mainly because money remains essentially alien to it. In this respect, the analysis set out by the Classics is much more fruitful, particularly when money is defined as a form of value and labour expressed in wage rather than in time units.

In Marx's *Grundrisse*, we can read that '[p]roduction is not only concerned with simple determination of prices, i.e. with translation of the exchange values of commodities into a common unit, but with the creation of exchange values' (Marx 1973: 217). Thus, if we remember that money is the form of value, 'the form in which all commodities equate, compare, measure themselves; into which all commodities dissolve themselves' (ibid.: 142), we immediately realise that for Marx the analysis of production merges with that of money. Since its creation, money identifies itself with the physical output it is integrated with. This identity is the fundamental peculiarity of money defined as a form of value. It is thanks to it that value acquires its social dimension and that bank money acquires its purchasing power. Marx is therefore right in claiming that, dissociated from real goods, money is 'a mere phantom of real wealth' (ibid.: 234). Hence, money finds its *raison d'être* only with regard to the output it defines, so that 'its independence is a mere semblance; its independence of circulation exists only in view of circulation, exists as dependence on it' (ibid.: 234).

Let us start from the process of production. Consistently with his predecessors, Marx claims that matter and energy are transformed into economic output by human labour, with the aid of capital and land. He then adds, referring back to Adam Smith's distinction between value and use value, that the economic process of production distinguishes itself from a process of physical transformation in that it defines a *creation of value*. Production is thus immediately assimilated to a process of creation of which labour is the unique factor. This logical priority of labour, however, can be socially established only when it is possible to express it in a standard common to every kind of individual work. As the attempt to reduce complex to simple, undifferentiated labour on any material basis whatsoever is doomed to failure, value cannot be socially expressed in terms of labour time. This is the conclusion implicit in Marx's refusal of the theory, supported by Owen and Proudhon, of time chits. Faced with the impossibility of expressing labour in a dimensional unit, Marx has the great intuition of introducing money as the form of value. 'Labour on the basis of exchange values presupposes, precisely, that neither the labour of the individual nor his products are directly general; that the product attains this form only by passing through an *objective mediation*, by means of a form of *money* distinct from itself' (ibid.: 172). Thus, the social definition of physical output implies the passage from the output–labour relationship to the money–output relationship because money is the form of value and value is determined by human labour.

It is here that money wages are introduced as the monetary definition of current output. In a monetary economic system, '[l]abour must directly produce exchange value, i.e. money. It must therefore be *wage labour*' (ibid.: 224). Let us repeat that the definition of current output in terms of wage units is a logical requirement that can only be disavowed at the cost of leaving output totally undetermined. For example, if we persisted in distinguishing labour from labour power and in claiming that wages do not define the totality of produced output but only that part which corresponds to the labour power, we would be unable to determine both labour and output. In fact, if wages merely define the commodity 'labour power', labour itself is bound to remain undetermined, which would make it impossible to determine value and, as a consequence, output.

Thus interpreted, Marx's analysis leads us to the conclusion that economic output is literally created by human labour and that this creation of value is expressed monetarily through the identity output $\equiv$ wages. By allowing money to take the place of real goods and services, the payment of wages defines an *absolute* exchange investing money with a purchasing power corresponding to its real content. Production is concerned '[n]ot merely with positing the form, but also the content' (ibid.: 217).

Keynes is another great economist who has developed his analysis of production along the lines sketched above. As is well known, Keynes repeatedly petitioned for the choice of labour as the sole factor of production. 'It is preferable to regard labour, including, of course, the personal services of the entrepreneur and his assistants, as the sole factor of production, operating in a given environment of technique, natural resources, capital equipment and effective demand' (Keynes 1973b: 454). Likewise, it is unanimously acknowledged that he is the first economist to have explicitly introduced the concept of wage units. 'We shall call the unit in which the quantity of employment is measured the labour-unit; and the money-wage of a labour-unit we shall call the wage-unit' (Keynes 1973a: 41).

Now, as we have briefly observed in the first chapter, the concept of wage units has often been misunderstood, Keynes himself being partly responsible for its misinterpretations. To cite but an example, let us refer to Joan Robinson's paper on the production function. In this text, Robinson considers the wage units as being the price of labour expressed in terms of output. 'We take as the wage units the price of an hour's labour in terms of the composite unit of product, no matter whether the worker who performs an hour's work is paid in cash or in peanuts' (Robinson 1953–4: 86). Thus interpreted, Keynes's concept of wage units leads inevitably to a vicious circle in which output is expressed in terms of a unit that is itself expressed in terms of product. The originality of Keynes's message is entirely lost, and his analysis is assimilated to that developed by the neoclassical school. And yet Robinson should have realised that if labour is the sole true factor of production it cannot logically belong to the category of produced output and cannot therefore have a price.

But this is not all. In the same paper, we are told, in fact, that wage units are units of standard labour: 'we may cost the capital goods in terms of wage units, that is, in effect, to measure their cost in terms of a unit of standard labour' (ibid.: 82). Robinson's thoughts seem to vacillate between a classical and a neoclassical theory of value, wandering between a definition of the wage unit in terms of real product and one in terms of standard labour. Yet, Keynes's analysis is far from being confined to these two theories of value. The importance he gives to bank money is symptomatic of his attempt to do away with both of them by introducing a monetary definition of produced output. True, he did not provide a complete answer to the way in which output relates to money. His suggestion of expressing labour (the source of value) in terms of wage units, however, is a clear sign of his refusal to measure real goods and services either in labour time or in relative prices. As soon as wages are no longer perceived 'as a kind of price' (Bradford and Harcourt 1997: 118), the way is open to a process of integration between real product and money taking place on the labour market through the payment of wages.

If we go back to Keynes's main insights into the nature of economic production, namely that output is expressed in wage units and results from a process of which labour is the sole factor, we soon realise that the monetary theory of production is very closely related to that of monetary expenditures (actually so closely that the two theories define the complementary aspects of one and the same reality). Hence, production is a creative process whose result can indifferently be referred to as real product or as money income, each of these concepts necessarily implying the other. Output is in fact the very object (or content) of money income, whereas money income is precisely the result of real product being given its monetary form. Determining current output is therefore equivalent to determining current national income.

Let us relate expenditures to the distinction between stock and flow variables. Traditionally, it is maintained that 'a stock is time-dimensionless, while a flow has the dimension of 1/time' (Patinkin 1972: 1). The relationship between income and wealth is considered to be emblematic of this distinction. Thus, while in continuous analysis the rate of flow of income over time is represented by a continuous function and wealth is calculated as its integral, in period analysis income is considered to be a stock, and wealth results simply from the addition of successive incomes weighted by the rate of interest. As pointed out by Patinkin, in period analysis 'there cannot – by definition – be variables with the dimension of a flow with respect to time' (ibid.: 6). Hence, the choice seems to be restricted between an analysis in which variables have the dimension of a flow (continuous analysis) and one that is time-dimensionless and whose variables have the dimension of a stock (period analysis). The problem is complicated by the fact that book-keeping entries in banks' balance sheets are stocks, so that empirical evidence seems to contrast, for example, with the theoretical assumptions that expenditures are a function of time. In the real world, variables such as income are timeless, whereas in theory their time dimension seems to be essential. Let us consider the formation of income R_1 of period p_1. Observation shows that the payment related to this event is instantaneous. Patinkin himself is prepared to concede that 'the time-dimensionlessness of R_1 and R_2 is also reflected in the fact that these payments must be considered as if they were concentrated at *instants* of time' (ibid.: 3). Reality is even more compelling: payments *are necessarily* concentrated at instants of time. This would be true also if money were material, every payment taking place at the very moment that the payer is debited and the payee credited. Payments being carried out by banks (even if money is convertible into gold as in the gold standard), each of them implies the destruction of a deposit and the simultaneous creation of another of the same amount. The fact of payments being instantaneous is obviously more evident nowadays, money being no longer assimilated to any particular commodity. Facts seem thus to confirm that income is a stock variable. What shall we infer from this contrast between theory and facts? Is it still correct to consider income as a flow? Is it possible to avoid the difficulty by claiming that income is a flow that can be converted into a stock simply 'by dividing this flow by the rate of interest' (ibid.: 4)? The answers to these questions depend on the nature of payments and on their relationship with produced output.

As seen in the previous section, production is not a function of time but an instantaneous event whose result is the positive creation of current output. The analysis of income allows us to get a better understanding of this process. The determination of income, in fact, is also an instantaneous event with a positive result with regard to time. If we refer the formation of income to the payment of wages, as suggested by Keynes, we can easily observe that the result of this instantaneous action (a flow) is the creation of a bank deposit (a stock) whose real object is the currently produced output. It appears, thus, that production is an economic process that coincides with the payment of wages. Output is therefore the result of an *emission*, in the sense that it is 'economically' determined at the very instant that it is given its monetary form.

The payment of wages is both an emission of nominal money (a simple numerical form) and of real money (defined by the unity of the monetary form and its real content). The payment itself is a flow (instantaneous as any other expenditure) and its result is a stock. This is so because '*wages are not merely the result of an expenditure of money but the product of an expenditure of labour*' (Schmitt 1984b: 95; our translation). In other words, 'workers emit real output and their wages are the result of the emission' (ibid.: 95; our translation). This clearly means that current output is issued as a sum of wages of which it defines the real object or content. This is the meaning of the *absolute* exchange on which the modern quantum approach to monetary macroeconomics is based. Through the payment of wages, output is exchanged against itself, in the exact sense that it is transformed into a sum of money that defines it economically. Wages *are* the product, and not its monetary counterpart: output being created as a sum of real money, product and wages are not two distinct objects. Through labour, matter and energy are given a new form, and they acquire their economic identity (in this new utility-form) through the payment of wages. Hence, current wages take (momentarily) the place of current physical output, their absolute exchange defining the conversion of real into monetary product. 'La formation des salaires est l'échange absolu, la *conversion*, du produit réel en produit monétaire' (ibid.: 96).

From the point of view of its relation with time, it appears that the formation of current income is a time-dimensionless event (the instantaneous expenditure corresponding to the payment of wages) whose result defines the finite period of time during which workers transform matter and energy in order to give it a new utility-form. Production and income creation are one and the same event. Thus, 'as real output, wages have the dimension of the time quantized by production' (ibid.: 106; our translation).

Schmitt's concept of quantum time is of particular significance for the understanding of production. It derives from his economic analysis of this process and not, as a superficial reader might be tempted to think, from yet another attempt to introduce physical concepts into economics. The quantisation of energy proper to quantum physics has nothing to do with that of time, an original concept related to production, even though in both theories – physical and economical – emissions are analysed in terms of their corpuscular and wave-like aspects. Let us try to summarise the main points of Schmitt's analysis. Being an instantaneous event that refers to a positive period of continuous time, production is said to 'quantize time; that is, *to capture instantaneously a slice of continuous time*: the first result of production is therefore the definition of a quantum of time. Output is not deposited in time; it *is* time' (ibid.: 54; our translation).

Let us note in passing that the idea of entities being made up of time instead of being merely deposited in time or being the result of activities taking place in time is not unfamiliar to physicists and philosophers. As clearly observed by Price, the traditional conception of time is actually contrasted by 'the *block universe view*, the point being that it regards reality as a single entity of which time is an ingredient, rather than as a changeable entity set *in* time' (Price 1996: 12). What Schmitt is able to prove is that, in economics, production is an instantaneous event relating to a finite and indivisible period of time (a quantum of time) and that its result, the product, is nothing other than this quantum. '*Le produit n'est rien d'autre qu'un quantum de temps*' (Schmitt 1984b: 55). This means that, albeit instantaneous, production defines a positive displacement in time. How can this be? How can a timeless event define a finite portion of time? Of course, this could never happen if production were a function of continuous time. In this case, however, it would be impossible to consider production as a creation, and no net output could ever be explained. As soon as it is understood that production creates its own space – unlike the displacement of a moving body, which takes place in a pre-existing space – it appears that '*production is not a displacement in space but in time*' (ibid.: 40; our translation). This particular kind of displacement pertains to the category of wave-like movements. At the very instant that production occurs, the whole period of time, $t_0 - t_n$, during which matter and energy are physically transformed is covered in both directions, from t_n to t_0 and from t_0 to t_n: 'à l'instant t_n, la production est une onde, un mouvement dans le temps, constaté de t_n à t_0 et identiquement de t_0 à t_n' (ibid.: 58).

The quantum nature of production is not easy to grasp. This is particularly true of its relationship with time. The idea that production quantises time or that output is a quantum of time will probably sound weird to most readers. Yet, it is a fact that production and product are the terms of an identity. This necessarily implies that production can be positive only if it is referred to a positive period of time. Now, analysis shows that production cannot be referred continuously to this positive period of time (otherwise its value could only be zero or infinity). The only possibility is therefore that of conceiving of production as an emission, an instantaneous event whose wave-like aspect is the displacement in time and whose corpuscular aspect is the quantum of time defined by it.

When money is introduced into the analysis, it becomes relatively easy to show that, like production, expenditures are not a function of time. In particular, the payment of wages is also an instantaneous event which, defining a positive income formation, refers to a finite period of time. Hence, it is through the payment of wages that the quantum of time defining current output is given its numerical expression. Wages themselves take the place (through conversion) of output and become the very definition of the quantum of time issued by production. From a book-keeping point of view, this corresponds with the fact that wages are a bank deposit (created or emitted by labour and not by banks) defining the real product entered on the assets side of banks' balance sheets. Thus, production leads to a positive creation of income, which clearly confirms that output is net in its entirety. What is created is not a new substance, of course (Lavoisier's law would never allow it); yet, it is also not a mere numerical form. It is the unity of the new output and of its monetary form. When wages are paid, output is converted into money, i.e. it is issued as a sum of money. Clearly understood, this means that the creation of bank money is positive only when it is associated with produced output. In Schmitt's words, we would say that bank money can exist only if it merges with the money created by production (ibid.: 101).

Created by labour, wages are given their numerical expression through the intermediation of bank money, which is thus made to define a positive income. Output is the object of the bank deposit generated by the payment of wages. This results immediately from the observation of the banks' double-entry relating to this payment. Entered on the assets side of the banks' balance sheet, firms are indebted for the exact amount earned by their workers and deposited on the liabilities side. From an analytical viewpoint, it is output itself that is entered on the banks' assets side. Thus, the payment of wages establishes a close relationship (an identity) between income – earned by workers – and output – the very object of firms' debt. The analysis of production previously sketched is therefore perfectly in line with the empirical observation of double-entry book-keeping. The positive deposit of workers is exactly matched by the negative deposit of firms, so that the entire output – the object of the negative deposit – is actually converted into a sum of money income. 'A positive money subsists, facing the negative money of F (the whole set of firms), which is immediately "filled" with the product of workers. While physical output remains deposited within the negative money, workers own ... a positive money equal to the amount of wages emitted [through production]' (ibid.: 114; our translation).

It is with the introduction of bank money that quantum theoretical analysis reaches its most elaborate form. Thus, although physical output results from a quantisation of time occurring independently of the presence of money, its transformation into an economic output requires the real emission of production to be associated with the emission of money. When this is done, production becomes a monetary creation and output is determined in the form of wages.

Without human labour, no real emission would be possible and no output would exist. Without money the object of the real emission could not be measured and no true economic system would exist. Wicksell was certainly right in claiming that '[p]roduction is not a technical problem only, but technical and economic at the same time' (Wicksell 1934: 106). The duty of economists is to provide a consistent answer to the economic problem of production – a task that can be satisfactorily carried out only if we are able to account both for the real and the monetary aspects of this process and of its result. This can be done following the quantum theoretical approach to monetary macroeconomics.

To conclude, let us observe that even such a neoclassical economist as Morishima recognises the necessity of explaining production in monetary terms. In his book on capital and credit, he explains the transition from a phase of primitive accumulation to the beginnings of capitalist production by referring to certificates issued by capitalists and by firms in exchange for the initial stock of commodities and for an equivalent amount of dividends respectively. These certificates, introduced as a device by the Japanese economist, may be thought of as a first attempt to transform a real into a monetary economy. Of course, Morishima is well aware that a simple juxtaposition of certificates is not up to the task. Unfortunately, he fails to realise that, lacking a true process of monetisation, his model is bound to remain sterile. As a matter of fact, his theory rests on the assumption that market prices can be determined in purely real terms, an assumption that prevents him from setting up a true monetary theory of production. The fact remains that Morishima is one of the relatively few economists to have explicitly admitted that '[t]he existing tools for the analysis of production which orthodox GET employs are either useless or at least inappropriate' (Morishima 1992: 6). Time has come to share his concern with the elaboration of 'a model which takes minimum consideration for production time lags' (ibid.: 29), and to complete the project initiated by the Classics and carried on by Keynes to develop the theory of production in conformity with the principles of monetary macroeconomics.

5   Money and capital

'If we wish to interpret the divergent views regarding the concept of capital as a *testimonium paupertatis* of political economy, we shall not be wholly wrong' (Wicksell 1954: 106). Unfortunately, Wicksell's observation is still valid today. Economists are far from being unanimous about the significance of the concept of capital, and their analyses are often too broad to provide an accurate insight into the mechanism of capital accumulation. From Adam Smith onwards, capital has been conceived of as a means of production, a social relationship, a factor of production, a wage fund, a set of instrumental goods, an interest-bearing sum of money, etc. Some of these definitions are reciprocally consistent, others are not. Some rely on a microeconomic perception of economic reality, others are essentially macroeconomic. The aim of this chapter is to provide the elements for a modern macroeconomic analysis of capital in which all these definitions may find their right place (if any).

Labour, time and capital

In his 1975 book, Bliss starts his analysis of capital from the following statement: '[c]apital theory is concerned with the implications for a market economy, for the theory of prices, for the theory of production and for the theory of distribution, of the existence of produced means of production' (Bliss 1975: 3). Although the author himself affirms his intention not to make a fetish of precision, his definition of capital sounds rather too loose. In fact, before being concerned with the implications of the existence of instrumental goods, capital theory must account for their very existence. Bliss considers capital goods as given instead of explaining where they come from. The answer is not self-evident. Of course, like any other commodity, capital goods are the result of production. Yet, as we have seen, production is not merely a physical process of transformation. Likewise, capital cannot be reduced to a collection of instrumental goods.

Second, Bliss draws our attention to an important aspect of capital theory. 'The essential ingredient, it might be argued, is time. All outlays of labour or consumption foregone have a date and the benefits will accrue at different dates. What we must capture in our theory to have it encompass capital is this intertemporal aspect of production and consumption. In this view time is the essence of capital' (ibid.: 4). Referring back to the works of the classical and the Austrian schools of thought, he sets to work to show that 'capital does spring from time and that the central problem of the theory is to show how economic analysis can deal with cases where we have to take into account the extension of production, consumption and planning through time' (ibid.: 7). Since time plays a crucial role in capital theory, let us start our analysis from the possible effects of time on capital formation.

The classical approach to capital

Time is not just an optional attribute of production. In fact, time is always present in every economic process, so that a timeless model of economics is bound to be hopelessly unrealistic. Moreover, time enters the economic definition of goods at the moment they are produced. If a theory is unable to account for it at this stage, it is useless to try to extend it to time by referring to the delivery date of goods. In the same way as money must be closely associated with real goods and not simply tagged on them (for example, in the form of a supplementary equation), time must enter into an objective relationship with output at the very instant of its economic creation. This is done by the modern quantum approach to monetary macroeconomics, in which production is explained as an instantaneous event whose result defines a quantum of time, a new (economic) 'space' created by human labour and expressed in terms of wage units. This is also what classical economists attempt to do when measuring value in labour time. We know today that their attempt was bound to fail, mainly because value is not a substance, a physical dimension of produced output, but a relationship of a purely numerical nature. Yet, the Classics were right in believing that time plays a fundamental role both in the theory of value and in that of capital. Let us start from Ricardo's analysis of the way in which time enters the theory of capital.

In the *Principles*, Ricardo claims that value is not determined by labour alone. 'It is hardly necessary to say, that commodities which have the same quantity of labour bestowed on their production, will differ in exchangeable value, if they cannot be brought to market in the same time' (Ricardo 1951: 37). Depending on the time necessary to bring different commodities to market, their value grows proportionately with the gain that would have derived from the investment of the capital used in their production. 'The difference in value arises ... from the profits being accumulated as capital, and is only a just compensation for the time the profits were withheld' (ibid.: 37). The term 'profit' is used here by Ricardo as synonymous with interest on the assumption that receipts are reinvested into new productions. Thus, if a commodity can be brought to market and sold before another whose production requires the same quantity of labour, the producer of the second commodity has to face a greater cost because of the longer period of investment of his circulating capital. If we keep our analysis within the logical boundaries of one process of production and circulation, the value of the second commodity must rise to cover the greater cost of its overall production (where the time required for its circulation is added to its labour time). The longer period of time necessary to bring the second commodity to market justifies a difference in value from the first commodity because of the higher interest entailed by its production. For example, if the first commodity is ready to be sold after 1 year and the second after 2 years, the value of the second must be raised by the interest matured in 1 year.

The introduction of interest apparently contrasts with Ricardo's claim that labour is the only factor of production. Yet, before reaching any final conclusion we have to explain the genesis of interest, and why and when it enters the value of produced output. This is what we shall attempt to do in the next chapter. For the time being, let us observe that Ricardo's reference to profits is in no way accidental. The great Anglo-Portuguese economist is well aware of the fact that time alone cannot account for an increase in value. Hence, either time is considered to be related to labour – which explains the value generated directly by production – or it is related to capital. In the second case, value is derived from what may be obtained from the investment of capital during a given period of time. By referring to profits, Ricardo seems therefore to suggest that there is a strict correlation between profits and capital, and that the value derived from capital has its origin in a process of production. The theory of capital appears to be part of the theory of value and becomes essential for understanding the way in which the process of accumulation is related to those of production and circulation.

At this point of the analysis, it is useful to introduce Adam Smith's distinction between circulating and fixed capital. The Scottish economist defines as 'circulating' the capital corresponding to the stock of goods that may be either sold or invested, and as 'fixed' the capital corresponding to that part of current income that is definitively saved through its investment in the production of instrumental goods.

> There are two different ways in which a capital may be employed so as to yield a revenue or profit to its employer. First, it may be employed in raising, manufacturing, or purchasing goods, and selling them again with a profit. ... Such capitals, therefore, may very properly be called circulating capitals. Secondly, it may be employed in the improvement of land, in the purchase of useful machines and instruments of trade, or in such-like things as yield a revenue or profit without changing masters, or circulating any further. Such capitals, therefore, may very properly be called fixed capitals.
>
> (Smith 1974: 374)

Earlier on in his famous book on the wealth of nations, Smith had already claimed that '[a]s soon as stock has accumulated in the hands of particular persons, some of them will naturally employ it in setting to work industrious people, whom they will supply with materials and subsistence' (ibid.: 151). What Smith is telling us here is that capital initially takes the form of a stock of consumption goods. In the first place, firms accumulate a real wage fund, and it is only the subsequent investment of this fund 'in setting to work industrious people' that transforms it definitively into capital. Expressed in terms of circulating and fixed capital, this means that '[e]very fixed capital is both originally derived from, and requires to be continually supported by, a circulating capital. All useful machines and instruments of trade are originally derived from a circulating capital, which furnishes the materials of which they are made, and the maintenance of the workmen who make them' (ibid.: 378).

Smith's distinction between circulating and fixed capital was taken over by Ricardo and Marx. As far as Ricardo is concerned, it is interesting to observe that he was not satisfied with the habit of distinguishing between the two sorts of capital on the basis of the physical durability of the goods invested in production. In the second edition of the *Principles*, the traditional claim that '[a]ccording as capital is rapidly perishable, and requires to be frequently reproduced, or is of slow consumption, it is classed under the heads of circulating, or of fixed capital' (Ricardo 1951: 31) has the following footnote: 'A division not essential, and in which the line of demarcation cannot be accurately drawn' (ibid.: 31). Ricardo prefers to call circulating capital that employed 'in the support of labour' (ibid.: 32), and fixed capital that 'invested in machinery, implements, buildings, &c.' (ibid.: 32).

Marx's point of view differs from Smith's and Ricardo's in that he emphasises the distinction between constant and variable capital rather than that between fixed and circulating capital. As is well known, his main attempt was to show that surplus value is generated by labour power being exploited beyond the time required for the reproduction of its own value. According to Marx, the peculiarity of this 'commodity' is that its use or consumption creates value. One may therefore claim that a surplus value is formed any time that the value created by the use of labour power is greater than the cost of its purchase (which corresponds to the labour time required for its reproduction). The capital invested in labour power is thus said to be variable because its value is influenced by variations in the rate of (relative or absolute) surplus value. Consistent with his theoretical choice, Marx interprets the distinction between circulating and fixed capital rather differently from his predecessors. In particular, having observed that all capital circulates, and that '[a]ll capital that functions as productive capital is fixed in the production process' (Marx 1978: 241), he claims that '[t]he formal characteristics of fixed and fluid capital arise only from the different turnovers of the capital value or *productive capital* that functions in the production process' (ibid.: 246). In other words, the distinction between fixed and circulating (fluid) capital is related to the way in which value is transferred from productive capital to final output. If, as in the case of labour power, the value of productive capital completely transfers to final output, we are in the presence of a circulating capital. On the contrary, if productive capital transfers its value to the products only gradually, we are confronted with a fixed capital. It thus appears that, in Marx's theory, variable capital pertains to the category of circulating capital, while constant capital is either fixed or circulating according to whether it is entirely or only partially consumed in every process of production. As we have said, the crucial distinction remains that between constant and variable capital as it is to variable capital (i.e. labour power) that economic growth is due. Now, a thorough analysis of surplus value shows that Marx's distinction between labour and labour power encounters a major obstacle: the logical impossibility of explaining the monetary realisation of surplus value. Obtained by firms through the partly gratuitous use of labour power, real surplus cannot be sold in the absence of a monetary income available to this end. Yet, this is not the only shortcoming of Marx's analysis. The need to account for a distribution of profit proportional to the entire capital invested (variable and constant) is the source of another major difficulty known as the problem of transforming values into prices. While both of these problems are related to Marx's choice to take labour power as a commodity, their heuristic values are different. In particular, the transformation problem subsists even if we do away with the (metaphysical) distinction between labour and its power. Like Ricardo's concern with the period of time required to bring products to market, Marx's transformation problem is a clear example of the need to reconcile the principle according to which value is determined by labour alone with the existence of incomes other than wages. It is to the theory of capital that Ricardo and Marx committed the solution to this problem, and it is this theory that we must investigate further.

Today, the time has come to clarify the terms of the distinction introduced by Smith. Let us start with the classical concept of circulating capital. In a primitive state of society, where production is at a subsistence level and consists exclusively of consumption goods, capital can be accumulated only in its circulating form and at great sacrifice. To have a positive capital, in fact, it is necessary to save part of current income, which is possible only if the population is prepared (or forced) to refrain from consumption. If this is the case, some of the produced consumption goods are stocked and their corresponding income transformed into capital. According to Smith, '[w]hat is annually saved is as regularly consumed as what is annually spent, and nearly in the same time too; but it is consumed by a different set of people' (Smith 1974: 437–8). However, whereas consumption might frequently be unproductive (since it is often carried out by 'guests and menial servants' whose work is considered by Smith as unproductive), invested savings are spent 'by labourers, manufacturers, and artificers, who reproduce with a profit the value of their annual consumption' (ibid.: 438). Now, if by circulating capital we mean the capital used to support labour, we must be aware that wages are not initially paid out of a pre-existing income or capital. The payment of wages logically precedes the formation of capital. The idea that capital may be used to support labour is related to the formation of a stock of consumption goods. When firms realise a profit, they obtain an income whose object consists of the goods not yet sold that build up the firms' real stock. This profit may be either distributed as dividends and interests or invested in a new production. If it is distributed, it is spent and destroyed in the final purchase of the stock. In this case, it is not used to support any new activity and cannot be considered as a circulating capital. On the contrary, if it is invested it allows the stock of consumption goods to be used to support labour. Workers producing investment goods spend their wages for the purchase of the stock of consumption goods. It is only in this case that profit is transformed into circulating capital.

As the reader will not fail to note, the expression 'circulating capital' is unlikely to be the most appropriate to define the sum invested in the production of capital goods as this production leads to the formation of an entirely new capital without entailing the reconstitution of the initial stock of consumption goods. By contrast, when we consider production and sale from a financial point of view, we could get the impression that capital is indeed used circularly since, output having been sold, firms recover the capital initially invested in its production. In reality, the whole process does not require the investment of any capital. Income and capital are the results of production and not its necessary condition. It is true, of course, that there are firms that, instead of financing production by activating their line of credit with banks, have recourse to their own reserves. In this case, they use their capital as a revolving fund that must be reconstituted periodically. The term of circulating capital would appropriately describe this use of their financial resources. Yet, we should never forget that even in this particular case wages do not need to be paid out of a positive income. The use of capital as a circulating fund does not modify the fact that labour is the source of a positive value. Wages define a positive income because labour, and labour alone, allows for physical output to be 'couched' in its monetary (numerical) form. The use of a positive income as a circulating fund to be invested in the payment of wages does not introduce any new process of integration between money and output. In a way, the capital used as a wage fund is not essentially different from a sum of real money borrowed from the banks. In both cases, the initial monetary stock must be reconstituted through the sale of output, and its reconstitution implies the substitution of the income spent in the payment of wages with the income generated by the process of production.

As a matter of pure rationality, wages should be paid out of a sum of nominal money. If firms use, instead, part of their money income, they use as a wage fund a sum that should have been spent on the commodity market. This implies both the transformation of their money income into a capital-time and the formation of a (real) stock of (unsold) consumption goods. Now, if firms use their capital as a revolving fund for the payment of wages, this will lead either to a renewed production of consumption goods or to the formation of a fixed capital. In the first case, the consumption goods newly produced may (partially or totally) take the place of those initially stocked, and the process carried on through the reconstitution of the revolving fund and its renewed investment. If this is so, the real stock formed initially and constantly reconstituted through time is entirely useless. If wages were paid using nominal money, no such stock would be necessary, and firms would not be forced to delay the sale of their output. In the second case, on the other hand, the process requires the accumulation of a positive capital. The formation of a fixed capital is possible only if part of the current income is saved and invested in the production of instrumental goods. The initial stock of consumption goods defines the real aspect of saving and represents the real wage fund handed over by firms in exchange for the newly produced capital goods. As long as the term 'circulating capital' is used to distinguish capital-time from that part of current income that is invested in the formation of fixed capital, it must not be confused with the concept of revolving or circulating wage fund mentioned above.

As suggested by Marx, all capital is a circulating capital in the sense that, initially, all capital takes the form of a capital-time. In this same sense, all money income is a circulating capital because the totality of income is instantaneously transformed into capital from the outset. The fact is that, at the very instant it is formed, income is saved and therefore transformed into capital-time. It is because of the presence of banks that income is immediately saved and lent, giving rise to a financial capital and a stock of real goods. 'Le revenu est aussitôt détruit pour être remplacé par un capital net – financier (le titre aux revenus déposés) et réel (les stocks)' (Schmitt 1984b: 161). Acting as financial intermediaries, banks lend to firms the income generated by production and not yet spent by its holders. 'Après la transformation (instantanée) du revenu en capital, la banque ... *n'est plus qu'un intermédiaire financier: elle a un titre sur les entreprises et elle fait face aux titulaires de revenus qui, à présent, ont un titre sur elle*' (ibid.: 159). Now, part of this capital-time is retransformed into money income to be spent for the final purchase of the goods initially stocked with firms. In order to pass from capital-time to fixed capital, it is necessary that part of the income saved be of a macroeconomic nature. This condition is satisfied when firms realise a profit, which they invest in a new production instead of redistributing it as dividend and interest. Through the sale of current output, firms may benefit from a transfer of income, which is immediately transformed into capital-time. Of this capital-time, the part that is not redistributed to income holders – and which we have designated as circulating capital proper – is then transformed into fixed capital. This transformation takes place on the labour market and corresponds to the investment of circulating capital in the production of new instrumental goods.

The problem here is to understand the role played by the stock of consumption goods defining the real object of circulating capital, and that played by the profit earned by firms. Now, whereas the stock of real goods has been treated as a real wage fund, invested profits have not been properly analysed by classical economists. In particular, it has never been established whether or not profits are spent when invested, and what would be the consequences of their expenditure on the labour market. Let us suppose things to happen in the following way. In period p_1, by selling consumption goods to income holders, firms (F) earn a profit which they invest in period p_2 on the labour market, selling the remaining consumption goods to the workers producing capital goods. A numerical example could run as shown in Figure 5.1.

From a physical point of view, firms exchange their stock of consumption goods against an equivalent stock of instrumental goods. Still from a 'real' point of view, workers are paid with the stock of goods formed in p_1 when firms realise their profit. What the Classics do not tell us is what these transactions imply from a monetary point of view. Is it correct for profits (circulating capital) to be distributed as wages? How is it that income holders spend 120 units of money income and get in exchange commodities whose total value amounts to 100 wage units? Is the fixed capital thus formed in F of a 'pathological' nature? These and

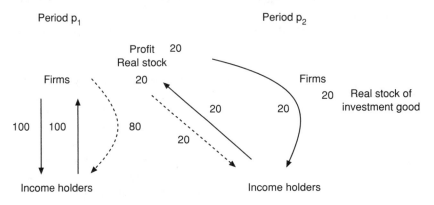

Figure 5.1 The investment of profit.

other questions must be answered if we are to provide a satisfactory theory of capital. Does the Austrian approach to capital help us in this task?

Böhm-Bawerk's approach to capital

As observed by Piffaretti (1994) in her dissertation, Böhm-Bawerk introduced the concept of the *average period of production* in order to integrate time, labour and utility in a unique model accounting for the measurement of capital. The idea is that capital may be integrated in the theory of value by considering the average period of time elapsing from each moment that a different investment of productive services takes place to the instant when production is completed.

Like the Classics', Böhm-Bawerk's point of departure is the constitution, through saving, of a circulating capital to be invested in the production of instrumental goods. In its first form, capital is a stock of consumption goods. Now, according to Böhm-Bawerk this stock may be assimilated to a reserve of 'productive power', or to a 'subsistence fund which makes circuitous production possible' (Böhm-Bawerk 1959c: 73). The constitution of a fund of saved up means of subsistence is thus the condition necessary for the production of capital goods proper, which Böhm-Bawerk defines as 'an aggregate of intermediate products' (ibid.: 73). The implementation in time of the productive power deriving from the workers' subsistence fund gives rise to a production of capital goods (i.e. to the transformation of circulating into fixed capital), which in turn leads to a production of finished goods. At this point, Böhm-Bawerk is faced with two problems: how to determine the value of fixed capital and how this may be transferred to final output. Having claimed that capital is not the source of value, the Austrian economist maintains that it is through labour (or, more generally, through the services of the factors of production) that capital transfers its value to current output. 'Capital does not independently deliver an impulse, it merely transmits an impulse delivered by originary productive forces' (Böhm-Bawerk 1959b: 95). Fixed and circulating capitals are considered to be intermediate goods in a process of production that leads to final output. As his aim is to reconcile the theory of value with the existence of different production periods, time plays a central role for Böhm-Bawerk. His concept of the average production period was elaborated with the precise intent to account for these differences and thus to avoid the difficulties that so deeply affect Ricardo's and Marx's theories of value. The period of investment of capital varying from one industry to another, value cannot be determined by labour time alone. Hence, Böhm-Bawerk proposes replacing the classical measure of value (in terms of directly incorporated labour) with a measure in which each individual capital – productive power – is referred to its period of investment. The average of these investment periods defines the average period of production.

According to Wicksell, 'free capital, by its very nature, consists of a sum of means of subsistence, i.e. consumption goods which are advanced to the workers and the owners of the forces of nature [land]' (Wicksell 1954: 115). The greater the stock of consumption goods, the longer the period of production of capital goods. Hence, the degree of productivity of roundabout methods of production increases with the increase in the stock of consumption goods (circulating capital) that is invested in the production of fixed capital. The more capital goods available, the greater the use value finally produced. As clearly noted by Böhm-Bawerk, the crucial problem here is to go from the increase in use value to the increase in exchange value. No one doubts that the use of instrumental goods leads to a greater production of finished (physical) goods. It is less obvious whether this greater quantity of goods defines also a greater economic value. Far from being sidetracked by physical or psychological considerations, Böhm-Bawerk rejects the traditional argument of the productivity theory and sets out to prove that the use of fixed capital has a positive impact on exchange value because of the longer period of production it involves. '[Capital is] indirectly productive because it makes possible the adoption of new and fruitful roundabout methods of production' (Böhm-Bawerk 1959b: 101).

As unanimously stressed by every economist interested in the theory of capital, Böhm-Bawerk's great merit is to have clearly perceived the close correlation existing between capital and time. This is what his roundabout methods of production are all about. As for the role played by capital, it is important to note that no increase in value can be attributed to its use. If one roundabout method of production leads to a more valuable output than another, it is not because the capitals invested in the two methods have different productivities in terms of value, but because their average periods of production differ. Böhm-Bawerk's reasoning is not easy to follow. To put it simply, we might say that it amounts to a sophisticated attempt to show that value is the result of the services of labour and land, as well as of time. Instead of considering capital as a factor of production, Böhm-Bawerk incorporates it (as an intermediate good) in the roundabout process of production, and makes time the element explaining the increase in value traditionally attributed to capital. Through his theory of interest – investigated in the next chapter – he tries to show that time allows us to explain value in terms of utility, and then applies his results to the theory of capital. This procedure leads Böhm-Bawerk to the conclusion that, because of the impact of the flow of time

on utility, every roundabout method of production has a result that depends both
on the utility (or services) of labour and land and on the period of their investment.

The point that we would like to emphasise is Böhm-Bawerk's refusal to treat
capital as being on the same footing as labour (and land). While labour has a
direct impact on value, capital's influence derives from the period of time elapsing
between the moment that savings are invested and the moment that final output is
ready to be sold on the market. However, the use of capital increases value because
of the difference between the value of present and that of future goods, and not
because of a hypothetical direct productivity of capital. This is the gist of Böhm-
Bawerk's message. If capital were a factor of production, interest would be its
remuneration and it would measure the increase in value owing to its use. Having
proved that the increase in physical productivity is not the necessary and sufficient
condition for an increase in value, Böhm-Bawerk maintains that we prefer present
over future goods since '[*w*]*e systematically undervalue our future wants and
also the means which serve to satisfy them*' (ibid.: 268). Thus, undervaluation of
future goods is the cause of a premium in favour of present goods and value
appears to depend on the length of the roundabout production period. '[T]he
premium or agio which present goods enjoy in comparison with future goods
belonging to periods of varying temporal remoteness attains proportions which
constitute a regular ratio *in accordance with the length of the intervening period
of time*' (ibid.: 288). Since investment is carried out in the present, its cost is
evaluated on the basis of the value of present goods. Obviously, investments take
place if their cost is not greater than the value of their outputs. Now, as future
goods are undervalued, a difference is bound to appear between the value of future
goods (once they become available) and their costs of production. This is not the
case, however, if investments were to be carried out in the future. Even if we
maintained that the cost of these investments calculated today turned out to be
smaller than the value of final output because the latter is underestimated, it is
clear that the effective cost of future investment will also be greater than its present
(under)valuation. Hence, an agio is possible only if a positive period of time
separates investment from the sale of final output.

Let us try to summarise the fundamental steps of Böhm-Bawerk's analysis. To
solve the problem of the relationship between value and capital, Böhm-Bawerk
considers production to be a roundabout process during which labour and land
are implemented at different dates and in different ways. Both circulating and
fixed capitals enter this process as intermediate products requiring labour and
land to be invested for different periods of time. If we abstract from land, we
could thus be led to think that Böhm-Bawerk's analysis is essentially a clever
attempt to reconcile the classical labour theory of value with the need to account
for differences in the composition of capital. In reality, Böhm-Bawerk's aim is
more ambitious than that. What the Austrian economist attempts to do is to prove
that, even though capital is not a factor of production, its use increases value not
in terms of incorporated labour but in terms of utility. To achieve this, he emphasises
the role played by time and assumes that individuals prefer present to future goods.
Because of this preference, future goods tend to be undervalued, which explains

the difference between the future value of future goods and their present estimated value. According to Böhm-Bawerk's psychological principle, the increase in value related to the flow of time would thus be more the effect of a generalised misconception than an objective variation of value itself. Now, this last consideration leads us to think that the roundabout method of production does not really succeed in reconciling the theory of value with that of capital. In particular, it does not seem correct to suppose – as Böhm-Bawerk does – that the effect of time may be accounted for only if we go from the future to the present. Piffaretti is right when she claims that, if future utility can be brought to the present, there are no logical reasons to exclude the possibility of present consumption increasing future utility. 'Böhm-Bawerk ne maîtrise pas l'analyse du temps et ne comprend pas que rapporter le futur vers le présent implique que le présent soit rapporté vers le futur: les effets de l'écoulement du temps, s'il y en a, doivent alors s'annuler réciproquement' (Piffaretti 1994: 131).

Other critiques have been addressed to Böhm-Bawerk's analysis. Among the most significant are those according to which the period of production is just a reformulation of the classical theory of labour-value. 'It is possible to claim that period of production and labour embodied in capital goods are two ways of accounting for or describing the same method of measurement of capital' (Garegnani 1972: 28; our translation). Another shortcoming of Böhm-Bawerk's theory can be seen in the logical impossibility of associating every single capital – particularly fixed capital – with precisely every single finished good it gives rise to. Thus, according to Hicks, Böhm-Bawerk's theory of capital cannot be accepted as such because 'roundaboutness' does not work when production must account for the presence of fixed capital. 'For the determination of a Period of Production, we must be able to associate particular inputs with particular outputs; and it is in the very nature of the use of durable instruments that this cannot be done' (Hicks 1973: 9).

Despite Böhm-Bawerk's failure to provide an entirely satisfactory analysis of the relationships existing among production, capital and time, it is a fact that '[e]ven today, the great name in this department of economics is the name of Böhm-Bawerk' (Hicks 1946: 192). His refusal to consider the physical productivity of capital as a necessary source of value together with his distinction between social and private capital – which we shall analyse in the next chapter – and the emphasis put on the role of time are just two of his great contributions to economic theory. Every attempt to provide a thorough analysis of capital must take them into account and show how they can be incorporated into a modern approach to monetary economics.

The neoclassical approach to capital

Walras's impasse

Part V of Walras's *Elements of Pure Economics* is devoted to the theory of capital formation (and credit). Consistent with the approach followed throughout the book, the first problem tackled by Walras is that of the determination of the prices of capital goods. The question of where capital comes from is only partially raised by Walras, who merely assumes 'that there are land-owners, workers, and capitalists who *save*' (Walras 1984: 42) and 'that over against those who create savings, there are entrepreneurs who produce new capital goods in lieu of raw materials or consumers' goods' (ibid.: 42). Thus, like consumption goods and services, capital goods are assumed to be given from the start. The determination of their prices is then the result of their sales and purchases on the capital goods market. 'So now we must contemplate a market which we shall call a *capital goods market*, where capital goods are bought and sold' (ibid.: 267). A few lines later, Walras specifies that '[t]he price of a capital good depends essentially on the price of its services, that is to say, on its *income*' (ibid.: 267). But how is income itself determined? Being the price of capital goods services, it is logical to suppose that income, like the price of any other good or service in neoclassical theory, is determined by supply and demand. Yet, Walras distinguishes between *gross* and *net* income and points out that it is net income (i.e. what remains of gross income after deduction of depreciation charges and insurance premium) that sets the condition for the capital goods market to be in equilibrium. At equilibrium, in fact, 'the rate of net income is the same for all capital goods' (ibid.: 268–9), so that:

> [w]hen we determine *i* we also determine the prices of all landed capital, personal capital and capital goods proper by virtue of the equation
>
> $$p - (\mu + v)P = iP$$
>
> or
>
> $$P = \frac{p}{i + \mu + v}$$
>
> (ibid.: 269)

where P is the price of a capital good, p is this capital good's gross income, i is the rate of net income, μP is the depreciation charge and vP is the insurance premium.

Now, the problem is that the price of capital goods depends on their net incomes, which depend on the price of capital goods. The circularity of this process is evident. This is not surprising, of course, as the entire theoretical framework of general equilibrium analysis is based on circularity. Walras's aim was to elaborate a mathematical theory of economics, and in mathematics the simultaneous solution of a system of equations accounts for circularity. Indeed, if economics were a branch of mathematics, Walras would be perfectly right. General equilibrium would be a consistent theoretical framework for economic analysis, and it would be impossible to 'understand without mathematics why or how current equilibrium prices are arrived at not only in exchange, but also in production, capital formation and circulation' (ibid.: 43). The fact is, however, that Walras's premise is far from evident. On the contrary, unless we accept Debreu's axiom that goods are numbers

– an assumption that is verified neither conceptually nor empirically – we cannot develop an economic theory on mathematical grounds. But if we do accept Debreu's axiom, then we must be prepared to end up with a theory that might well tell us nothing about the economic reality: 'the theory, in the strict sense, is logically entirely disconnected from its interpretations' (Debreu 1959: x). The question has nothing to do with the possibility of introducing mathematical formalisation into economics. Indeed, economics can enter the realm of science only if its object of enquiry can be measured, a condition that requires the use of numbers. The real problem is whether the introduction of numbers is the result of an economic process or of a mathematical definition. If – as we have endeavoured to prove so far – goods and numbers are associated through production, it becomes clear that economics stands on its own feet. Hence, it should also be clear that simultaneity cannot be postulated simply because it is implied by the mathematical solution of a system of equations. The circularity implicit in Walras's determination of prices has thus to be refuted on logical (and not on mathematical) grounds. Let us say it once again. Real goods and services derive their numerical expression from their association with money, an operation that defines an *absolute* exchange taking place on the factors market. This result, which is not obtained from a mathematical but from an economic analysis of production, does not warrant the introduction of any functional relationship between input and output, and definitely limits the competence of mathematics within economics. As a consequence, general equilibrium can no longer be retained as a fruitful theoretical framework for economic analysis.

Walras's analysis of capital determination is developed along the same lines as his theory of relative prices and production. Exchange plays a central role, together with the condition of equality between prices and costs of production. As observed by Walras, capital goods would neither be sold nor purchased if they 'could only be exchanged for one another in ratios proportional to their net incomes' (Walras 1984: 269). If this were the case, prices could never be determined for lack of any rational motive for exchange. To avoid this difficulty, and to find a sufficient number of independent equations, Walras assumes that, in a progressive economy, income exceeds consumption, and he introduces the equality between this surplus and the value of capital goods as a new condition of equilibrium. The following quotation shows with great clarity Walras's choice for a mathematical approach to economics and for a theory of capital based on (relative) exchange.

New capital goods are exchanged against the excess of income over consumption; and the condition of equality between the value of the new capital goods and the value of the excess gives us the equation required for the determination of the rate of net income and consequently for the determination of the prices of capital goods. Moreover, new capital goods are products; and the condition of equality between their selling price and their cost of production gives us the equations required for the determination of the quantities manufactured. Once again we have to describe this equilibrium mathematically and then show how it is automatically realized in the market.

(ibid.: 269–70)

Once again, the entire exercise amounts to determining a system of independent equations in which there are as many equations as unknowns. On the whole, Walras's analysis leaves the economic process of capital accumulation unexplained. While it is correct that positive saving is a prerequisite for the formation of capital, it is difficult to see how saving might be determined by the difference between the price of the services of capital (what Walras calls income) and consumption. Logically, saving precedes the production of capital goods and cannot, therefore, depend on them or on the price of their services. The problem is again one of circularity. Economics being a science on its own, it must provide a theory capable of explaining where capital comes from and how capital goods relate to the production of final output.

Let us approach Walras's analysis from a slightly different point of view. The crucial point to verify is whether or not the price of the service of capital is determined independently of the price of capital. According to Walras, it is through a system of general equilibrium that prices of goods and productive services are established. Hence, for example, the price of the services of labour is determined by referring the supply of labour to the demand for it, that of land by referring the supply of land to the demand for it, etc. Wages per unit of labour and rent per unit of land are the variables to be determined, the price of services being then calculated by multiplying wages and rent by the quantity of labour and land actually used in a given period of reference. What about capital? If by capital we mean capital goods, their services must consist of the newly produced real goods that can be directly attributed to their use. Now, the problem is how the price of these services may be determined. Supply and demand for capital goods are of no help here because Walras maintains that the price of capital is derived from that of its services. Let us then suppose capital to stand for financial capital. This is perfectly in line with Walras's own analysis since he explicitly claims that '[n]ew capital goods are exchanged against the excess of income over consumption' (ibid.: 269). In this case, the supply of and demand for financial capital determine the rate of interest, and the price of capital goods is obtained by multiplying the capital invested in their production by the rate of interest (times the period of time taken into consideration) and adding it to their value. At this point, Walras introduces another constraint into his system, requiring the (selling) price of capital goods to be equal to their cost of production: 'new capital goods are products, and the condition of equality between their selling price and their cost of production gives the equations required for the determination of the quantities manufactured' (ibid.: 269–70).

As there are no reasons to believe that the prices determined by a system based on consumers' preferences are necessarily proportionate to the costs of production, Walras is forced to introduce this relationship as a condition of equilibrium by his decision to consider the quantities of capital goods available in his system as given. This decision itself is imposed by the unavoidable fact that, for a general equilibrium to exist, it is necessary that all markets be simultaneously cleared. If we accept Walras's analytical framework, we are faced with a system of relative prices in which every variable must be determined in real terms. This implies that the rate of interest must also be conceived of as a relative price, which means that it would usually be impossible to determine a unique rate of interest for the whole system. There would be as many rates of interest as there are different kinds of capital goods. Thus, the assumption that quantities are given as initial endowments of the system becomes a theoretical necessity of Walras's general equilibrium. Unfortunately, as clearly shown by Garegnani, accepting this hypothesis amounts to accepting that equilibrium is already known before being determined since 'Walras's equations of capitalisation can be simultaneously satisfied only when some of the given quantities are those compatible with the situation of equilibrium that has to be determined; this amounts to saying that the theory is bound to circularity' (Garegnani 1972: 113; our translation).

From Böhm-Bawerk to Wicksell

The main attempt to transpose Böhm-Bawerk's analysis of capital into a neoclassical framework is Wicksell's. In *Value, Capital and Rent* (Wicksell 1954), the Swedish economist takes over the concept of the average period of production and tries to work out a theory of distribution in which a central role is played by the theory of the marginal productivity of capital. His attempt is that of reconciling the measurement of capital in terms of the average period of production with the use of the concept of marginal productivity. As shown by Garegnani, however, the restrictive conditions that have to be introduced to bring about this reconciliation – simple rate of interest, absence of fixed capital and presence of just one factor of production besides capital – are too strong to be realistic. To overcome this difficulty, in his *Lectures on Political Economy* Wicksell (1934) abandons the use of the average period of production and maintains that capital must rather be measured in terms of its (relative) value. By doing so, however, he falls into a contradiction that consists in determining the remuneration of capital by using a theory (of marginal productivity) which has to be applied to a measure of capital that is itself dependent on this remuneration. In Garegnani's words, by measuring capital in terms of (relative) value, Wicksell 'contradicts the requisite that capital be conceived of as being independent of variations in distribution' (Garegnani 1972: 185; our translation).

As brilliantly shown by Bliss (1975), the marginalist theory is not essential to the neoclassical approach. It seems perfectly legitimate to maintain, then, that Wicksell's impasse is due to the use of the concept of marginal productivity, a neoclassical theory of capital being well within our reach if we are prepared to drop this concept. In reality, this is not the case. The logical shortcomings that we have tried to highlight earlier in this chapter and in Chapter 2 are unrelated to the marginalist principle. Thus, whether we give it up or not, the neoclassical approach to capital appears to be doomed to failure. Does this imply that the whole of

Wicksell's analysis of capital must be rejected on logical grounds? This would be a rather drastic and unfair conclusion. The work of the Swedish economist deserves a more sympathetic appraisal: its deep insights into the theory of capital are still today a source of inspiration in this complex and controversial field. As an example, let us refer to the way in which Wicksell defines the means of production and their use in the process of capital accumulation.

'[I]f the means of subsistence have not yet passed over into the hands of the workers, but are still (directly or indirectly through money) in the possession of the capitalist, then they are undoubtedly means of production, *because they serve for the purchase of labour*' (Wicksell 1954: 102–3). Wicksell is here defining capital as a real wage fund. The idea is that firms can make up such a fund through profits, and use it as a real wage for workers. The recourse to profits is necessary to avoid any confusion between the means of subsistence that belong to the category of circulating capital and those that do not. The distinction cannot be made by referring to their physical characteristics, but calls for an unambiguous economic principle. It is the working of monetary economies that provides this principle. Commodities qualify as consumption goods if they are bought through the final expenditure of money income; they pertain to the category of capital goods if they are purchased through the investment of profits (actual or advanced). Now, the first form of investment is the initial purchase by firms of that part of the means of subsistence that is not immediately sold to workers. Thus conceived, circulating capital is made up of a stock of real goods and their monetary counterpart (profit). This is how Wicksell's claim that the means of subsistence owned by firms are undoubtedly means of production should be understood in the light of modern monetary analysis.

Firms own part of the consumption goods currently produced only if they earn a positive profit. It is only in this case that the still unsold stock of consumption goods may be considered as a real wage fund. It must be clear, however, that firms are only the initial holders of this stock, which is bound to be finally purchased by wage-earners as soon as the corresponding profit is invested in a new payment of wages. The concrete transformation of the means of subsistence into means of production requires, thus, a new production whose result is the substitution of the initial stock of consumption goods (circulating capital) with a final 'stock' of investment goods (fixed capital). As they are paid through the investment of profit, workers receive the consumption goods previously stocked by firms in exchange for their new production of investment goods. Wicksell is perfectly entitled to claim that the means of subsistence in the hands of firms are transformed into means of production because they serve for the purchase of labour. It is precisely because they pay wages out of their profit that firms acquire the final possession of investment goods *on the labour market*. The expenditure of a positive income (profit) within the payment of wages defines the purchase of labour itself and, therefore, of the products resulting from its activity. In exchange for their new products, workers receive a drawing right over the initial stock of consumption goods, which is the proof that the means of subsistence making up the real wage fund are bound to be transformed into investment goods and can thus be considered as means of production by destination. The idea that capitalisation works its way through a purchase of labour is far-reaching and deserves all our attention. As we shall see in the last chapter, today's pathological process of capital accumulation is entirely the result of this mechanism of direct appropriation of fixed capital goods. It is one of the great merits of Wicksell to have pointed it out.

Of course, this is not the only example of Wicksell's contribution to the theory of capital. For the sake of brevity, let us simply remember that – having claimed that 'Böhm-Bawerk's really epoch-making idea … was to recognize in the *capitalistic production process* itself … the simple, primary concept, of which capital in all its guises is then only derived or secondary' (Wicksell 1997: 18) – Wicksell maintains that 'capital itself is almost always a product' (Wicksell 1934: 149), thus refusing to identify it with a factor of production. Despite his predilection for neoclassical analysis, Wicksell is aware that capital goods are produced means of production, so that their productive capacity must be referred back to labour and land and to their period of implementation in time. Together with time, saved up labour becomes a key element in the theory of capital. This was, of course, Böhm-Bawerk's essential message. Wicksell takes it over, trying to show that it is eventually compatible with the concept of marginal productivity. This has often been interpreted as being the mark of Wicksell's attempt to reformulate Böhm-Bawerk's theory along the lines of neoclassical analysis. Now, although this interpretation is largely substantiated by Wicksell's use of the neoclassical framework of analysis, it seems possible to suggest an alternative way of looking at the relationship between capital and its physical productivity. Even though capital is not directly at the origin of a positive value, nobody has ever denied that its use leads to an increase in physical output. Thus, the problem is to determine whether and how this physical increase can be transformed into an increase in value. As we know, Böhm-Bawerk's solution was to refer labour and land to the average period of production. Wicksell's attempt to evaluate the increase in physical productivity was also related to the possibility of attributing it to the use of saved up labour and land, and not directly to capital. Since capital is made up of produced instrumental goods, and since it is not itself a factor of production, it seems reasonable to maintain that the value added by the use of capital must derive from labour and land.

Following Schumpeter, let us consider labour alone. How can we explain the increase in value due to the increase in physical productivity by referring to labour? Is it not true that labour-value is independent of physical productivity? That labour can only account for the exchange value of final output irrespective of its value-in-use? This would obviously be the case if we were to reason within a classical theoretical framework. Wicksell, however, is not a supporter of the classical labour theory of value. He believes instead that value must also be related to factors other than labour, and particularly to time. But if we do not take on board Böhm-Bawerk's roundabout methods of production – as Wicksell decided to do on second thought – how are we to account for the role played by time? Moreover, as time itself is not a factor of production, how can its combination with labour be the source of value? Although it cannot be claimed that Wicksell has provided a definitive answer to this question, his solution – together with Böhm-Bawerk's – has the merit of clarifying the terms of the problem. In particular, it clearly shows that value is the result of the economic process considered as a whole, from production to capital accumulation. Wicksell's definition of interest as a form of income deriving from the implementation of saved up labour in time is, in fact, symptomatic of an overall vision of the economic process in which capital and interest are tied up with labour and time. It is true that Wicksell explains interest as a difference between marginal productivities (ibid.: 154) and that the link between the increase in physical productivity and the increase in value remains essentially unexplained. Nevertheless, as we shall see in the next two chapters, his analysis provides the elements for a new approach to the theory of capital, of interest and of the present pathological process of capital accumulation. For the time being, let us dwell a little longer on the main difficulties faced by the traditional approach to capital, with particular attention being paid to the problem of its measurement.

On the measurement of capital

As generally admitted by economists, social capital is made up of produced means of production. The problem of measuring social capital is therefore that of determining the value of these means of production. Now, whether we choose the classical or the neoclassical point of view, we are confronted with the difficulty that – like that of any other good – the value (price) of capital goods depends on distribution and on the rate of interest. Joan Robinson puts forward some key elements of this problem in her paper on the production function and the theory of capital. As stressed by Harcourt, 'Joan Robinson's article thus links the modern discussion on capital to an old puzzle: is there a unit in which aggregate or social capital may be measured, a unit that is itself independent of distribution and prices?' (Harcourt 1972: 3). Now, as Harcourt again points out, the solution provided by Robinson is not independent of distribution and prices. Is it because 'it is impossible to conceive of a quantity of "capital in general", the *value* of which is independent of the rate of interest and wages' (ibid.: 20)? Let us try to clarify the terms of the problem.

The argument advanced by Robinson is that a neoclassical production function cannot be constructed unless capital enters it as an independent magnitude. Thus understood, her claim is set against the neoclassical belief that economic variables may result from the solution of a set of simultaneous equations. The debate is part of the well-known controversy between the economists who consider co-determination to be a viciously circular process and those who maintain that the search for a simultaneous solution of a set of equations is a perfectly legitimate procedure in the field of economics. Now, if it were true that capital can only be determined simultaneously with the rate of interest and prices, we would almost be forced to share the neoclassical point of view. As much as we would like to sympathise with Robinson's approach, we would have no rationale to embrace an argument that leaves capital totally undetermined unless we introduce the unrealistic assumption of perfect foresight and lack of uncertainty. Yet, things are not as they appear to be. The problem of measuring capital is not that of establishing its equilibrium value. The whole argument needs to be put on the right track. Capital is a monetary entity with a real object. This means that it cannot be determined only in real or monetary terms. The measure of capital in labour-units is not a viable solution since, besides being confronted with the problem of labour heterogeneity, it does not allow for the monetary determination of capital. The same conclusion applies to the neoclassical attempt to express the value of capital in terms of relative prices. It thus appears that the true problem is not that of establishing whether or not capital may be measured independently of distribution and prices, but instead that of explaining the origin of capital in its twin aspects.

As already pointed out by Solow, the theory of capital still remains a controversial subject, and 'when a theoretical question remains debatable after 80 years there is a presumption that the question is badly posed – or very deep indeed' (Solow 1963: 10). Solow believes that the question of capital has been badly posed and tries to show that, despite being 'very complicated and very difficult' (ibid.: 11), capital theory may be mastered by referring to the concept of rate of return on investment. According to the Massachusetts Institute of Technology Professor, 'we really want a theory of interest rates, not a theory of capital' (ibid.: 16). Contrary to his famous predecessors, Solow maintains that interest rates can be explained without having previously worked out a theory of capital. According to his definition, the rate of return on investment is simply the ratio between the extra units of consumption, k, that will be earned tomorrow and the units of consumption saved and invested today, h, minus 1 ($k/h - 1$). Solow claims that this way of looking at the theory has the advantage of avoiding the problem of measuring capital. Yet, he seems to forget that in his approach he is faced with a similar difficulty, namely the problem of measuring consumption. Admittedly, Solow is 'concerned with the rate of return the stock of real capital goods is able to provide and how it depends on changes in technology and the cumulation of past saving' (ibid.: 28). Because saving–investment decisions are dependent on 'the durability of the structures and equipment involved' and on 'the complementary inputs of labor and materials required' (ibid.: 28), he maintains that 'the rate of return is a useful indicator of the choices facing society, while capital–output ratios are not' (ibid.: 28). However, in order to calculate the rate of return on investment, it is necessary to refer present (extra) consumption to past saving, a ratio that is meaningful only if its two terms are homogeneous. Obviously, Solow believes they are, and he would certainly be right if, as he assumes, output could be determined through a production function. But the production function itself requires its elements to be homogeneous. It is a matter of elementary logic that equations can be formulated only if constants and variables pertain to the same homogeneous set. This would indeed be the case if labour and consumption goods (in the example chosen by Solow) were expressed in money. Yet, his approach being fundamentally neoclassical, Solow never mentions this possibility. We are thus bound to conclude that his analysis suffers from the same shortcomings as the theory it stems from. The logical indeterminacy of relative prices does not allow for working out a theory of production in mathematical terms, so that Solow's claim that the rate of return on investment is 'a dimensionless number (per unit of time) and one which will have meaning no matter how we choose to idealize the process of capitalistic production in our models' (ibid.: 36) can only be considered as a *petitio principii* of no heuristic value.

In fact, Solow's analysis is germane to that of Sraffa. The attempt to derive the rate of return on investment from a comparison between current extra consumption and past saving rests on the implicit assumption that commodities are produced by means of commodities, and that the rate of return itself 'is primarily a technological concept' (ibid.: 69). Unfortunately, as pointed out by Harcourt, Solow's 'analysis is an illegitimate extrapolation of results that hold only for a one-commodity, malleable capital world in which the short run and the long run collapse into one and perfect foresight and realized expectations are guaranteed' (Harcourt 1972: 117).

Solow's belief that the rate of return on investment may be positive and increase with the aid of technical progress is all the more surprising as he himself very lucidly observes that, conceived of as a residual, net output may be positive only if inputs are incompletely accounted for.

> The rate of growth of output usually exceeds what one can reasonably attribute to the specific list of inputs at hand. And the difference is what we call the rate of increase of output per unit of input or, more picturesquely, the rate of technical progress. Now it is obvious that the more complete the list of inputs, the smaller will be the residual.
>
> (Solow 1963: 38)

The net product, defined as the difference between output and inputs, is thus considered by Solow as a residual that is reduced to zero when we are able to refer output to the complete set of inputs. In this case, the effects of technological progress would 'be imputed back to resources used in research activity and hours worked by scientists and engineers' (ibid.: 39).

Is Solow not contradicting himself? Setting out his model in the case of disembodied technical progress, he calculates a one-period rate of return by relating the saving of a marginal quantity of output at time t_0 to the additional consumption at time t_1 – which is equal to the increment in output plus 'the surviving part of the originally-saved capital' (ibid.: 45). His conclusion is here that 'the one-period rate of return r_1 is the net marginal product of capital, *at the level of technology ruling in period 1*' (ibid.: 45). He reaches a different conclusion when analysing the case of embodied technical progress, the rate of return on saving being now smaller than the net marginal product of capital. Yet, despite this difference in amounts, it seems correct to claim that Solow has essentially the same definition of the two concepts: his rate of return is basically related to a net increase in output derived from saving and technical progress. His whole analysis rests on the possibility of determining a net product as the difference between output and inputs. According to his own observations, however, this possibility cannot be taken for granted. On the contrary, to assume the existence of a net real product is to argue against Lavoisier's principle of conservation of matter and energy, unless we are prepared to replace the traditional (physical) conception of capital and product with a truly economic conception based on a monetary macroeconomic approach. This is not the path followed by Solow. Although he claims that capital is a very complex concept, he fails fully to realise the importance of its monetary component. He is certainly right in claiming that 'only someone who is naively identifying all the many aspects of capitalistic production with one of them, it does not matter which, would believe that the theory can be summed up by defining something called "capital" and calling the interest rate the marginal productivity of it' (ibid.: 14). Nonetheless, he identifies capital with the different aspects of its real components, thus forgetting that the concept of capital defines a reality that is simultaneously real and monetary.

Like his fellow neoclassical economists, Solow considers capital to be far too complex to be reduced to a single entity. At the same time, he is well aware of the difficulty of accounting for this complexity by means of mathematical modelling. This is why he tries to set out what he calls a 'surrogate production function', his aim being to provide an instrument capable of greatly simplifying both the theory and its econometric formulation. Now, the point is that production functions require aggregation, which is precisely what modern programming techniques attempt to avoid. Since production functions are elements of the static models of GEA, and since 'the problem of accumulation of capital goods or inventories is naturally or intrinsically ruled out in the static theory' (Morishima 1992: 27), it seems difficult to accept Solow's suggestion that simple production functions should be used in the interest of empirical measurement and approximation. In his paper, Fisher (1969) observes, in fact, that aggregate production functions rest on foundations that seem 'solid only insofar as relatively small changes are concerned' and concludes that 'the conditions for the existence of aggregate production functions, at least when widely diverse industries are included, seem very, very strong' (Fisher 1969: 576). In this respect, Samuelson's claim that a rigorous analysis of capital relies 'upon a complex–heterogeneous–capital programming model' (Samuelson 1962: 193) sounds to be more a logical necessity than a preferable alternative. The famous American economist has been consistent in claiming that the neoclassical approach to capital theory consists in applying modern programming techniques to heterogeneous capital goods models.

> Repeatedly in writings and lectures I have insisted that capital theory can be rigorously developed without using any Clark-like concept of aggregate 'capital', instead relying upon a complete analysis of a great variety of heterogeneous physical capital goods and processes through time. Such an analysis leans heavily on the tools of modern linear and more general programming and might therefore be called neo-classical.
>
> (ibid.: 193)

But is it realistic to believe that a model could ever account for a complete analysis of such a great variety of heterogeneous physical capital goods and temporal processes existing in the real world? Moreover, is it not true that physical goods remain economically heterogeneous unless they are associated with numbers? Hence, only two possibilities are actually available to us. Either we are able to show how real goods are related to numbers – in which case there is no longer any need for linear and non-linear programming models – or we stick with heterogeneity, hoping that mathematics will help us to create a model of the real world. Samuelson opts for the second alternative in order to avoid the problems of capital aggregation. By doing so, he seems to forget that no scientific theory can exist if its object cannot be measured, which is precisely what happens for capital if capital goods remain heterogeneous.

This is a point that Hicks did not miss. In fact, perfectly aware that the need for homogeneity is as true of capital goods as it is of any other real good, he argued in favour of aggregation. 'All that we get from the physical goods is a list – so much of this, so much of that; for macro-economics there must be aggregation' (Hicks 1973: 151). Hicks analyses the attempt to solve the problem of aggregation by measuring capital in value terms. In particular, he claims that, as the capital–output ratio is usually taken to be a real concept, the money values of output and capital must be deflated by the index of output prices. The interesting point here is that he maintains both that the capital–output ratio 'is to be kept as a pure number' and that real capital is 'the value of capital in terms of final output' (ibid.: 152). Correctly understood, this means that in order to compare capital and final output it is necessary to determine their money values first. The index of output prices is introduced to evaluate output and capital at constant prices, but it is not essential to the point that we are making here. What really matters is that the capital–output ratio could never be a pure number unless its two terms were homogeneous. Money values allow capital and output to be expressed in the same unit. It is only once money values are determined that the capital–output ratio may also be used to express the value of capital in terms of output. The relevant fact is that capital and output are bundles of goods physically heterogeneous. Money values are the only means by which they can be made homogeneous. If money values could not be determined, the capital–output ratio could neither be 'written down' nor 'kept as a pure number'.

Since the heterogeneity problem arises also when capital goods alone are considered, a major difficulty seems to bar the way to the monetary valuation of capital. It could be argued, in fact, that 'it is necessary even for the value measure that it should be possible to set a market price on each item in the capital goods stock' (ibid.: 154), and that, since 'there is no reason why that should be so' (ibid.: 154), we are locked in a serious impasse. Hicks's problem lies in the fact that there may be goods that are not traded on the market and whose prices would thus remain undetermined according to neoclassical principles. (One of the difficulties met by neoclassical theories of capital is, in fact, that of valuing intermediate goods for which there are no markets, so that it is impossible to value them at market prices.) Looking for a solution compatible with the theory of relative prices, Hicks claims that a forward-looking measure 'enables us to generalize the value measure to cover goods that have no market' (ibid.: 158). This solution, consisting in 'a capitalization of the marginal stream of net outputs which disposal over the marginal unit will permit' (ibid.: 157), is not particularly satisfactory. The weakness of this procedure is that value is assumed to be determined by the stream of future net outputs expected from the stock of capital goods. Even if this assumption were on the whole acceptable, it would be impossible to attribute the stream of net outputs (whatever this is supposed to mean) to the different goods of the capital stock. Moreover, as observed by Hicks himself, the forward-looking measure of capital has the annoying consequence that a change in technology causes a variation in the measure of capital (equal to the variation in the stream of future net outputs) even if the physical stock of capital goods remains unchanged. To avoid it, Hicks introduces the volume measure of capital, which he considers as a backward-looking measure 'derived by accumulating past net inputs' (ibid.: 159). His aim is to give a measure of capital, which he calls *capital at cost*, that 'will behave in the way that we should expect from a volume index' (ibid.: 159). The problem with this kind of backward-looking measure is that the process of accumulation could be continuously made to start at earlier points in time. To avoid reducing capital at cost to the capital goods accumulated over centuries, Hicks suggests that it be considered essentially as an index number measure. This means that, even in the volume measure case, capital has to be measured in value. At the starting point of the process of accumulation that we are interested in investigating, capital is measured in value terms. According to Hicks, 'it is perfectly consistent to use the *value* of capital at the base date as the initial *volume*' as what we have to do is 'simply to adopt the convention that *at the base date* value and volume are the same' (ibid.: 159–60). But is it really just a matter of convention? Is it logically consistent to maintain that value and volume are the same at the base date and that, as we move forward, 'value changes in one way, volume in another' (ibid.: 160)? If they change in different ways, they will never be the same at any subsequent date, and if we decided to start our analysis from another base date no convention could really make them equal. The degree of arbitrariness becomes so high that the entire approach is seriously undermined. Hicks's considerations about the difficulties introduced in the value measure of capital by aggregation and expectations confirm this malaise. The time has come to face the problem from a different footing. What is wrong with the traditional way of measuring capital is not the intent to express it both in value and in physical terms. Capital goods are monetised real goods, and must therefore be considered in both their monetary and physical aspects. This does not mean, however, that they can be measured in either monetary or real terms. Like any other produced good, capital goods are defined by the identity between a monetary form and its real content, and it is from this twofold point of view that they must be grasped.

Income, capital and time

As we have already observed in the previous chapter, in his 1992 book Morishima claims that, static models of GEA being timeless, traditional neoclassical theory is unable to account for capital accumulation or even for production. According to the Japanese economist, the failure of GET is mainly due to the fact that '[neoclassical] economists never seriously ask what is capital, or what is a capitalist' (Morishima 1992: 28). More precisely, he rightly maintains that the capitalist process of production and accumulation must be explained by taking into consideration both its monetary elements and time. Despite his efforts, Morishima's attempt to integrate money and time into the neoclassical framework fails, mainly because his theory rests on the assumption that market prices can be determined in purely real terms. Notwithstanding this, Morishima is one of the few contemporary economists to have lucidly recognised the need for a theory of capital in which money and time are called upon to play a central role.

As we have seen in previous sections of this chapter, classical and Austrian economists have already attempted to incorporate time into their theories. On the other hand, Hicks has insisted on the need to distinguish physical from financial capital.

> If it is capital in the volume sense that is being measured, capital is physical goods; but in the value sense capital is not physical goods. It is a sum of values which may conveniently be described as a Fund. A Fund that may be embodied in physical goods in different ways. There are these two senses of Real Capital which need to be distinguished.
>
> (Hicks 1977: 152)

Other economists have since worked hard to incorporate money into GE models. Unfortunately, as recognised by Orphanides and Solow (1990: 258), '[t]he fundamental difficulty is that we do not yet have any clearly preferred way to introduce money into models of the real economy, especially those that feature durable productive assets as well. Models of a monetary economy without real capital cannot be taken seriously as vehicles for the study of money-and-growth'.

As we have attempted to prove in Chapter 2, money has not yet been satisfactorily integrated into models of the real economy. The neoclassical dichotomy between monetary and real variables has proved too difficult an obstacle to be overcome by traditional analysis. Now, the point is that either money is integrated from the beginning into the real world of production or it is bound to remain a mere device, entirely alien to the real world.

From money to capital-time

The privileged starting point of macroeconomic analysis is bank money. In its initial form of a unit of account, money is issued by banks as an acknowledgement of debt with no other object than itself. Thus, money as such is a purely numerical form with no proper value. Its function is to count (real) goods, to monetise them. As we have seen, this monetisation takes place on the factors market, through the payment of the macroeconomic costs of production (wages). As a result of this payment – which implies the instantaneous reflux of money to its point of emission where it is immediately destroyed – a positive bank deposit is formed to the benefit of wage-earners. This means that the payment of wages defines the purchase of current output (in its monetary form) by workers and not by firms, by which physical goods are simply stored waiting for their final sale on the commodity market. Workers' bank deposits define a positive purchasing power precisely because their object is current output. Hence the payment of wages is an instantaneous event occurring through a circular money-flow, giving rise to a money-stock formed as a bank deposit and having current output as real content.

From a monetary point of view, the result of production is the formation of a positive money income deposited by wage-earners on the liabilities side of the banks' balance sheets. Now, it is in the nature of double-entry book-keeping that what is entered as a liability is immediately matched by an equivalent entry on the assets side of the balance sheet. The money income deposited by wage-earners is thus immediately lent by banks to firms – which is perfectly in line with the fact that firms get indebted to the extent that banks pay their costs of production. This is tantamount to saying that the money income generated by production is immediately saved by workers, lent to firms and transformed into capital until its final expenditure on the commodity market (for the purchase of the physical output stored by firms). Its existence being limited to the period elapsing between the formation of money income and its final expenditure, this first kind of circulating capital is closely related to time and might be called – following Schmitt – *capital-time*. 'Le premier capital, la "forme-mère" de toutes les autres formes-capital, est simplement le temps séparant le revenu actuel de sa dépense future. Même le capital en son aspect le plus "solide", le capital fixe ou instrumental, est logiquement réductible au capital-temps' (Schmitt 1984b: 151).

Capital-time is a first kind of circulating capital in the sense that its real object is a stock of consumption goods, part of which might become the real object of a true circulating capital (in the classical sense) if an identical part of the initial money income (only momentarily saved and transformed into capital-time) were to be saved once for all. To the extent that workers (or, more generally, income holders) dispose of their bank deposits in order to purchase current output, capital-time is retransformed into money income and destroyed. Yet, only that part of money income is destroyed that covers the costs of production of the consumption goods actually purchased by income holders. If, as is usually the case, consumption goods are sold at a market price greater than their cost, part of the money income spent for their purchase is transferred as profit to firms. Here again, we are confronted with a positive saving of money income and with its transformation into capital-time. But this time, the stock of current output is not simply stored but also owned by firms (their stockholders) since profit is their own income. The difference between the two cases becomes significant, however, only if profit is invested instead of being redistributed to income holders. It is only in this case, in fact, that capital-time defines a circulating capital – a circulating fund – whose investment gives rise to a fixed capital.

From circulating to fixed capital

Keynes is certainly right in relating (fixed) capital to investment. 'We shall mean by the rate of investment the net increment during a period of time of the capital of the community' (Keynes 1971: 114). He is also right in claiming that the value of investment does not correspond to 'the increment of value of total capital, but [to] the value of the increment of capital during any period' (ibid.: 114) since, while it is increased by investment, the value of total capital is decreased by wear and tear. Hence, any new production is (at least) partially devoted to restoring the initial value of social or fixed capital. This is what we used to call amortisation, a process that is best defined as the production of replacement goods and whose output, although it does not increase the value of total capital, pertains entirely to the category of capital goods. In the same passage of Keynes's *Treatise*, we find another interesting claim, namely that 'the value of current investment ... [is] equal to the aggregate of savings and profits' (ibid.: 114). As the reader knows, in his *Treatise* Keynes considers 'that profits are not part of the community's income' (ibid.: 111). This means that from the outset Keynes conceived profits as an income that firms derive from 'the earnings of the community [households]'. Now, if we bear in mind that profits are partially transformed into interests and dividends or lent on the financial market, it is easy to observe, with Keynes, that net profits actually nourish current investment. Likewise, saving being that part of current income that is not spent on current consumption, it is obvious that they are bound to be lent to firms and invested, together with current net profits, in the production of new capital goods.

Before taking our analysis a step further, it is worth preventing a possible misunderstanding. A cursory reader may suggest, in fact, that Keynes's claim that current investment is equal to aggregate savings and profits is no longer supported in his later work, the *General Theory*, where he repeatedly asserts the necessary equality between saving and investment. In reality, Keynes did not change his mind. As is shown by the following quotation taken from a draft of the first chapter of his *Treatise*, even before publication of his 1930 book he had no doubts that the production of capital goods is nourished by savings. 'A supply of *new* capital, whether in the form of finished goods or of goods in process, can only come into existence in so far as those who have claims on the community's flow of income are willing to *defer* their claims, i.e. out of "savings" ' (Keynes 1973b: 19). The claim that capital goods result from the investment of savings is only apparently in contrast with the claim that they result from the investment of profits. Resulting from a transfer from consumers to firms, profits too pertain to the category of those incomes that are not spent for the final purchase of consumption goods. In this sense, profits are part of saving. Thus, the term 'saving' can be meant to incorporate both individual savings and profits. Global macroeconomic saving is that part of current income that is saved by the economy as a whole, and is equivalent to that part of current income that is saved by consumers plus net profits, i.e. plus the part of income that is definitively transferred to firms. The production of capital goods derives from the investment of global saving, and is thus financed both by individuals' savings lent to firms and by profits. As suggested by Schmitt, it may even be claimed that capital goods result from the investment of profits only, since savings lent to firms can be conceived of as an advance of (future) profits. 'Thus investment is the expenditure of a current profit (already realised) or of an advanced profit (which, although it will be realised in the future, is already available, since it is exchanged with the income actually saved and lent to firms). In conclusion, investment is always the expenditure of a firm's profit' (Schmitt 1984b: 166; our translation).

As analysis and facts confirm, any new production of capital goods requires the investment of an equivalent amount of current income. In other words, the production of capital goods is the transformation of circulating into fixed capital. The circulating capital relevant here is that earned by firms as net profit. Let us start from a period, p_0, in which only consumption goods are produced by firms, F. Let us suppose further that firms are successful in earning a positive profit out of their sales of current output. At the end of p_0, firms own a circulating capital – resulting from the transformation of their profit – whose real object is a stock of consumption goods. As a numerical example, let us suppose current production to be defined by 100 wage units. If, for the purchase of current output, consumers spend the totality of their income and obtain in exchange consumption goods up to a value of 80 units (wage units), F's profit amounts to 20 units. A financial capital of 20 units is thus formed, whose real object is an equivalent stock made up of the consumption goods still available to F. The circulating capital formed in F defines a macroeconomic saving and is still, in its essence, a capital-time. Fixed capital results from the transformation of this stock of consumption goods into instrumental goods. In period p_1, in fact, firm F invests its profit by asking part of its workers to produce an equivalent amount of investment goods. Supposing that total employment is unaffected by this change in production, workers are still paid 100 wage units, 80 wage units for their new production of consumption goods and 20 wage units for their production of investment goods. Leaving aside any new formation of profit in period p_1 – which will merely reproduce a situation analogous to that of p_0 – we observe that consumers have at their disposal the exact amount of income required for the purchase of the consumption goods currently produced in p_1 and of those stocked by F in p_0. As a result of the whole process, 20 units of investment goods are formed as fixed capital.

If workers had been employed in both periods for the production of wage goods only, consumption would have reached 200 units. Production of fixed capital reduces it to 180 units. This simply means that production of instrumental goods requires consumers to save part of their current income, which, through F's investment, is definitively transformed into fixed capital. Instead of producing and consuming 200 units of wage goods, society opts for the 'productive consumption' of 20 units of wage goods, giving rise to an equivalent amount of instrumental goods. The formation of profit and its corresponding stock of consumption goods is the first step in the process of capitalisation. It is thus possible to maintain that the stock formed in p_0 is the first definition of the fixed capital of p_1.

> La formation du profit détermine la création équivalente d'un stock de biens-
> salaires. Ce stock est la première définition du capital *fixe*. En effet, le capital
> fixe remonte dans son existence jusqu'à la formation du profit monétaire,
> dont il n'est que l''avatar'. Le premier 'contenu' du capital fixe est donc une
> collection de biens-salaires stockés, autrement dit un pur capital-temps.
>
> (Schmitt 1984b: 170)

It is because 20 units of the current income of p_0 are transformed into fixed
capital that they are definitively saved, and that society gives up definitively an
equivalent part of its consumption of wage goods, substituting it with a production
of instrumental goods. 'Les biens-salaires convertis en capitaux fixes sont une
épargne fixe, dont la dissolution est à jamais reportée, jour après jour' (ibid.:
171).

Böhm-Bawerk's suggestion that capital is time finds here a new corroboration.
His intuition is right for the twofold reason that capital-time is the initial form of
every capital and that the transformation of circulating into fixed capital *fixes*
capital-time in a form – instrumental goods – that will never allow for its
consumption. In this context, roundabout methods of production are significant
inasmuch as they give rise to a greater production of capital goods. It is the
investment of profit, in fact, that allows an exact evaluation of fixed capital. In
our numerical example, capital goods result from the productive investment of
20 units of profit, i.e. from the conversion of 20 units of wage goods into equivalent
instrumental goods. Consistent with Keynes's analysis – but not necessarily with
that of his self-styled followers – labour is the sole source of value, which is
consequently expressed in wage units independently of the nature of produced
output. Hence, capital goods derive their value directly from production and, like
consumption goods, are defined in wage units.

In period p_0, production consists of consumption goods only and takes place –
economically – when wages are paid out to workers. At that very instant, an income
appears that is immediately transformed into capital-time. The double result of
production is therefore a financial capital (a bank deposit) and its corresponding
stock of consumption goods. Supposing that final purchases of consumption goods
are all carried out within the period, at the end of p_0 households have spent the
totality of their capital and firms benefited from a transfer of 20 units of income
that make up their profit. Again, this income is transformed into capital-time and
has as its real object an equivalent stock of consumption goods stored within F. In
period p_1, instrumental goods are produced up to an amount of 20 wage units.
This time the income earned by workers producing capital goods is spent for the
purchase of the consumption goods stocked in p_0. Once this purchase has taken
place, we observe that a new 'stock' of instrumental goods has actually replaced
the previous stock of consumption goods. 'La production de la nouvelle période,
qui suscite les biens-capitaux, chasse les biens-salaires et les remplace aussitôt,
dans le "stock" inchangé, par des capitaux instrumentaux' (ibid.: 175). Now, if
the physical aspect of fixed capital is perfectly accounted for by this substitution
of instrumental for consumption goods into F's stock, the financial aspect may be

troublesome. Having been spent on the final purchase of the stock of consumption goods of p_0, the income earned by the producers of fixed capital goods cannot be transformed into the financial counterpart of the new 'stock' of instrumental goods. The only way to guarantee perfect correspondence between the physical and financial aspects of fixed capital is to grant that profit is transformed into a fixed financial capital. Does the investment of profit achieve this result? This is the crucial question that must be answered if we are to understand the origin of present monetary disorders. Before attending to it, let us conclude our 'positive' analysis of capital by briefly investigating the problem of interest.

6   Money, capital and interest

'For centuries men have asked why interest is paid, whether it should be regulated or prohibited, what makes the rate of interest high here but low there' (Bliss 1975: 327). These questions are still partially unanswered today. Most economists have even given up the search for the origin of interest, their main efforts being conveyed towards the determination of the rate of interest. However, is it actually possible to determine the rate of interest if the interest itself is not? Attempts at determining the rate of interest directly without inquiring about its origin seem to suggest a positive answer. On the contrary, more classical analyses tend to call for a negative answer. In this chapter, we shall try to account for the main contributions to the theoretical investigation of interest, with the explicit aim of providing elements for a new macroeconomic analysis of this concept.

Interest, exchange and credit

Interest, time and credit

Many economists define interest as a risk premium related to the use of securities, which are considered less perfect than money: '[m]oney appears simply as the most perfect type of security; other securities are less perfect, and command a lower price because of their imperfection … of their imperfect "moneyness" ' (Hicks 1978: 163). The lack of general acceptability is thus seen as the cause for 'those bills which are not money … to stand at a discount' (ibid.: 166). At close scrutiny, however, these reasons do not seem to hold their ground. Why should 'moneyness' as such be a quality? Banknotes are the most liquid form of money claims, yet if they are lost or stolen their initial holder suffers from a loss that cannot be repaired. Had he maintained his claims against the banking system in the form of bank deposits, he would not have definitively lost his right over current or future output. Is it possibly to praise his rational behaviour that a positive interest is paid on his bank deposits and none is paid on banknotes? Are banknotes 'more intensely' money than bank deposits? The reader already knows that, in reality, neither banknotes nor claims on bank deposits are money. They both define a claim over a given amount of money income, not money itself, which is simply a numerical vehicle whose existence is limited to the instant that payments actually take place. Why should the most secure and modern of these two claims lead to a positive payment of interest to his holder? If interest was a risk premium related to the nature of securities held, why should the holder of banknotes not be compensated for the high risk he is taking by switching from bank deposits to banknotes?

Banknotes apart, it may be argued that there are securities (mostly long-term bills) that would never be purchased if they did not bear a positive interest. This is obviously true, as it is true that the level of risk differs from one security to another. Yet, this is not the point. The level of risk could at most explain the need for a microeconomic compensation between the borrower and the lender. In this sense, interest would simply define a transfer of money income from the borrower to the lender, and not the formation of a positive, new macroeconomic income. But then the justification of interest would derive from a comparison between advantages and disadvantages of lending (borrowing). A priori, this means that interest might have to be paid by lenders if it were proved that they derive a net advantage from saving and lending their present income in order to spend, after recovery of their loan, the borrowers' future income. This would indeed be the case in the absence of inflation, technological progress leading to a decrease in prices and (often but not always) to an increase in quality. Lenders would thus be able, once reimbursed, to purchase more and better than they would have done had they spent their income in the first place. As compensation for a disadvantage, interests would have to be paid by lenders to borrowers, and not vice versa. Obviously, this is only one of the several possibilities arising from this microeconomic conception of interest.

An analogous way to explain interest is by relating consumption to the flow of time. From a microeconomic point of view, for instance, interest might be derived from the exchange between present and future consumption. Within this framework, the rate of interest would define the equilibrium price between the supply of and demand for current saving. Interest could thus derive from a partial redistribution of income from future to present savers. When loans fall due, borrowers of today's income will have to transfer to lenders a sum increased by the amount of interest. Time is involved not as a source of value but only insofar as its flow – associated with banks' financial intermediation – allows borrowers to spend today their income of tomorrow. In this context, however, it is not possible to justify the existence of a positive interest. For what reason would borrowers of present saving have to pay interest on top of their future reimbursement? Perhaps because today's consumption has a greater value than tomorrow's? Other elements might also be considered (e.g. risk, subjective preferences and expectations). Yet, none of them is apt to explain interest as an additional income due from borrowers to savers.

Interest is often defined as a charge for the use of credit or borrowed income, and the interest rate as the price paid for the use of a loan per unit of time. According to this definition, 'it seems natural to analyse the determination of the rate of interest in terms of the demand for and supply of loans' (Patinkin 1972: 124). The supply of loans is related to saving and reflects the behaviour of income holders with respect to variations in the rate of interest. Wealth effects notwithstanding, a rise in interest rates is likely to decrease current consumption and increase current saving. The determinant factor here is the marginal rate of substitution between present and future consumption. Then, similarly to what happens in the case of relative prices, the rate of interest is determined when the demand for and supply of loans balance each other. The analysis very briefly sketched here refers, of course, to the neoclassical theory of interest. The interest rate is considered as a relative price to be determined on the financial market through the interplay of the supply of and demand for loanable funds. Now, even though it is reasonable to claim that interest rates represent a determinant element in the decision to invest and to save, this does not explain why a positive interest exists at all. As clearly pointed out by Patinkin, referring to the demand for consumption loans does not help to find a solution. In fact, 'it is a much better approximation of the truth to say that interest must be paid on consumption loans because the potential lender has the alternative of lending money at interest on productive loans than to say that the demand for consumption loans is the reason for the existence of interest' (ibid.: 129).

The best attempt to provide a theory of interest by referring to time is that of Böhm-Bawerk. In his analysis, the Austrian economist explains the origin of interest on loans (*Leihzins*) by assuming that future goods are generally undervalued. Intertemporal exchange between present and future goods is thus said to generate a premium that is distributed to lenders in the form of interest. Now, the problem is that every exchange occurs between equivalents. As cogently argued by Piffaretti (1994), this means that Böhm-Bawerk's intertemporal exchange must in fact refer to two full transactions taking place at two distinct points in time. Since each of these transactions – corresponding to lending and reimbursement – occurs between equivalents and since each of them has a term in common with the other (the claim on future goods), there can be no numerical difference between them. The exchange between present goods and the claim on future goods is necessarily equivalent to that between this same claim and the future goods, so that no premium can ever appear between these two exchanges. Nor is it possible to argue that undervaluation of future goods may be numerically determined since the first exchange, for the increasing demand to borrow present goods leads to an increase in the price of the claim on future goods. It is logically impossible, in fact, for a single exchange to determine two variables simultaneously, i.e. the price of present goods and that of future goods. 'Comment serait-il alors possible que, dans le même échange, les agents puissent soit déterminer la valeur des biens soit déterminer la valeur du titre correspondant [aux biens futurs]?' (Piffaretti 1994: 78).

Böhm-Bawerk's theory of income holders' preference for present over future commodities is also drastically rejected by Patinkin, who correctly observes that:

> the fact that individuals in such an economy insist on receiving interest in order to save is no evidence of a systematic preference for present goods over future ones. More generally, the fact that an individual will, at the margin, insist on receiving more than one unit of future goods to compensate him for

foregoing one unit of present goods is not necessarily the *cause* of the existence of interest but its *effect*: he insists on receiving more because he has the alternative of obtaining more by lending out at interest the money that would be released from current consumption by saving.

(Patinkin 1972: 129–30)

Yet, Böhm-Bawerk's analysis is not limited to the *Leihzins*, and we shall soon come back to it. For the moment, let us observe that no true justification for the existence of a positive interest on consumption loans can be found unless we are prepared to refer time and credit to production. If credit is merely related to consumption, it seems impossible to explain how a positive interest may derive from exchange. Even if it is recognised that in this case interest is not a new income, it is still unclear why the exchange between present and future consumption must involve a premium for the seller of present consumption goods. Shall we thus conclude that the origin of interest cannot be accounted for by exchange only?

In his reply to Brisman's critique of Böhm-Bawerk's theory of capital and interest, Wicksell rejects as superficial the idea that interest is a common phenomenon of price formation, saving having a price in exactly the same way as any good has a price. 'It is no doubt somewhat easier to understand that wood and meat cost money, than that money costs *more* money, or that "savings have a price" – besides, the latter expression is quite unclear and somehow invites contradiction' (Wicksell 1997: 21). The great Swedish economist gets straight to the core of the problem. To define interest as a price is tantamount to considering saving as a real good, a rather curious claim since it implies the transformation of money income into an object of exchange whose price has nothing to do with its cost of production. In fact, besides Wicksell's argument – which epitomises the absurdity of defining interest as the money price of money – it may also be noted that if interest were the price of saving then saving would have a price entirely different from its value. For example, given an interest rate of, say, 10 per cent, saving of 100 units of money income would have a yearly price of 10 units. Does it make any sense to claim that a real good of value 100 units has a price of 10 units? In reality, if saving amounts to 100 units of money income, its price is 100 units of money income, neither more nor less. As pointed out by Wicksell, interest is a difficult phenomenon to explain, a phenomenon that cannot be understood by referring to the market for loanable funds only.

This refers to interest on pure consumption loans. In a private economic sense, the lender's claim is capital, and thus far, as well as in everyday language, his income can, of course, be called interest. But it is not part of the return on social capital; instead it only *parasitizes*, so to speak, on one of the large social income categories: wages, rents and (with respect to the whole economy, as derived from social production) interest.

(Wicksell 1997: 23–4)

At this point, a distinction seems necessary between interest on consumption loans and interest on investment loans. Further analysis is also required to establish whether interest may be considered as a relative price or – in Wicksell's words – as a net income derived from social production. Let us start by investigating the role played by interest in GEA.

Interest and relative prices

According to Walras's first definition, interest is the current price of the services yield by capital and is determined through the adjustment of supply and demand on the services market. 'The current contract price of capital-services in terms of *numéraire* will be called the *interest charge [l'intérêt]*' (Walras 1984: 223). Now, in Part V of his *Elements of Pure Economics*, Walras establishes a close relationship between the price of capital services and that of capital goods. 'The price of a capital good depends essentially on the price of its services, that is to say, on its *income*' (ibid.: 267). It thus appears that, at equilibrium, the rate of interest equals the rate of net income, which 'is the same for all capital goods' (ibid.: 269). Hence, the price of the services yield by capital defines both interest and net income and goes to determine capital goods, a determination that is made to depend on the equalisation between saving and the value of capital goods: 'the condition of equality between the value of the new capital goods and the value of the excess [of income over consumption] gives us the equation required for the determination of the rate of net income and consequently for the determination of the prices of capital goods' (ibid.: 269).

Walras's framework is not a monetary one. He explicitly maintains that the money market (*marché du capital*) must be kept separate from the capital goods market, and his excess of income over consumption is to be understood in terms of real goods. However, there are no reasons to avoid interpreting the concept of income in the usual sense and to refer interest to the *marché du capital*. Walras's equality between the value of capital goods and the excess of income over consumption may thus be expressed in terms of saving and investment. 'Thus equilibrium in capital formation will first be established *in principle*. Then it will be established *effectively* by the reciprocal exchange between savings to be accumulated and new capital goods to be supplied' (ibid.: 282–3). Following this path, we end by considering the adjustment between saving and investment as the process determining the rate of interest. In fact, this is precisely what Walras does when he assumes that savers lend their savings to manufacturers so that 'the market for services will be wholly or partly replaced so far as the renting of new capital goods is concerned, by a *market for numéraire-capital*, where the unit price of the hire of *numéraire*-capital, which goes under the name of *rate of interest*, will be determined' (ibid.: 289).

An interesting feature of Walras's analysis, which has not always been sufficiently emphasised, is that interest is closely related to production (of new capital goods) rather than to consumption. Thus, the rate of interest is not seen as the ratio allowing the equalisation between the supply of and demand for present and future consumption, but as the price resulting from the exchange between capital saved and capital invested. Symptomatically, Walras considers the equality between rate of interest and rate of net income as a necessary condition for equilibrium. 'But it is evident that this rate of interest, when determined by the operations of bidding and by the law of offer and demand, always tends to coincide with a rate of net income like the one we have just defined' (ibid.: 289).

The process of capital accumulation plays a central role in Walras's conception of interest. It is on the market for new capital goods that the rate of net income is determined, and it is the rate of net income that eventually sets the value for the rate of interest. The following quotation shows Walras's clear distinction between how the rate of interest manifests itself and how it is actually determined.

> Thus the rate of interest, which is the ratio of net profit to the price of securities, manifests itself, to be sure, in the market for *numéraire*-capital, that is to say in the banking system, though actually it is determined in the capital goods market, that is to say in the stock exchange, as a rate of net income which is the common ratio of the net price of services to the price of landed capital, personal capital as well as capital proper.
>
> (ibid.: 290)

Now, the concept of net income is related to that of capital productivity, the services yielded by capital being more valuable than capital itself only if the value of final output is increased through the use of capital goods. It would not be surprising, therefore, to find Walras's followers dealing mainly with the problem of justifying interest by referring to capital productivity. Yet, this is not precisely what happens. Contrary to Walras's line of approach, they start by considering the exchange between present and future consumption and attempt to prove that, because of positive time preference, interest derives from intertemporal exchange rather than from the process of capital accumulation.

Time preference, which reflects intertemporal preference and whose rate defines the marginal rate of substitution between present and future consumption, is a key element in the neoclassical determination of interest. In particular, equality between the rate of time preference and the market rate of interest is seen as the condition allowing for market equilibrium. '[Neoclassical economists] consider that, once the market rate of interest is set equal to the time preference rate corresponding to market-clearing consumption, market equilibrium obtains directly' (Ono 1994: 9). Like Fisher and Böhm-Bawerk, neoclassical authors assume that economic agents manifest a relative preference for present over future consumption so that interest rate is determined through intertemporal exchange. As a matter of fact, two different approaches stem from Böhm-Bawerk's analysis of capital and interest. According to those economists who refer back to Fisher's theory of waiting, interest results from the increase in productivity caused by a scarce factor: the inducement to save (or wait). Thus, interest is seen here as 'the reward received by investors to induce them to provide waiting' (Kirzner 1996: 136). The fundamental aspect of this analysis is that it attempts to explain how the rate of interest is determined, leaving aside the problem of its origin. This approach had already been criticised by Böhm-Bawerk, who maintained that determining factors of the rate of interest should not be confused with originating causes of interest itself and who showed that waiting does not transform a physical increase in productivity into an increase in value. Contrary to what Kirzner believes, the question of whether or not waiting is a productive factor is not a 'strictly "philosophical" question' (ibid.: 137). The claim that labour is the sole economic factor of production is not a matter of philosophical choice but the unavoidable result of the monetary analysis of production. It is because income is created as a bank deposit and because any new bank deposit results from a payment of wages (see Chapters 3 and 4) that capital itself cannot be identified with a factor of production. What is true of capital is also necessarily true of waiting as waiting (or saving) is essentially what explains the formation of capital as capital-time. Modern monetary analysis thus confirms that of Böhm-Bawerk. What remains to be explained is the increment in value accounting for the very existence of interest. If waiting cannot give rise to any increase in value, it cannot be the source of interest. Yet, it cannot be entirely dismissed as illogical or counterfactual either. Although neither time nor waiting is a factor of production, it might still be possible to show that, because of fixed capital accumulation and through interest payment, they allow for an increase in value thanks to an increase in the physical productivity of labour. Of course, this would take us a long way from Fisher's original theory of waiting. Nevertheless, it would make Fisher, together with Ricardo, Böhm-Bawerk and Wicksell, one of the authors who has most contributed to a theory of interest, accounting for its origin as well as for its measurement.

Let us momentarily abandon the productivity theories of interest and move to the second approach derived by neoclassical authors from Böhm-Bawerk's concept of time preference. According to those economists who emphasise the role of exchange, interest is merely the result of intertemporal exchange between present and future goods given widespread positive time preference. Following Böhm-Bawerk, they dismiss physical productivity as the true origin of interest. 'PTPT [pure time preference theory] exponents often drive home the irrelevance of physical productivity by pointing out that physical productivity is neither necessary nor sufficient for an explanation of interest' (ibid.: 147). They claim instead that time preference alone can account for value-productivity, regardless of the presence (or not) of physical productivity. As noted by Kirzner, this is not to say 'that a change in the conditions of physical productivity would invariably leave the rate of interest unchanged' (ibid.: 147). Physical productivity could indeed enter the determination of the rate of interest – so they maintain – yet positive time preference remains the sole interest-originating cause.

Now, whether or not interest is referred to productivity (of time, waiting or any other factor of this kind), the common feature of neoclassical models is that they rest on the principle of time preference and on the mechanism of intertemporal exchange. Whether interest is seen as a productivity return or not, time preference plays a central role because it is through the adjustment of consumer preferences that Neoclassics attempt to evaluate the set of relative prices of which the rate of interest is an element. As we have already seen (and both Fisher and Böhm-Bawerk refer to it explicitly), the principle of time preference is based on the undervaluation of future goods that explains interest on loans, either consumption or production loans. The underlying assumption, of course, is that future goods are different from present ones; an assumption that may easily be accepted if we refer to production, namely to the exchange between present productive services and future produced output. In particular, the present saving of consumption goods giving rise to a circulating capital defines a stock of goods entirely different from that resulting from the roundabout process of production in which labour operates with the aid of fixed capital. In a pure exchange economy, however, this does not seem to be the case. Unless we consider time to be productive in terms of value – a hypothesis rejected by neoclassical economists – how can we justify a positive difference in value between future and present goods? True, what is claimed on the basis of time preference is that the difference is not an objective one, future goods being undervalued for purely psychological reasons. Yet, it is not at all clear why consumers should value differently the same goods according to an asymmetric time relationship. If it is realistic to suppose that the same goods may provide different 'utilities' to their consumers at different points in time, there is no reason to believe that households will constantly derive from future goods a greater utility than from the ones they value at present. Let us suppose that a consumer of a given commodity values it at 10 units today. Why should he necessarily value at less than 10 units the utility he will derive from the same commodity tomorrow? It could well be that he gives up consumption today simply because he is already fully satisfied and that he hopes to have a greater need for consumption (of the same goods) in the future. Would he not be inclined to overvalue future goods in this case? The time asymmetry implicit in the concept of time preference is an assumption that is not corroborated, either by facts or by logic, and that seriously undermines the neoclassical attempt to explain interest in a pure exchange economy. Moreover, even in this case, the origin of interest cannot be explained by resorting to undervaluation of future goods. If it is conceivable to maintain that future goods will provide a greater utility than today's, it is not because of psychological undervaluation but rather because we can increase the quantity and quality of future output thanks to technological improvements and roundabout methods of production.

Let us set aside the difficulty related to time preference and analyse again the concept of intertemporal exchange on which the neoclassical theory of interest rests. Briefly, intertemporal exchange is the substitution between present and future goods that consumers carry out on spot and forward markets. Given the two agents A and B, if agent A prefers future to present consumption of good a and if B prefers present to future consumption of this same good, an intertemporal exchange is likely to occur between good a and a claim on another similar good (a′) to be produced in the future. Agent A gives up his present consumption in exchange for B's future savings. In fact, intertemporal exchange between goods a and a′ is composed of two exchanges taking place, one in the present, say at t_1, and the other in the future, say at t_2. At t_1, good a is exchanged against a financial claim having a′ as its object, while at t_2 the financial claim is surrendered in exchange for a′. Each of these two exchanges is a self-contained transaction defining a relative price. Now, since every exchange defines the perfect equivalence (the identity) between its two terms, no difference could ever be found between the prices of goods a and a′ if the two exchanges were to be considered as the two complementary components of a single intertemporal exchange. In this case, however, no interest could be determined as being the intertemporal substitution rate between goods a and a′. A difference between the prices of goods a and a′ can arise only if the two exchanges, at t_1 and t_2, are independent transactions leaving consumers free to adjust at their will their rate of exchange in order to maximise their utilities. The whole body of neoclassical analysis supports this second alternative. Unfortunately, this means that no intertemporal exchange can ever occur between goods a and a′.

The neoclassical attempt at explaining interest by referring to time preference and intertemporal exchange is thus flawed on two counts. First, because time preference is a subjective principle that cannot be substantiated on either logical or factual grounds; second, because intertemporal exchange is a transaction inconsistent with the principle of direct real exchange on which the neoclassical paradigm is based. Consumer preferences and utility maximisation cannot determine a number of variables that tends to infinity. It must not be forgotten, in fact, that '[s]ince people have different preferences for the consumption of different commodities, the time preference rate for each commodity differs across commodities, and depends on their consumption schedules' (Ono 1994: 19). This amounts to saying that a specific rate of time preference may be established not only for each single commodity but also for each single agent interested in it (as a buyer or seller). The task faced by neoclassical economists is certainly not an easy one. Starting from individuals' changing preferences, they want to determine a series of time preference rates, which must then be equalised to the market rate of interest (at each point in time) in order to reach an optimum market equilibrium. Once again, even before tackling this problem from a mathematical point of view – which neoclassical authors do with great technical ability – we should ascertain whether (relative) exchange might indeed provide a logical setting for the determination of prices. If it is proved that this is not so, coherence will demand that we abandon the neoclassical paradigm and look for an alternative approach to economic analysis. The logical impossibility of determining intertemporal exchanges is part of this evidence. We have briefly referred to the other clues in Chapters 2 and 3. Developed by Schmitt in a series of manuscripts yet to be published, they represent the most serious debunking of neoclassical economics to date. What is fundamentally wrong with the neoclassical attempt at determining prices is that through direct confrontation between (real) goods it is impossible to determine simultaneously the rate of exchange and the quantity exchanged. The fact is that relative prices (the rates of exchange) are not independent of the quantity exchanged. Hence, the independent equations of supply and demand required for the determination of relative prices are far more numerous than the unknowns: the system of general equilibrium is inevitably overdetermined.

The argument is too important and complex to be dealt with in a few paragraphs. Waiting for Schmitt's latest manuscripts to be published, readers unfamiliar with his analysis may find some useful hints in *Inflation, chômage et malformations du capital* (Schmitt 1984b), as well as in his contributions to Deleplace and Nell (1996) and to Cencini and Baranzini (1996). As for our present concern, let us note that, even if we stick to neoclassical analysis, the traditional Walrasian general equilibrium framework is not well equipped to explain interest rates in a world marked by persistent stagnation. As pointed out by Ono, the assumptions that:

1 the marginal utility of money eventually becomes zero as real balances expand,

and that

2 markets are cleared at each point in time,

'are postulates rather than properties derived from rational behaviour' (Ono 1994: 2). According to the Japanese economist, a better understanding of interest rate determination could be achieved by assuming – along Keynesian lines – that money has a direct utility and that '[t]he adjustment speed of flow prices is finite' (ibid.: 4) while 'stock prices adjust immediately' (ibid.: 4). Ono's intention is to describe the workings of a dynamic monetary economy by reconciling 'the conventional law of demand and supply under Walrasian price-taking (or competitive behaviour)' (ibid.: 3) with Keynes's concept of liquidity preference. Instead of referring to a (Walrasian) system of perfect price adjustment or to a (non-Walrasian) system of market disequilibrium, Ono considers a sluggish price adjustment model and tries to show that 'full market equilibrium does not exist if the utility of money is insatiable, and that "persistent" stagnation occurs even if prices do adjust' (ibid.: 12). With respect to interest, he claims that liquidity preference gives rise to an infratemporal rate of interest deriving from the 'utility that people seek from the liquidity of money at the cost of lost opportunities for earning interest on other assets' (ibid.: 19). In this context, equilibrium would require both the intertemporal (time preference) and the infratemporal (liquidity) rates of interest to be equal to the (financial) market rate, the optimising behaviour of households resulting in 'the equalization of all the rates of interest to the market rate of interest at each point in time' (ibid.: 20).

Is Ono's attempt to account for the determination of interest rates successful? A preliminary – and perhaps definitive – answer to this question requires a careful analysis of Keynes's concept of liquidity preference. This is what we shall attempt to do in the next section.

Interest, income and production

Interest, saving, investment and Keynes's liquidity preference

Following Wicksell, Keynes defines the natural rate of interest as 'the rate at which saving and the value of investment are exactly balanced' (Keynes 1971: 139), and claims that interest rate fluctuations have an impact on production and employment through their influence on the rate of investment and prices. For example, according to Keynes, a rise in the rate of interest 'discourages investment relatively to saving, and therefore lowers prices which, by causing the receipts of entrepreneurs to fall below the normal, influences them to offer less employment all round' (ibid.: 171).

Now, it is all-important to observe that Keynes's own analysis does not substantiate the idea that saving and investment are made equal through the fluctuation of the rate of interest. As a matter of fact, the relationship between saving and investment is conceived of rather differently in the *Treatise* and in the *General Theory*. Although in the *Treatise* (Keynes 1971) Keynes's conception is mainly microeconomic, in the *General Theory* (Keynes 1973a) it is essentially macroeconomic, emphasis switching from behavioural considerations to the analysis of the economic system as a whole. In the *Treatise*, 'saving is the act of the individual consumer and consists in the negative act of refraining from spending the whole of his current income on consumption' (Keynes 1971: 155), and investment 'is the act of the entrepreneur ... and consists in the positive act of starting or maintaining some process of production or of withholding liquid goods' (ibid.: 155). In the *General Theory*, his approach changes. As he clearly states in his preface to the French edition, 'for the system as a whole the amount of income which is saved, in the sense that it is not spent on current consumption, is and must necessarily be exactly equal to the amount of net new investment' (Keynes 1973a: xxxii). Apparently, then, in his general theory of employment published in 1936 there is no role to be played by the rate of interest as the balancing factor in the relationship between saving and investment since this relationship is transformed from a condition of equilibrium into an identity. At closer examination, however, Keynes's analysis has a more articulated result.

> The amount of aggregate income and of aggregate saving are the *results* of the free choices of individuals whether or not to consume and whether or not to invest; but they are neither of them capable of assuming an independent value resulting from a separate set of decisions taken irrespective of the decisions concerning consumption and investment.
>
> (ibid.: 65)

Keynes's statement is clear: although consumers and producers are free to save or to invest, from a macroeconomic point of view saving is necessarily equal to investment. Hence, although the rate of interest influences the decisions to save and to invest, the equality between saving and investment is reached independently of the level of the interest rate. For example, a higher rate of interest may induce consumers to save more and producers to invest less, yet it cannot prevent macroeconomic saving being always equal to macroeconomic investment. Let us try to illustrate this by referring to modern monetary analysis and by bearing in mind that Keynes defines current investment as 'the current addition to the value of the capital equipment which has resulted from the productive activity of the period' (ibid.: 62), and also as 'the value of that part of current output which is not consumed' (ibid.: 63).

The two definitions of current investment (one referring to production and the other to the expenditure of current income) are complementary, and a correct interpretation of the relationship between saving and investment requires the use of both. Let us distinguish two cases according to whether production consists of consumption goods only or of consumption and capital goods. In both cases, we assume saving to be positive. Since saving is that part of current income that is not spent on consumption, when production is made up of consumption goods only saving defines that part of currently produced output which is not purchased on the commodity market. Thus, in the first case that we are considering, saving is that part of income which is still available in the form of a bank deposit and which is necessary for the purchase of the consumption goods that have not yet been finally sold. Now, if the goods still to be purchased on the commodity market are bound to remain unsold (if they are unsaleable *de facto* since nobody will ever want to buy them), saving will never be absorbed into consumption. However weird this may appear at first sight, investment is not nil. On the contrary, saving defines an equivalent, although useless, investment that takes the form of the consumption goods forcibly purchased by the producing firms. The income saved and deposited with the banks, in fact, is necessarily lent to firms, which, by covering the cost of production of the unsold consumption goods, are their first purchasers. Having been purchased by firms, consumption goods unsold on the commodity market are the form initially taken by investment. In the very particular case that we are examining, the initial purchase of firms is bound to become final, so that investment is in fact a loss that, being perfectly balanced by saving, leads to the destruction of the income saved by consumers and inevitably spent by firms. The interesting conclusion here is that, even under the most unfavourable circumstances, saving and investment are necessarily equivalent.

The same result is obtained, quite obviously, when the consumption goods accumulated in period p_0 are purchased in p_1 in the absence of a new production of capital goods. In this case, it can be maintained equally well that there has been no macroeconomic saving at all, or that the initial investment in the form of consumption goods (in period p_0) has been entirely absorbed by an increase in consumption (in period p_1). Unlike in the previous case, firms do not suffer from a loss, the whole of consumption goods produced in p_0 being purchased (partly in p_0 and partly in p_1) by consumers. The equivalence of saving and investment is thus respected even in this instance, albeit for an amount of investment (and of saving) equal to zero.

The last occurrence that we are considering here is by far the most interesting as it corresponds to the situation in which saving evolves into a process of capital accumulation. Current output of period p_0 is still supposed to consist of consumption goods only, but this time firms enter a new production of capital goods in period p_1. Now, modern monetary analysis shows that saving and investment are always at equality, in period p_0 as well as in period p_1 and for the two periods taken as a whole. In the initial period, p_0, a positive saving is formed that is matched by an equivalent investment taking the form of a circulating fund of consumption goods. As in the cases previously analysed, the income saved by consumers is spent by firms and gives rise to a circulating capital made up of consumption goods. Before capital goods are produced, investment is positive and equal to the amount of current income saved by consumers. Consistent with Keynes's definition of investment as 'the value of that part of current output which is not consumed' (Keynes 1973a: 63), the consumption goods purchased by firms define an amount of circulating capital exactly equal to the amount of savings. Then, in the following period, the circulating capital formed in p_0 is replaced by an equivalent production of capital goods. The consumption goods 'saved' in p_0 are definitively sold to consumers in p_1 and, in exchange for them, firms obtain the newly produced capital goods. Now, the production of these capital or investment goods leads to the formation of a new current income that cannot be spent for their purchase (for the simple reason that capital goods have already been purchased by firms). We thus observe that the investment, in p_1, of the saving formed in p_0 (and provisionally invested in consumption goods) entails the substitution of a new current income – spent by firms for the purchase of capital goods – for an old one – previously saved and now available again for the purchase of the consumption goods accumulated in the circulating fund of firms. In other words, the income saved by consumers and momentarily spent by firms in p_0 is now changed into a new income definitively spent by firms (and, therefore, saved by consumers) in the production of new investment goods. Saving and investment are thus perfectly equal, both in p_0 and in p_1, and, consequently, also in the two periods taken together.

The necessary equality of saving and investment is no reason for considering them to be the two terms of an equation that is satisfied at equilibrium only. Likewise, that is no reason for considering the rate of interest to be their equilibrating factor. At its deepest level, Keynes's theory teaches us that saving and investment are bound to be equal whatever the decisions taken by consumers and producers. Yet, as we have noticed already, individuals are free to save as they please and their decision to save is quite independent of any decision to invest. The fact is that once the decision to save a given amount of income becomes a positive act of saving, the latter simultaneously finds its counterpart in an equivalent investment. Saving and investment are twin results of the set of decisions taken by the economic system as a whole.

The rate of interest plays a role insofar as it influences the decisions to save or invest. Let us refer back to our last example and suppose that the rate of interest increases, thus encouraging consumers to save a greater part of their current income. The increase in saving occurring in p_0 is matched by an equivalent increase of the consumption goods making up the circulating fund of real goods accumulated by firms. 'The value of that part of current output which is not consumed' being increased to the same extent as saving, investment is immediately brought to the level of saving. A first conclusion may be, therefore, that in period p_0 a higher rate of interest increases saving and investment simultaneously. However, the analysis has not reached its end yet. There remains for us to consider, in fact, what happens in period p_1. Let us suppose that the increased level of the rate of interest pushes firms to reduce their production of capital goods. In this case, investment in p_1 is lower than saving in p_0. Not being transformed into capital goods, part of the income saved in p_0 remains invested in the form of consumption goods. Hence, if it is true that the increase in the rate of interest does not cause saving to diverge from investment, it is true also that only part of the investment defines a new production of capital goods.

As we have already observed, in the *General Theory*, Keynes (1973a) abandons the traditional idea that the rate of interest is the equilibrating factor between saving and investment. His new idea, which he reiterated on several occasions after publication of his 1936 book, is that 'it is not the rate of interest, but the level of incomes which ensures equality between saving and investment' (Keynes 1973c: 212). For the time being, let us leave aside the problems related to the logical possibility (or impossibility) of reconciling a necessary equality – which holds good at any instant in time – with a conditional one – which is realised for a given level of income only. Our attention here is fully devoted to the determination of the rate of interest, and on this subject Keynes maintains that 'the rate of interest is determined by the total demand and total supply of cash or liquid resources' (ibid.: 230). The desire to hold wealth in the form of cash derives from what Keynes calls *liquidity preference*. The necessary condition for the existence of a liquidity preference is 'the existence of *uncertainty* as to the future of the rate of interest' (Keynes 1973a: 168), and the motives inducing people to hold cash are classified 'as the income-motive and the business-motive, the precautionary-motive and the speculative-motive' (ibid.: 195). Among these, the speculative motive is considered by Keynes as being 'particularly important in transmitting the effects of a *change* in the quantity of money' (ibid.: 196) as 'experience indicates that the aggregate demand for money to satisfy the speculative-motive usually shows a continuous response to gradual changes in the rate of interest' (ibid.: 197). In an article published in June 1938 in *The Economic Journal*, Keynes (1938) renews his attempt to persuade Robertson of his theory and specifies that the total demand for cash is made up of 'the inactive demand due to the state of confidence and expectations on the part of the owners of wealth, and the active demand due to the level of activity established by the decisions of the entrepreneurs' (Keynes 1973c: 230).

How does Keynes's analysis fit in with modern monetary macroeconomics? An immediate observation is that the demand for cash bears little relation to the real world. Transactions may easily take place without the use of a single unit of cash, and the same is true for speculation, whose impressive increase is closely tied to the possibility of forward sales and purchases carried out through the intermediation of banks. The precautionary motive also is not a good enough reason for holding cash, since sudden expenditures and 'unforeseen opportunities of advantageous purchases' (Keynes 1973a: 196) may very often be carried out using bank facilities such as cheques or credit cards. This first observation is then substantiated by a rigorous analysis of bank money, of its book-entry nature and of the laws governing its emission and its association with output. One of the conclusions reached by the modern analysis of bank money is that cash is not directly money, but rather a highly liquid claim, an easily transferable bond giving its bearer a right on the issuing bank. As IOUs of the central bank, banknotes are an acknowledgement of debt, a fact confirmed by their being recorded on the liabilities side of the central bank's balance sheet. The holders of banknotes own a claim on a deposit whose object is an equivalent measure of current output. Holding a claim in the form of cash does not yield interest and is riskier than holding it in the form of a current (or deposit) account. The advantage, however, is its extreme liquidity. The fact remains that, substantially, banknotes are a claim on current or future output, as are current or deposit account certificates. Now, in our monetary systems, the amount of cash is not arbitrarily determined by the central bank – so that its supply might not match the demand exerted by consumers and entrepreneurs. In reality, banknotes are issued by the central bank and distributed to commercial banks on the ultimate request of their clients. Income holders have the choice to hold a claim on their banks in one form or another, and banks must be ready to provide them with the amount of cash that they are entitled to. On the basis of the foreseeable behaviour of their clients, banks ask for the creation of banknotes. Should the amount of notes thus created be insufficient to satisfy public request, banks would have to ask for more, their demand being necessarily satisfied by the central bank. On the contrary, if the public were to decide to use less cash, the plethoric amount of banknotes would be transferred back to the central bank and replaced by an equivalent sum of other forms of claims on bank deposits. As in the first case, the adjustment between demand for and supply of cash would not affect the rate of interest.

Keynes reasons as if banknotes were material money whose relative price – the rate of interest – was determined through its supply and demand. What is even more astonishing is that, having placed bank money at the centre of his theory, he cannot help identifying it with cash. At the end of Chapter 13 of the *General Theory*, in fact, he claims that:

> [i]t is impossible for the actual amount of hoarding to change as a result of decisions on the part of the public, so long as we mean by 'hoarding' the actual holding of cash. For the amount of hoarding must be equal to the quantity of money ...; and the quantity of money is not determined by the public.

> (Keynes 1973a: 174)

In this passage, Keynes maintains that the quantity of money is nothing other than the actual holding of cash and that its amount is determined autonomously (albeit not arbitrarily) by the central bank. That this is not so is particularly evident today, owing to the evolution of the banking system itself and to our increased understanding of monetary laws. Even if we define cash deposits as current accounts – as Keynes did in his *Treatise* – it is erroneous to reduce money to cash. The mistake is twofold because neither banknotes nor current account certificates are money (but claims on bank deposits) and because bank deposits themselves do not define an amount of money but of income. Keynes himself recognises that commercial banks issue money as a spontaneous acknowledgement of debt: 'the bank may create a claim against itself in favour of a borrower, in return for his promise of subsequent reimbursement' (Keynes 1971: 21). This is precisely what happens in the real world. Money is entirely created by commercial banks to be used as a numerical vehicle of produced output. Keynes's point of view is therefore doubly misleading; first, because he identifies money with cash and, second, because he considers cash as having a value in itself. Both assumptions are mistaken. As a pure numerical form, money has no proper value, and banknotes are a claim on a bank deposit whose object is not money itself but its real content. Keynes seems to misunderstand the role played by the central bank, which is not to create *ex nihilo* a sum of money already endowed with a positive value (money proper) but to regroup into a single system all the banks operating within the nation. This is done through interbank clearing, and has the effect of transforming the different acknowledgements of debt issued by each bank into a common unit called central or national money. The substitution of commercial banks' monies with central bank's money, however, does not imply any additional creation of money by the central bank. Interbank clearing is a mechanism through which commercial banks' monies are changed into (not exchanged with) central bank's money; in Schmitt's words, it is a process of catalysis of which central bank's money is the main agent (catalyst). Put differently, the creation of a given sum of central bank's money implies the destruction of an equivalent sum of commercial banks' money.

As a matter of fact, Keynes's analysis is rich in arguments that, if followed through, may lead to an articulated theory in which bank money plays a crucial role. Unfortunately, as in the case of his analysis of overdraft facilities, Keynes has not developed his intuition far enough to free himself entirely from the old ideas 'which ramify, for those brought up as most of us have been, into every corner of our minds' (Keynes 1973a: xxiii). Why did Keynes hold on to the orthodox belief that interest rate is determined as a relative price through the adjustment of the demand for and supply of a real asset called cash? One may suggest that he did so as part of his attempt to show that saving and investment are made equal through the fluctuation of income rather than of the rate of interest. Indeed, this is a plausible guess as Keynes himself has often maintained this to be the core of his theory of employment. Besides, the multiplier theory rests precisely on this assumption. Now, it may be interesting to note that, in reality, the theory of the multiplier leads to the opposite result. Let us observe first that, for the (horizontal) multiplier to determine a decreasing (as opposed to infinite) process in time, saving must correspond to hoarding since an autonomous investment has the alleged (decreasing) effect on employment only if the part that has been saved in a given period is no longer available for consumption later. The second observation is that, according to Keynes, the propensity to hoard defines the same concept as liquidity preference. 'The concept of *hoarding* may be regarded as a first approximation to the concept of *liquidity-preference*. Indeed if we were to substitute "propensity to hoard" for "hoarding", it would come to substantially the same thing' (ibid.: 174). Then, since liquidity preference determines the demand for cash, the same must be true of the propensity to hoard. At this point, let us recall that, again according to Keynes, it is through fluctuations of the interest rate that the demand for cash is brought into equality with the supply of cash. This means that the interest rate influences the propensity to hoard. Moreover, because of the postulated equality between saving and hoarding, the propensity to save is equal to the propensity to hoard, so that the rate of interest determines also the propensity to save – and, since they are complementary, the propensity to consume. Hence, other things being equal, the rate of interest determines saving. But if this is actually the case, then the rate of interest becomes the factor whose fluctuation brings saving into equality with investment. It is not difficult to realise that this result patently contradicts Keynes's claim that equality between saving and investment is determined through fluctuations of income and not of interest rate. But there is more. This result having been reached by starting from the analysis of the multiplier, we are bound to conclude that the theory of the multiplier is self-defeating. If the equality between saving and investment is reached without any need for a fluctuation of income, there is no longer any reason to believe that an increase in investment may have more than one effect on employment over time.

Although it does not oppose the equivalence between saving and investment, a variation in the rate of interest may modify the composition of investment. In particular, an increase in the rate of interest may decrease the production of investment goods and lead to a fall in employment. This last consideration opens the way to a further development of the analysis. The decision to invest in the production of capital goods, in fact, is not related to absolute variations in the rate of interest, but rather to its variation with respect to the rate of profit. The problem of interest is closely connected to that of profit and capital accumulation. Emphasis must then be switched from the analysis of the rate of interest to that of capital accumulation and interest. In particular, it must be established whether or not interest is an additional income, and whether it is the result of the physical productivity of capital, the marginal efficiency of capital or the peculiar characteristics of the process of capital accumulation. Let us take each of these different points one after the other, from the analysis of the marginal efficiency of capital to that implied in the modern theory of capital.

Interest and marginal efficiency of capital

As clearly pointed out by Pasinetti, Keynes's concept of marginal efficiency of capital 'was destroyed almost immediately after the publication of the *General Theory* by being reduced to, and confused with, the orthodox notion of the "marginal productivity of capital" '(Pasinetti 1997: 198). In his attempt to re-establish the modern marginal efficiency of capital in its own rights, Pasinetti starts by showing that saving is conceived of quite differently by Keynes and by the orthodox economists of neoclassical vintage. In particular, he maintains that, while for the latter saving has no consequences on global demand, for Keynes saving may alter global demand since decisions to save and decisions to invest are essentially independent of one another. 'Any decision to save is simply a decision *not to spend*, with the desire to hold a corresponding amount of abstract

Figure 6.1 Savings and bank deposits.

purchasing power to be exerted in the future, without, however, any commitment either to demand any specific commodity or to demand it at any specific time' (ibid.: 201–2). This is an astonishing claim for an economist who has always favoured a macroeconomic approach to economics. It is even more surprising, of course, that Keynes himself provides the arguments for such a claim. Global demand is a macroeconomic concept and, as such, it should not be submitted to the randomly changing behaviour of individuals. The decision to save is certainly independent of the decision to invest, but both of these actions relate to microeconomics and can have no impact on global demand. What Pasinetti fails to perceive is that global demand is not determined on the commodity market alone. Once the financial market is introduced into the picture, it becomes evident that saving is not that part of income which is not spent, but rather that part of current income which is spent for the purchase of financial claims. We must not forget, in fact, that Keynes's point of departure is bank money and that, according to double-entry book-keeping, saving is necessarily deposited within the banking system and, precisely because it is formed as a deposit, it is immediately spent on the financial market. Let us look at the balance sheet displayed in Figure 6.1.

The meaning of this double-entry is straightforward. Their income being deposited with the banking system (BS), income holders are the owners of a financial claim whose object is the current output physically deposited with firm F. This amounts to saying that, by purchasing BS's financial claim, income holders lend to F the exact amount of money necessary to cover the costs of production of current output. Thus, the entire amount of income saved is spent by F for the (intermediate) purchase of current output. Obviously, this does not imply the final destruction of income, but its transformation into capital-time, i.e. into a capital that will either be spent (for the final purchase of produced output) or invested at a later date.

Another way of proving that saving does not decrease global demand is to refer to available income. It should be clear, in fact, that at a macroeconomic level demand is determined by the amount of available purchasing power. Now, if saving reduced available income, we would be forced to conclude that it equally reduces global demand. The notion of hoarding having nothing to do with the modern conception of bank money, it is rather the opposite conclusion that imposes itself. Every income that is not spent defines a deposit with the banking system. This necessarily implies that every income saved is an income that is still entirely available, i.e. an income that does not fail to feed an equivalent demand. It is only if saving could literally destroy a money income that positive saving would decrease demand. Yet, the only operation leading to a destruction of income is its final expenditure, an operation that defines a positive demand. Saving leaves the amount of available income unaltered because it is not spent for the final purchase of current output. It is thus proved that saving does not reduce global demand both because it does not entail a destruction of purchasing power and because it feeds a positive expenditure on the financial market, i.e. a positive demand for financial claims.

While Pasinetti is certainly right in pointing out that 'we do not live in a barter economy' (ibid.: 201) but in a monetary economy of production, he goes too far in his attempt to do away with orthodox (neoclassical) theory. His perception of economic reality is partial and only apparently a monetary one. In fact, he misses a crucial point that has been repeatedly stressed by Keynes, namely that our monetary economies encompass both production *and* exchange. Modern macroeconomic theory must account for two complementary processes – production and circulation – and it can do so only if it has money as its starting point. As soon as bank money is introduced into the picture, the whole perception of reality changes. In particular, saving can no longer be identified with hoarding and considered as an income that, not being spent on the commodity market, cannot be spent on any other market either. Financial intermediation is a fundamental activity performed by banks, and one that is implicit in the use of bank money. Whatever the amount entered on the liabilities side of a bank's balance sheet, it is necessarily lent since it is entirely needed to cover the credit entered on the assets side. Saving defining a positive deposit with the bank, it follows that, as soon as it is formed, it is spent for the purchase of a financial claim whose object is the product (financially) deposited by the debtors with the bank. If analysis is unable to account for financial as well as for monetary intermediation, it is bound to offer a faulty view of economic reality, leading us astray from the correct understanding of the real world.

Let us go back to Pasinetti's attempt to rehabilitate the marginal efficiency of capital as opposed to the marginal productivity of capital. Having analysed the concept of saving, he moves on to investment and to a criticism of the orthodox theory of the investment-demand function. His starting points are Keynes's claims that 'it is preferable to regard labour, including, of course, the personal services of the entrepreneur and his assistants, as the sole factor of production' (Keynes 1973a: 213–14), and that the marginal efficiency of capital is concerned 'with the increment of value due to the employment of one more value unit of capital' (ibid.: 138). Pasinetti then goes on to show that 'the downward-sloping investment-demand function, *to the extent* that it relies on a continuous process of substitution of capital for labour, as the rate of interest falls, is theoretically unsound; it has no logical foundations' (Pasinetti 1997: 204). His main argument is that the reswitching of technique controversy in capital theory has definitively proved that 'a "well-behaved" aggregate neoclassical production function, in general, does not exist' (ibid.: 203–4), so that, if a downward-sloping relation exists, it 'must be explained by something else – by some *other* theory or circumstance' (ibid.: 204). Keynes's originality, then, consists in having analysed investment and the marginal efficiency of capital without referring to the neoclassical production function.

Now, despite its originality, Keynes's theory of capital and investment is not entirely immune to criticism. For example, he claims that the marginal efficiency of capital is 'equal to that rate of discount which would make the present value of the series of annuities given by the returns expected from the capital-asset during its life just equal to its supply price' (Keynes 1973a: 135). But this is hardly consistent with his choice to consider labour as the sole factor of production. In fact, how can the use of capital produce an increment in value if the whole value is determined by labour alone? This is a difficult problem. To define labour as the sole factor of production is not an arbitrary assumption but the necessary result of a rigorous analysis of value. Keynes is inevitably led to this conclusion by his own monetary theory of production. He is thus trapped in the same dilemma as the Classics: either to stick to his theory of labour-value and face the arduous task of explaining how capital may increase the value of output without being productive at all or to disown the main tenets of his theory of production and assume – this time arbitrarily – that capital is a factor of production on its own merits. The failure of the Classics to elaborate a solution consistent with their labour theory of production is emblematic of the difficulty inherent in the choice of the first alternative. Yet, Keynes's theory of production and value differs substantially from that of the Classics as it is constructed on monetary terms (wage units) rather than on real terms (labour time units). This is a difference of the utmost importance because, although a material conception of labour-value does not explain the economic impact of capital, Keynes's monetary analysis might indeed lead to a satisfactory solution of this problem. Unfortunately, Keynes himself did not develop such a solution. His concept of the marginal efficiency of capital is either too embedded in traditional (neoclassical) analysis or too vague to be truly helpful. If we consider it to be the orthodox concept of the marginal productivity of capital, we enter the imaginary world in which capital has the metaphysical property of creating value. This world – as claimed by Pasinetti – clashes with the logical impossibility of determining an aggregate physical measure of capital independent of the rate of interest. On the other hand, if we take it to refer to the marginal efficiency of investment, we abandon – unsolved – the original problem of explaining the link between capital and value.

Pasinetti's article on Keynes's concept of the marginal efficiency of capital has the great merit of clarifying the terms of the problem and clearing the path for an alternative solution. By interpreting Keynes's concept as referring to the marginal efficiency of *investment*, he maintains that a central and independent role is played by the rate of interest, which '*determines* what the marginal efficiency of the last investment project is going to be' (Pasinetti 1997: 208). Besides the relevance of the statement that 'the relation between the marginal efficiency of investment and the rate of interest is not one of interdependence; it is one of causality' (ibid.: 209), the emphasis placed on the rate of interest seems to be extremely fruitful, not least because of the problem of the 'productivity' of capital in terms of value. Quite disappointingly, however, Keynes's analysis of the rate of interest is less than ideal. His definition of it as 'the "price" which equilibrates the desire to hold wealth in the form of cash with the available quantity of cash'

(Keynes 1973a: 167) is reminiscent of neoclassical analysis in its simplest terms, and the introduction of the concept of liquidity preference does not substantially alter its microeconomic character. Pasinetti claims that Keynes's originality is that he considered the rate of interest as 'a truly *independent* variable, i.e. a variable that is independent of both basic forces – technology and utility – that are traditionally considered to be at the foundation of economic variables' (Pasinetti 1997: 212). This is an unconventional way of dealing with the problem. Unfortunately, it leads nowhere because liquidity preference does not explain the origin of any new macroeconomic income called interest. There can be little doubt, in fact, that the rate of interest is an economic concept to be explained in economic terms. Likewise, it is certain that the rate of interest exists only if interest itself exists, and, since interest is a macroeconomic concept only if it is explained in relation to production, it is clear that Keynes's microeconomic analysis of the rate of interest fails altogether to explain it. Although it is true that the rate of interest is independent of technology and utility, it is incorrect to treat it as a microeconomic concept. A new theory of the rate of interest is needed, but it must be macroeconomic in nature.

Interest and fixed capital

The source of interest

Economists have never stopped looking for a satisfactory answer to this age-long question. Adam Smith was the first to have related interest to the process of capital accumulation. In Chapter 6 of Book I of the *Wealth of Nations*, he explicitly stated that economic growth requires the accumulation of a stock in the hands of particular persons who 'will naturally employ it in setting to work industrious people, whom they will supply with materials and subsistence' (Smith 1974: 151). He then adds that '[the entrepreneur] would have no interest to employ them [workmen], unless he expected from the sale of their work something more than what was sufficient to replace his stock to him; and he could have no interest to employ a great stock rather than a small one, unless his profits were to bear some proportion to the extent of his stock' (ibid.: 151). Smith's use of the term 'profit' should not mislead us. As already pointed out by Böhm-Bawerk, it is perfectly legitimate here to take profit to mean interest on capital. If we thus interpret Smith's analysis, we can immediately relate interest to the stock of circulating capital invested in the production of new capital goods. 'They [profits on stock, i.e. interests] are regulated altogether by the value of the stock employed, and are greater or smaller in proportion to the extent of this stock' (ibid.: 151). At this point, the problem faced by Smith is that of explaining how a positive interest may derive from a stock of capitalised goods. His main difficulty lies in the necessity of reconciling the fact that labour is the only source of value with the need to include interest in the definition and measurement of value. Thus, on the one hand, he claims that '[l]abour measures the value not only of that part of price which resolves itself into labour, but of that which resolves itself into rent, and of that which resolves itself into profit' (ibid.: 153). On the other hand, he maintains that '[w]ages, profit and rent, are the three original sources of all revenue as well as of all exchangeable value. All other revenue is ultimately derived from some one or other of these' (ibid.: 155).

In Chapter 4 of Book II of his most famous work, Smith refers directly to interest and rightly observes that '[t]he stock that is lent at interest is always considered as a capital by the lender. He expects that in due time it is to be restored to him, and that in the meantime the borrower is to pay him a certain annual rent for the use of it. The borrower may use it either as a capital, or as a stock reserved for immediate consumption' (ibid.: 450). Although interest is paid in both cases, whether the sum lent is spent for immediate consumption or invested as capital, it is in the investment of saving that its source can be found. It is when Smith's stock is used as a real fund in the production of new capital goods that the sum lent to firms (or earned by them as profit) is definitively transformed into capital. And it is in this process of fixed capital accumulation that the logical justification of interest is to be found. 'If he [the borrower] uses it [the stock] as capital, he employs it in the maintenance of productive labourers, who reproduce the value with a profit. He can, in this case, both restore the capital and pay the interest without alienating or encroaching upon any other source of revenue' (ibid.: 450). Hence, interest is derived from labour but not from wages. Labour increases the value of final output by the amount of interest without 'encroaching upon' wages. This is the difficult message conveyed by Smith's succinct analysis of interest.

Another important contribution to the understanding of the origin of interest is that of Ricardo. Besides claiming that commodities 'will differ in exchangeable value, if they cannot be brought to market in the same time' (Ricardo 1951: 37), he maintains that differences in value arise 'from the profits being accumulated as capital, and [are] only a just compensation for the time that the profits were withheld' (ibid.: 37). The fundamental element here is time. Yet, time alone cannot be considered as a source of value and, therefore, of interest. How are we to justify the appearance of a new value unless we think of time as a metaphysical category? Ricardo's idea of 'compensation for the income accumulated as capital' might prove extremely useful. Although he did not take it far enough, Ricardo's intuition contains all the elements required to explain the very formation of a macroeconomic income called interest. As may be observed by any economist familiar with the subject, one of these elements is time. Now, time is a crucial element on two accounts: first, because it leads to the transformation of current income into circulating capital, thus allowing for the exchange between current and future consumption; second, because part of current income may be 'fixed' in time through its investment in the production of capital goods. It is to fixed capital that Ricardo's intuition must be referred. When this is done, interest appears to be a compensation for the income actually saved by the community as a whole in the form of fixed capital.

Before picking up again Ricardo's suggestion of analysing interest in terms of 'compensation', let us consider Böhm-Bawerk's contribution to the search for the origin of interest.

Böhm-Bawerk views interest (*Urzins*) as being related to production and to the difference between the present value of subsistence goods distributed to workers and the future value of the goods that will be produced by these workers. At time t_0, workers are paid an amount of wages equivalent to the stock of consumption goods accumulated by firms as the real content of their circulating capital. At time t_1, firms sell the output produced by their workers and realise a benefit equal to the difference between the value of output and that of the initial stock of consumption goods. But how is it possible for labour to give rise to a value greater than its own? If we discard – as done by Böhm-Bawerk – Marx's distinction between labour and labour power, it is hard to believe that labour may create a measure of value greater than the one it gives up. The task is even beyond our reach if – following Böhm-Bawerk – we rule out the possibility of considering the increase in the physical productivity of labour as an increase in value. Yet, Böhm-Bawerk is right in distinguishing between original interest (*Urzins*) and interest on loans (*Leihzins*) and in trying to explain the first on the basis of production, time and capital. As we have already pointed out, the main difficulty here is to reconcile the formation of a new income (interest) with the fact that only human labour can generate a positive value. Capital goods do not create any positive value and yet interest is a macroeconomic income derived from fixed capital. To explain interest is to solve this apparently insoluble dilemma.

Böhm-Bawerk refuses the old productivity theory, according to which interest is the result of the increase in physical productivity allowed by capital. He is perfectly aware of the fact that the true problem lies in explaining interest in terms of value and not in physical units. It is the interest derived from the very existence of capital that accounts for a net increase in value. It is because society endures a sacrifice that capital can be accumulated, and it is in this macroeconomic saving that interest has its source. Böhm-Bawerk's attempt to explain interest as a positive increase in value owing to capital is related to his concept of a roundabout process of production and his claim that future goods are undervalued. According to his analysis, the length of the period of production modifies the valuation of capital goods since individuals tend to underestimate future as opposed to present goods. Thus, the use of capital and the flow of time together lead to an increase in the value of present relative to future productions. Underestimation of future goods and technical superiority of present goods determines a premium on present goods that explains the origin of interest.

Schumpeter's analysis of interest seems to develop along the same lines as Böhm-Bawerk's. He starts by defining interest as 'a premium on present over future purchasing power' (Schumpeter 1955: 157) and claims that productive interest originates in new enterprises and 'has its source in profits' (ibid.: 158). Referring to Böhm-Bawerk's concept of roundabout methods of production, Schumpeter maintains that interest springs from entrepreneurial activity and relates to the finance required for innovations. He also claims that interest on capital 'is a permanent net income' (ibid.: 159) and sets out to explain where it comes from and why it is permanent. According to Schumpeter's theory of profit, innovation is indeed a source of net income; yet competition has the annoying consequence of reducing the formation of net income to a temporary phenomenon. In order to account for the permanent character of interest, Schumpeter is thus led to claim that 'the capitalist would first have to lend his capital to one entrepreneur and after a certain time to another, since the first cannot be permanently in a position to pay interest' (ibid.: 208).

Despite this curious conclusion, it is important to notice that Schumpeter does not accept the idea that interest may be defined as a premium on concrete goods. He maintains instead that 'we cannot move away from the money basis of interest' (ibid.: 184). Interest is thus derived from the control over capital goods allowed by the investment of current saving. But how is it that the productive investment of current saving leads to an increase in value greater than that generated by the new production itself? How is it possible to derive a positive interest on top of the income generated by the production of capital goods? In other words, for what reason must 'present purchasing power ... regularly be at a premium over future purchasing power in the money market' (ibid.: 188)? According to Schumpeter, new combinations of productive forces can account for an increase in the sum invested in production and thus justify the fact that 'a present sum will be normally valued more highly than a future sum' (ibid.: 190). However, even if entrepreneurs 'have a higher estimation for present as against future purchasing power' (ibid.: 191), this does not mean that technological progress leads necessarily (and regularly) to an increase in produced value. If it does not, some entrepreneurs may obtain a profit only at the expense of others, and it would be possible to explain interest only as a transfer from borrowers to lenders. In this case, interest would spring from current income and would not define a positive increase in value. Apprehended 'as a tax upon profit' (ibid.: 175), interest does not pertain to the category of net incomes and is reduced to 'a market phenomenon' (ibid.: 187).

As suggested by Böhm-Bawerk, however, interest on loans (*Leihzins*) must be distinguished from productive interest (*Urzins*). The true justification of interest lies in the demonstration that it defines an increase in value. Interest has its source in the value invested in fixed capital. Schumpeter claims that 'saving which is actually observable is in part a consequence of the existing interest' (ibid.: 200). In fact, it is the other way round: it is interest that is a consequence of macroeconomic saving, i.e. of the saving definitively transformed into fixed capital. Admittedly, interest is paid on current deposits too, and in this respect it is possible to claim that it has an influence over the amount of savings lent to consumers (which is not that part of saving that Schumpeter refers to in the above quotation). Yet, interest on loans is merely a transfer of income from borrower to lender that would probably not even exist if the accumulation of fixed capital were not at the origin of a positive value (the interest on capital). It is because current income is partly transformed into fixed capital and thus definitively subtracted from consumption that interest is formed. In a sense, interest is the compensation that a society is entitled to because of its (macroeconomic) saving. The income lent to consumers does not give rise to the formation of interest. On the contrary, it is because a positive interest is generated by the accumulation of fixed capital that consumers wanting to borrow part of current income are forced to pay a price in order to encourage savers to lend to them (and not only to capital). 'Thus interest forces its way into the business of people who have not themselves anything to do with new combinations' (ibid.: 202). Hence, interest on consumption is of a microeconomic nature, whereas the only true macroeconomic interest is that on capital. Whereas the former implies a simple transfer of (future) income between borrower and lender, the latter defines a positive increase in the value of current output because of capital accumulation.

The theory of interest is a further example of the all too frequent confusion between micro- and macroeconomics. Schumpeter himself does not always avoid it, his analysis being founded both on a macroeconomic conception of interest and on microeconomic considerations concerning entrepreneurial behaviour. He correctly distinguishes between productive interest and interest on ordinary loans, but then seems to be at a loss when he is to explain interest as a permanent net income. Now, a satisfactory solution may be found only if interest is related to fixed capital accumulation. Both Böhm-Bawerk and Schumpeter have greatly contributed to the elaboration of this solution, mainly by stressing the fundamental role played by time and production.

Interest as a macroeconomic cost

Although Böhm-Bawerk had convincingly argued for the necessity of transforming physical productivity into a productivity in value if interest in terms of a net increase in current income was to be explained, several economists have attempted to show that interest may be derived directly from an increase in physical productivity. Arguing against Schumpeter's argument that in equilibrium interest decreases necessarily to zero, Samuelson, for example, maintains that time may be the direct cause of an increase in physical productivity that does not necessarily need to be expressed in terms of value. His case rests on the apparently obvious observation that seeds ripen into a greater quantity of crops, the difference being imputable to the productivity of seeds through time. Referring to rice, Samuelson maintains that the whole ripening process leads to a net increase in final output that explains interest without recurring to the dubious concept of time preference. His example would thus have the double advantage of avoiding Böhm-Bawerk's critique – everything being expressed in terms of rice – and the need for any assumption regarding time preference. As claimed in Chapter 4, however, no net output can be determined on purely physical grounds. Samuelson's increase of 10 units of rice is not a net increase due to a miraculous productivity of rice itself. Once all the physical factors entering the process of growing are taken into account, it appears that the increase in rice is entirely due to a process of physical transformation, and that no net product can be related to the physical productivity of rice and time. On the whole, Samuelson's example does not provide an explanation of interest either in real or in monetary terms. The necessary equality between physical inputs and outputs is too great an obstacle to derive interest directly from physical productivity. Moreover, as observed by Kirzner, there are no logical reasons for excluding the possibility that Samuelson's increase in productivity is entirely anticipated so that no increase in value is obtained that could account for the existence of a positive interest. 'Why does not the market bid up the price of all the "machines" (in which the individual might plan to invest his capital) so that no net annual yield remains?' (Kirzner 1996: 141).

The relationships among physical productivity, value and interest are not easy to grasp. Böhm-Bawerk consistently tried to reconcile his critique of traditional productivity theories of interest with the possibility of defining an increase in value as a result of roundabout processes of production. Unfortunately, his attempt was spoilt by the search for a subjective cause of an increase that has to be objective if interest is to define a net social income. Wicksell is another great economist to have uncompromisingly discarded measuring capital in physical units. His attempt at providing an unambiguous theory of capital and interest is not less effective than his rigorous critique of the work of his predecessors. To avoid circularity, he maintains that interest may be explained as '*the difference between the marginal productivity of saved-up labour and land and of current labour and land*' (Wicksell 1934: 154). Instead of referring interest to the physical productivity of capital itself, Wicksell emphasises the greater efficiency of saved up labour and land with respect to 'current labour and land directly employed in the production of consumption-goods' (ibid.: 150). The source of interest is thus to be found in the fact that, being employed in the production of capital goods, labour (and land) acquires a greater efficiency. Wicksell's reasoning is subtle and requires careful reading. At first sight, it may even be misleading, the productivity of saved up labour (and land) being closely related to that of capital (which Wicksell refuses). If it is maintained that capital is 'a single coherent mass of saved-up labour and saved-up land, which is accumulated in the course of years' (ibid.: 150), then it seems obvious to infer that the value-creating power of capital has to be attributed to its productivity. Yet, another interpretation is possible, in which time plays a fundamental role in accounting for the existence of interest and in which the increase in productivity results in an increase in value due rather to labour working with the aid of capital than to capital directly. 'In the real sense, of course, ... only the original factors – man and nature [are productive]. But the productivity of both becomes, or at any rate may become, greater if they are employed for more distant ends than if they are employed for the immediate production of commodities' (ibid.: 150). As stressed by Wicksell, time is a key element in the process of capital accumulation. It is through saving that labour and land are transformed into capital, their investment in the production of investment goods defining their irreversible passage from circulating to fixed capital. The increase in physical productivity deriving from the use of instrumental goods must then be referred to labour and land, the only original factors of production and value. This means that if the increase in physical productivity must define a positive increase in value this can only come from an increase in the value created by labour (and land). Interest is a net income whose source is the transformation of labour into fixed capital and whose amount is determined by the increase in value – expressed in terms of labour (wage units) – obtained by labour working with the aid of capital goods. 'This marginal productivity [of capital], and the share in the product which it determines, provides in the first place, a recompense for the actual capital used up in production' (ibid.: 153).

Like Senior's (1854) theory of abstinence, Wicksell's analysis suggests here that interest is a compensation for the capital invested in the production of instrumental goods. Modern monetary macroeconomics confirms this intuition.

Let us start from interest paid on consumption loans. An important point here is that even in this particular case interest is related to capital. The income saved being immediately transformed into capital-time, it is a capital that is lent. However, this capital is not positive for society as a whole. Positive for lenders, it is in fact negative for borrowers (who spend their future income for the purchase of present consumption goods). It is for this reason that interest on consumption loans is not a net income. When borrowers pay an interest to lenders, they simply transfer to them part of their income. No net value is added to final output because of this transfer. Things change when interest is paid on production loans. This time the capital lent (or transferred as profit) to firms is invested in a new production of instrumental goods and hence definitively transformed into fixed capital. The part of capital-time thus invested defines a positive, macroeconomic capital. As underlined by Schmitt, fixed capital is irreversibly lost by income holders. 'L'ensemble des épargnants et même, plus généralement, l'ensemble des titulaires de revenus perd définitivement tout revenu fixé dans le capital' (Schmitt 1984b: 561). It is because of this loss suffered by income holders that fixed capital accumulation is the source of a positive interest, which becomes 'the compensation [obtained by income holders] for the income lent and definitively lost as capital' (ibid.: 562; our translation). Now, since 'the final absorption of income into fixed capital is a cost of production for the entire nation ... it follows that interest is a macroeconomic cost assumed by society as a whole' (ibid.: 565; our translation). This explains the origin of interest as a macroeconomic income but seems at odds with Schmitt's claim that national income is entirely made up of wages. Let us briefly show how the French author manages to reconcile the cost of production definition of interest with the fact that wages are the only source of value.

Value is the numerical form in which current output is integrated. Since labour is the unique, macroeconomic factor of production, wages are this numerical form and define the value total of national output. Capital and land do not share the same logical status as labour. They cannot integrate output in its monetary form, and are therefore neither factors of production nor an original source of value. Although capital goods increase physical productivity, they are not directly the cause of any increase in value. If output goes from 10 to 100 physical units because the use of fixed capital increases productivity, this does not allow us to infer that its value is also increased ten times. As the Classics had clearly understood, the increase in use values does not define an equivalent increase in exchange values. Does this mean that the use of fixed capital has no consequence at all on the value of final output? Even if capital itself is not a source of value, is it not possible to maintain that its use increases the value produced by labour (which remains the sole factor of production)?

Indeed, if interest is a cost of production, value is necessarily increased to the extent that a positive interest is paid to capital lenders. We should thus infer that interest measures the increase in efficiency due to the use of capital. Yet, wages are the only measure of value. Hence, capital can be at the origin of a new value only if it increases the efficiency of *labour*. It seems possible to maintain, then, that wages measure interest that measures the increase in capital efficacy. This sounds all the more weird as wages and interest are two complementary categories of national income. As observed by Schmitt, however, this is only apparently so. In fact, it is perfectly conceivable to maintain that interest is included in (nominal) wages and that (real) wages and interest are complementary in the measure of national income. Let us suppose (nominal) wages to be equal to 100 wage units and interest rate to be equal to 10 per cent. Even though total value is equal to 100 wage units, part of it is represented by interest. Expressed by 10 wage units, interest defines a positive value generated by labour but attributed to capital (to its owners). Part of the workers' activity is thus devoted to themselves – for the production of wage goods – and part to capital owners – for the production of interest goods. Once interest has been paid, we know the amount of value generated by the production of interest goods, i.e. the part of global output produced on behalf of capital owners. The integration of current output in its numerical form is thus operated by labour alone, but partly on behalf of wage-earners and partly on that of security holders. Things happen as if output were emitted jointly by capital lenders and wage-earners. 'Tout se passe comme si l'épargnant était, au prorata de son revenu investi, le co-émetteur du produit, à concurrence exacte de l'intérêt perçu' (Schmitt 1984b: 566).

As we have seen, the origin of interest is to be found in the compensation that lenders derive from their loss of current income to the benefit of fixed capital. Its measure is determined on the financial market. This means that the rate determined on this market influences the total amount of interest goods produced in the system irrespective of the physical productivity of capital. In our numerical example, the value of the increase in labour efficiency is of 10 units, which is also the value of the interest goods produced during the period considered. What is difficult to reconcile is the fact that interest is a new, macroeconomic income derived from fixed capital with the need to identify it with a sum of wage units. Being derived from the income invested into instrumental goods, interest is not directly produced by labour; yet it is human labour that measures interest goods as only human labour can give a monetary form to physical output. If interest were not a cost of production and if it were not measured in wage units, it would not be a positive income. The whole of current output is measured in wage units. Hence, the entire output is initially issued as a sum of wage goods. If interest were nil, households would benefit from a real wage corresponding to total output. The presence of a positive interest diminishes real wages to the benefit of security holders. Current output is thus partly made up of wage goods and partly of interest goods. Labour is still the sole macroeconomic factor of production, yet part of the value that it creates has its origin in fixed capital. Operating with the aid of capital, labour produces a set of goods that it gives up – as a compensation – to the owners of capital. It is in this respect that interest is a cost of production. To produce with the aid of capital requires the previous transformation of circulating into fixed capital. This transformation defines a macroeconomic saving and implies a sacrifice that will be compensated later by a positive production of interest goods.

One of the great merits of Schmitt's analysis is to show that the creation of interest as a net income is perfectly consistent with the measure of value in wage units. This is done by referring to the quantum dimension of the processes defining production and consumption (final purchase of produced output). As the reader will remember, in Chapter 4 it was pointed out that – according to Schmitt's revolutionary discovery of quantum time – each production is an instantaneous event defining a precise quantum of time. Hence, each production and its final purchase coincide in quantum time even if they take place at different instants of continuous time. This peculiarity of quantum economics allows Schmitt to infer that the final purchase of current output may modify the formation of current income. In the case we are analysing, the expenditure of a positive interest must be interpreted as a final purchase of interest goods occurring on the labour market. From the moment that wages are paid, part of the goods produced by workers is definitively purchased on behalf of capital owners. 'Since interest is positive, the emission of x units of wages includes a purchase, equal to y, of interest goods on behalf of their holders, the savers' (Schmitt 1984b: 563; our translation). Interest is thus included in wages as a joint expenditure reducing the amount of real wages. 'L'analyse moderne saisit les intérêts *dans les salaires*, comme une "catégorie-gigogne" ' (ibid.: 563). Being present simultaneously on the commodity and on the labour markets, interest can therefore be explained as a net income even if it does not correspond to the remuneration of a factor of production. If interest were confined to the commodity market, no economic theory could ever account for it. It is on the labour market that income is created, and it is here that interest must be formed if it is to define a net income. Now, since capital is not a factor of production, interest is actually formed at the moment that current output is sold and not when it is produced. How can we reconcile these apparently contradictory statements? As claimed by Schmitt, because sale and production are in fact simultaneous in quantum time, a positive expenditure of income may take place within the payment of wages. Hence, interest is formed and spent simultaneously on the two markets. It is because interest is spent in the payment of wages taking place on the labour market that workers' activity gives rise to a positive amount of interest goods, and it is for this very reason that interest is indeed a net income.

The analysis of interest briefly sketched here in value terms needs to be widened in order to account for banks' intervention and for the expression of interest in terms of prices. Although this has already been partly done by Schmitt in his latest manuscript on the monetary origin of unemployment (Schmitt 1998), a complete theory of interest is still in the making. The fundamental elements required for its achievement are provided by the quantum theoretical approach to macroeconomics. They are the mark of a new conception of bank money and of the monetary process of production and circulation. They are also the best confirmation of Böhm-Bawerk's and Wicksell's intuitions as to the origin of interest and its relationship with capital and time. Now, Wicksell's contribution shows that interest plays a major role in the explanation of the pathological functioning of our monetary systems. His distinction between natural and monetary rates of interest now acquires its full meaning and – as we shall see in the following chapter – its reappraisal throws a new light on the problem of unemployment.

The idea conveyed by Schmitt's quantum theoretical approach to monetary economics is that what happens at a later date in continuous time – the final purchase of current output – can modify what happened earlier – the payment of wages. Far from being a metaphysical concept of no practical interest, temporal reversibility or time symmetry is a serious concern even within the realm of such a rigorous science as physics. As suggested by Price in his book on time's arrow, there can be events that modify the past if our knowledge of what happened in the past is directly influenced by our present information. 'The past which might coherently be taken to depend on our present actions is the *inaccessible* past – that bit of the past which we cannot simply "observe", before we act to bring it about' (Price 1996: 180). Discovered and developed in economics, the concept of quantum time seems to fit perfectly Price's claim for backward causation. If wages paid at time t_0 are of 100 monetary units, we know for certain that at t_0 production is made up of wage goods and is measured by 100 wage units. Now, our knowledge of what happened at t_0 is liable to be modified by what happens at a later date. For example, if at t_1 the purchase of wage goods gives rise to a positive income transfer in favour of firms, we can infer that part of the goods produced at t_0 were in fact financed (in advance) by the profit formed at t_1. Our knowledge of what happens at t_1 allows us to reinterpret what actually happened at t_0. This is not to say that our first knowledge was wrong, but that it was incomplete. It remains true that production of t_0 has a value of 100 wage units, but we now learn that part of the wage goods produced (and whose physical form is obviously unchanged) was in fact profit goods by destination. 'Why shouldn't we suppose … that the real taxonomy is from our standpoint teleological: that is, that there are real distinctions between objects which turn on what is to happen to them in the future?' (ibid.: 189). This is precisely what happens in the case of interest. When a positive interest is paid to capital lenders, the result of the initial payment of wages must be reinterpreted. What presented itself as a production of 100 units of wage goods appears to be a production of wage *and* interest goods. Even if the use of capital does not directly increase the value of final output, the increase in productivity that labour derives from its working with the aid of instrumental goods takes the form of a re-emission of wages measured by the amount of interest. The payment of interest taking place at t_1 leads us to a deeper knowledge of what happened at t_0, namely that the goods produced have a total value of 110 wage units and that part of them (10 wage units in value terms) are interest goods.

7   Order versus disorder

The neoclassical approach to economic disorder

Walras's point of view

In Walras's *Elements of Pure Economics*, we find only a very brief reference to economic breakdowns, which are seen as equilibrium disturbances of unspecified origin. 'For, just as a lake is, at times, stirred to its very depths by a storm, so also the market is sometimes thrown into violent confusion by *crises*, which are sudden and general disturbances of equilibrium' (Walras 1984: 381). Nothing is said about the nature of these sudden and general disturbances, Walras's only suggestion being that '[t]he more we know of the ideal conditions of equilibrium, the better we shall be able to control or prevent these crises' (ibid.: 381). We are thus led to think that within the neoclassical theoretical framework anything that causes the system to depart from equilibrium is the source of an economic disorder. Now, as general equilibrium implies the equalisation of supply and demand on the commodity, services and financial markets, disorder results from consumers', producers' and/or asset holders' incapacity to agree about the terms of their relative exchanges. On the labour market, for example, an excess supply of labour that is not absorbed through a decrease in wages leads to unemployment. Whatever hampers the free fluctuation of wages is thus identified as the cause of this particular unbalance. Likewise, consumers' behaviour may oppose the determination of equilibrium on the commodity market, with negative consequences for the clearance of this market as well as for future decisions to invest and produce.

If we confined our analysis to this broad line of thought, we would have to conclude that economic disorder is the unavoidable mark of a system constantly trying to reach a state – equilibrium – which escapes every time it is approached.

> Such is the continuous market, which is perpetually tending towards equilibrium without ever actually attaining it, because the market has no other way of approaching equilibrium except by groping, and before the goal is reached, it has to renew its efforts and start over again, all the basic data of the problem, e.g. the initial quantities possessed, the utilities of goods and services, the technical coefficients, the excess of income over consumption, the working capital requirements, etc., having changed in the meantime.
>
> (ibid.: 380)

Unbalance would be the rule and we would have to live with it, in the constantly renewed attempt to reduce it as much as possible. This would be a very difficult attempt, for equilibrium market conditions rest mainly on the behaviour of economic agents, which is essentially unpredictable. Despite courageous and unrealistic assumptions, it can hardly be denied that human behaviour is often far from rational and certainly too complex to be expressed mathematically. Regardless of whether human behaviour can be expressed in mathematical terms, it is a fact that if equilibrium depends on households' and producers' behaviour the causes of unbalance are as various and unforeseeable as the reasons that may induce these economic agents to behave in a non-optimal way. In such a context, it is vain to look for a rigorous analysis of economic disorder and for a rational way to avoid it. At best, we may attempt to approach this changing world by introducing suitable assumptions into our models, hoping that they do not prove too unrealistic and that things work out the way that we want them to.

No other insights can be found in Walras's work. In particular, he does not provide any hints as to monetary disorders such as inflation and deflation. This is not surprising, of course, for Walras's analysis is not monetary. Other economists working along similar lines have nonetheless attempted to elaborate a monetary theory. The most famous attempt is that of the monetarist school. Let us analyse it critically.

Friedman's quantity theory

Friedman states that the quantity theory of money first developed as 'a theoretical approach that insisted that money does matter – that any interpretation of short-term movements in economic activity is likely to be seriously at fault if it neglects monetary changes and repercussions and if it leaves unexplained why people are willing to hold the particular nominal quantity of money in existence' (Friedman 1956: 3). An important feature of this approach is that it aims to integrate the quantity theory of money with the general equilibrium system of price determination. Unfortunately, the result is not in line with the ambitious research programme set up by the monetarists. Among the most serious shortcomings of this approach, we find the dichotomy between real and monetary sectors (also known as the homogeneity or the money neutrality postulate), the old-fashioned identification of money with a real good or an asset (epitomised by the use of terms such as 'quantity', 'mass', 'velocity of circulation' and 'hoarding') and the belief that people's behaviour may modify the relationship between supply of and demand for money and thus be the cause of monetary disorders. As the first two points have already been substantiated by the analysis developed in the previous chapters and in other publications, let us concentrate on the third.

'The quantity theory is in the first instance a theory of the demand for money' (ibid.: 4). Having thus stated the principle of his approach, Friedman investigates form and characteristics of the demand function for money on the assumption that 'to the ultimate wealth-owning units in the economy, money is one kind of asset, one way of holding wealth. To the productive enterprise, money is a capital good, a source of productive services that are combined with other productive services to yield the products that the enterprise sells' (ibid.: 4). It appears from the outset that Friedman has a blurred conception of the distinctions among money, income and capital. Although he is certainly aware of the classical distinction between nominal and real money, his interpretation of the two concepts is far less articulated than Ricardo's and Marx's. In particular, he does not seem to realise that real money is not simply the ratio between nominal money and the price level. Logically, money comes first, and it is only through its integration with current output that it is transformed into income and then into capital. By identifying it with an asset and with a capital good, Friedman avoids explaining how this integration may actually take place. Yet, his claim that the quantity theory 'is not a theory of output, or of money income, or of the price level' (ibid.: 4) is not good enough to justify this procedure. It is not because the quantity theory is confined to the study of the demand for money that we are entitled to assume money to be a capital good. As a matter of fact, capital goods are produced means of production and not a mere sum of money. If they can be expressed monetarily, it is because money is integrated as their numerical form and thus transformed into capital. Likewise, income is the result of the integration of money with physical output, a result that requires the simultaneous intervention of firms, banks and workers. If this process of integration is not properly understood, it is impossible to formulate any realistic and coherent hypothesis as to the relationship between supply of and demand for money.

Let us consider a very simple example of how the monetarist approach may lead us astray. Suppose current production gives rise to 100 units of money wages paid out by banks on behalf of firms. At the very moment that wages are paid, households own a monetary asset equal to 100 units temporarily deposited with their banks. Households' total wealth is thus held in the form of bank deposits so that, according to the monetarist approach, their demand for money is equal to 100 units. Now, productive enterprises also exert a demand for money of 100 units since this is precisely the amount they need to pay for their productive services. Consistent with the quantity theory, we should therefore infer that the total demand for money is equal to 200 units, twice the amount of money actually issued by banks. At this point, we could assume that a faithful disciple of Friedman's school would simply claim that consistency is assured if we assume each unit of money to circulate twice per unit of time. In the example, payments being instantaneous events, the money units issued by banks would instantaneously be given to firms and workers, 100 units being thus enough to satisfy their combined demand. However, is it correct to say that a single transaction – the payment of wages – defines a velocity of money circulation of 2 money units per unit of time? In reality, the money issued by banks and paid to workers on behalf of firms flows immediately back to its emission point. Hence, money's velocity is equal to infinity rather than to 2 money units per unit of time. This clearly means that money is not a stock but a flow, so that its 'velocity' – provided we may reasonably refer to this concept – has nothing to do with the velocity of circulation of a physical object. The payment of wages is a single transaction that satisfies simultaneously the demand for money of both firms and workers, it is true, but *not* because money circulates twice, first from banks to firms and then from firms to workers. Being of a book-keeping nature, bank money 'circulates' from and to its point of emission in a unique and instantaneous movement. Let us consider our example from the point of view of wealth. How is total wealth measured according to Friedman's monetarist approach? What are its component parts? The answer is much more complex than one would expect. If we tackle the problem as suggested by Friedman, we should start by claiming that '[f]rom the broadest and most general point of view, total wealth includes all sources of "income" or consumable services' (ibid.: 4). A curious start indeed, for it is not at all evident that wealth must be taken to be the *source* of income rather than the *result* of production. It is true that human productive capacity is a *potential* source of income, but this does not turn it into *actual* wealth. If no work is done, how is it possible for wealth to be positive? Now, even if we leave aside this initial difficulty, the problem remains intricate. Capital, for example, is a source of income and, therefore, must be considered as a form of wealth. But what about interest? As it is a source of income only if it is transformed into capital, how are we to classify it? Is capital wealth because it is a source of interest or because it is the result of labour, which is itself a source of income? Friedman claims that 'wealth can be held in numerous forms' (ibid.: 5) and considers 'five different forms in which wealth can be held' (ibid.: 5), namely money, bonds, equities, physical non-human goods and human capital. Here again, the confusion between *source* and *result* is striking. The first four forms of wealth considered by Friedman are the result of a productive process, whereas the fifth is one of its causes (unless, of course, one maintains that money and capital goods are themselves given before any production has actually taken place). But if production is still to occur, money can exist only as an empty numerical form of no value. How, then, might it be defined as wealth? It should also be obvious that in this particular situation physical non-human goods could only be a heterogeneous mass of raw materials that might only euphemistically be called wealth. On the contrary, when production is taken into consideration, money is transformed into income (and then into capital-time) and may therefore be defined as wealth. Likewise, raw materials are transformed into commodities and can also enter the category of wealth.

At this point, the problem is how to establish whether money (income) and commodities are two distinct elements of the set that defines total wealth or whether they are actually two aspects of the same element. Does production create a positive sum of money income and at the same time a positive amount of commodities? Let us suppose the costs of production to be equal to 100 money units. Is the total value resulting from the productive process equal to 100 or 200 units? Given the costs of production, the value of produced output is of 100 units. Hence, total value (or wealth) may equal 200 units only if 100 units of money income were created independently of the production of commodities. This *not* being the case, it should be clear that money income and physical output are one and the same result of production, one and the same element of wealth. It is as soon as money is conceived of as a numerical form and output as its real content that this reality becomes incontrovertible. Hence, the first four forms of wealth singled out by Friedman can be reduced to one, bonds and equities being simply different forms in which a claim on money income may be held.

The next question that has to be answered refers to the relationship between money income and what Friedman calls human capital. We have already observed that, considered as a 'productive capacity of human beings', human capital is only a potential source of wealth. If this source is indeed activated, a positive production occurs that leads to the formation of wealth. In our numerical example, labour gives rise to a money income of 100 units defining current output. Wages paid to workers are thus the measure of the wealth created by Friedman's human capital. Now, wages earned by labour are considered by Friedman to be just one form of wealth or, using his own formulation, just the income generated by one of the different forms in which wealth may be held. Money being another of these forms, shall we conclude that, on the whole, wealth amounts to 200 units: 100 owned by firms and 100 owned by workers? Would it be correct to maintain that, in our example, total wealth is made up of 100 units of money and 100 units of human capital? This would be so only if banks issued money as an asset, production notwithstanding. However, if we leave aside any metaphysical conception of banks, there is no reason to believe that money can have a positive value whatsoever independently of production. Human capital itself has no measurable value outside production. It is only through the payment of wages that human activity (and its result) is given its numerical form. Hence, it is only at the moment that wages are paid that a monetary capital is formed which corresponds to the activity of labour. It follows that wages measure simultaneously the income earned by workers through their activity and the capital invested by firms. What firms owe to banks is the very income earned by workers. As we have seen in the first two chapters, double-entry book-keeping implies a triangular relationship among banks, firms and workers, so that the income earned by the last is immediately deposited with banks and lent to firms. Finally, the demand for money acquires a different meaning in the light of the modern approach to bank money. Rather than a willingness to hold wealth in a particular form, the demand for money defines the amount of money required for banks to give a numerical form to production. This being so, does it still make sense to analyse monetary disorders in terms of unbalance between supply of and demand for money?

According to Friedman, '[t]he quantity theorist accepts the empirical hypothesis that the demand for money is highly stable' (ibid.: 16) and holds also 'that there are important factors affecting the supply of money that do not affect the demand for money' (ibid.: 16). Unbalances are thus likely to appear any time that an unexpected change occurs in the money supply. For example, inflation would result from a sudden increase in the money supply due to factors that leave the demand for money unaltered. Clearly, this explanation rests on the assumption that the supply of money may be determined independently of the demand for money. Perfectly consistent with the dichotomous conception of neoclassical analysis, this assumption breaks down as soon as money is considered in its fundamental relationship with production. The idea that money is a mass created by banks (or 'monetary authorities') independently of the mass of real goods resulting from production is far-fetched and entirely alien to our monetary economies. In reality, money is emitted simultaneously with the formation of physical output. The two masses hypothesised by monetarists are in fact the two faces of one and the same coin. Hence, if a difference is to be found between these two faces, it can certainly not result from the lack of coherence between the decisions taken by different economic agents, for instance by banks and firms. Since every production defines a perfect identity between supply (output) and demand (money income), no difference can be found between supply of and demand for money. As already claimed by Wicksell in his 1898 book on interest and prices, money has reached perfect mobility 'as a result of concentration in the hands of the banks of cash holdings and of the business of lending, and of the use of bills and notes, cheques and clearing methods' (Wicksell 1965: 110), so that it is 'no longer possible to refer to the supply of money as an independent magnitude, differing from the demand for money' (ibid.: 110). Yet, it cannot be denied that monetary disorders exist, or, in other words, that the identity between supply and demand is not necessarily respected in today's monetary systems. How is it possible for the money supply not to be equal to the demand for money, given that the latter is defined by the amount of money actually required by production and thus associated with current output? This is the question that must be answered if monetary disorders are to be explained at all. A numerical difference between the money supply and the demand for money (as defined above) is not impossible, yet it cannot be explained by referring to the dichotomous world of neoclassical analysis. Indeed, if Friedman were correct, monetary disorder would be the rule, the adjustment between monetary and real masses being dependent on the behaviour of two autonomous sets of agents. But if the two masses are independent, their equilibrium cannot even be defined. Whatever their relationship, it could be taken as a reference, thus leaving equilibrium totally undetermined. A correct understanding of disorder requires a rigorous definition of order, and this is what the monetary analysis of production provides. Monetarism is too blurred at the edges to represent a valid framework of analysis and too far from reality to be referred to empirically.

Our negative conclusion is not substantially different when analysis shifts from monetary theory to monetary policy. In his paper on the role of monetary policy published by *The American Economic Review*, Friedman (1968) argues in favour of a monetary interpretation of depression and against a policy based on public spending and tax reductions. His analysis rests on the distinction between nominal and real magnitudes and develops from a critical to a positive approach. He first explains what monetary policy cannot do, namely pegging interest rates and the rate of unemployment for more than very limited periods, and concludes this part of his paper by claiming that 'the monetary authority controls nominal quantities …. In principle, it can use this control to peg a nominal quantity … or to peg the rate of change in a nominal quantity …. It cannot use its control over nominal quantities to peg a real quantity' (Friedman 1968: 11). Perfectly in line with the dichotomous approach of neoclassical analysis, this conclusion is at odds with the actual workings of our monetary systems. In particular, it is not true that monetary authorities can modify at will the nominal rate of growth of the money supply. In most developed countries, central banks are autonomous with respect to political power and do not cover budget deficits simply by issuing nominal money. What is wrongly called the 'quantity' or 'mass' of nominal money is not issued under the control of central banks. As every banker knows, money is actually issued by commercial banks on behalf of the public, and double-entry book-keeping shows that nominal money is transformed into real money from the very moment that it is emitted. Contrary to what is usually thought, this transformation does not result from nominal money being related to the level of prices, but is the logical consequence of nominal money being integrated with current output. Hence, even though Friedman is right in distinguishing nominal from real money, he is wrong in believing that nominal money is issued by monetary authorities autonomously with respect to the real world of production and circulation.

A much more promising insight comes from the second part of Friedman's paper, in which he deals with what monetary policy can do. Referring to John Stuart Mill's metaphor for money – i.e. a 'machine' – Friedman claims that 'a positive and important task for the monetary authority [is] to suggest improvements in the machine that will reduce the chances that it will get out of order, and to use its own powers so as to keep the machine in good working order' (ibid.: 13). If we take the word 'machine' to mean the monetary system, we get the gist of what should be the goal of central banks in our modern economic settings. Instead of trying vainly to modify or control either nominal or real quantities, central banks should improve the structure of our monetary systems in much the same way as has been done in the past under pressure by some enlightened experts such as Ricardo – who was the first to suggest the distinction between monetary and financial departments later introduced by the Bank of England – and by private bankers – who developed the principles of interbank clearing. In this sense, it is correct to maintain that a 'thing monetary policy can do is provide a stable background for the economy' (ibid.: 13). In his critical appraisal of the role of monetary policy, Friedman refers also to major disturbances arising from exceptional sources such as a post-war monetary expansion or an explosive federal budget, and he maintains that monetary policy can contribute to offsetting them. Again, his claim would be right if he were suggesting that monetary authorities must intervene to create a structure that will never allow central banks to finance budget deficits. Regrettably, this is only a part of what is suggested by Friedman, who sees monetary policy as a means to counter these 'disturbances' rather than as a way of preventing them. As for minor disturbances, the American economist has no hesitations in claiming that monetary policy can do very little to avoid them. 'We simply do not know enough to be able to predict either what their effects will be with any precision or what monetary policy is required to offset their effects' (ibid.: 14).

On the whole, Friedman's analysis of the aims and limits of the monetary authorities' intervention may be fruitfully reinterpreted on the basis of the principles of modern monetary macroeconomics. This would take us a long way away from the quantity theory of money, of course. Yet, it is only fair to recognise that Friedman is one of the few authors to have coherently stressed the relevance of monetary analysis and attempted to set up a monetary theory of economic disorder. What strikes us today is that, despite his understanding of the complexity of our monetary systems, he still supports the simplistic idea that monetary order is a question of equilibrium and that monetary authorities can secure it through a rigorous control of the rate of growth of the money supply. 'I believe that a monetary total is the best currently available immediate guide or criterion for monetary policy' (ibid.: 15). Once again, it is the dichotomous conception of the economic world that hampers Friedman's analysis. This is confirmed by his definition of the 'natural rate of unemployment', in which monetary factors disappear altogether. 'The "natural rate of unemployment", in other words, is the level that would be ground out by the Walrasian system of general equilibrium equations, provided there is imbedded in them the actual structural characteristics of the labour and commodity markets' (ibid.: 8). If an author who has always stressed the importance of money is even led to emphasise the role played by direct, real exchange, it is not surprising that so many economists still believe money to be a veil. How far removed from reality this conception is should be evident. Yet, this does not seem to be so. Neoclassical theory is so much embedded in our discipline that it 'transforms' reality, making the world resemble our vision instead of helping us to understand it. Neoclassical theory seems convincing because it is apparently based on reality. Is it not true that exchange as well as production are a matter of supply and demand? Is it not also true that, similar to what happens in the physical world, shocks generate unbalances?

How can we seriously doubt that unemployment is a disequilibrium caused by the imperfect matching of supply and demand on the labour market when Keynesian economists, too, believe so? 'Involuntary unemployment is a disequilibrium phenomenon; the behaviour, the persistence, of excess supplies of labour depend on how and how fast markets adjust to shocks, and on how large and how frequent the shocks are' (Tobin 1972: 2). In fact, economic reality cannot be reduced to the simple mechanism of supply and demand. As maintained by the greatest economists of the past, Walras included, economics starts where goods are associated with numbers. Now, it is thanks to bank money that this association takes place at its best. Thus, far from being a simple veil, money becomes the peculiar object of economic enquiry, the key element for the understanding of the logical (as opposed to behavioural) laws governing our economic systems. Disorder can therefore be explained only by referring to the workings of the monetary system and to its compliance with these laws. To clarify this approach further, let us briefly analyse the way in which the Classics dealt with the problems of monetary disorder and crisis.

The classical analysis of monetary disorder and recession

Ricardo's approach

As observed by Schmitt in his introduction to the Italian translation of David Ricardo's monetary writings, the rigour exercised by the Anglo-Portuguese economist in his monetary analysis is already evident in his early 'monetarist' theses. Ricardo's rigour enabled him to avoid the confusions which so many supporters of the quantity theory of money would later fall into. In particular, since his paper on the high price of bullion (Ricardo 1810), Ricardo clearly distinguished between monetary creation and capital formation. As Marx subsequently confirmed, what is created by banks and lent to the economy is a sum of nominal money and not of capital. 'When the credit system is developed, so that money is concentrated in the hands of the banks, it is they who advance it, at least nominally. This advance is only related to the money in circulation. It is an advance of circulation, not an advance of the capital it circulates' (Marx 1981: 664). The increase in the 'quantity' of money issued by the Bank of England leads to a rise in the prices of currently produced goods and services and not to a rise in the value of income or capital. 'But however abundant may be the quantity of money or of bank-notes; though it may increase the nominal prices of commodities; though it may distribute the productive capital in different proportions; though the Bank, by increasing the quantity of their notes, may enable A to carry on part of the business formerly engrossed by B and C, nothing will be added to the real revenue and wealth of the country' (Ricardo 1951, Vol. III: 93). If we abstract from the physical support used to represent it, money as such has no intrinsic value, but as soon as it is created it derives a positive value from the real goods it is associated with. Thus, if a new emission of money were added to that already associated with current output, the result would be a nominal increase of the monetary units 'vehiculating' output. 'If banks create new money, the excess will immediately contribute with pre-existing money to convey *the same product* to final consumers' (Schmitt 1985: 18; our translation).

Let us repeat that according to Ricardo a monetary overemission does not increase income or wealth, but is reabsorbed through a nominal rise in prices. 'If the Bank were to bring a large additional sum of notes into the market, and offer them on loan ... neither the notes, nor the money, would be retained unemployed by the borrowers; they would be sent into every market, and would every where raise the prices of commodities, till they were absorbed in the general circulation' (Ricardo 1951, Vol. III: 91). Ricardo's first explanation of monetary disorder therefore refers to the activity of the Bank of England as the issuing bank. It is a partial and somewhat simple explanation that applies only to monetary systems still in the making (like the English system of that time), of course. In more developed monetary systems such as those of today, an inflation of this kind does not find any practical backing. The autonomy of central banks together with the principles guiding their monetary and financial intermediation is enough to ward off an overemission of national money. Yet, despite its limitations, this first

Ricardian contribution to monetary theory has the merit of reaffirming the numerical and vehicular nature of bank money already foreshadowed by Adam Smith in the *Wealth of Nations*. Thus, consistent with his theoretical choice and contrary to what is maintained by the followers of the quantity theory of money, Ricardo claims that the value of money is entirely derived from the real goods and services that it is integrated with and of which it defines the numerical form.

At this point, Ricardo provides a second explanation of inflation. The monetary unit loses part of its value if the Bank's emission is in excess with respect to its gold reserves. As noted by Schmitt, Ricardo has no difficulty in showing that the speculative gain that would appear in a regime of convertibility between commodity-gold and money-gold would lead the Bank of England to intervene by immediately reducing its emissions and thus suffocating any inflationary pressure from the start. Still following the analytical path suggested by Schmitt, let us point out that Adam Smith's distinction between nominal and real magnitudes allows Ricardo to substantiate the claim that money derives its value from produced output. It follows that prices are simply 'the expression and name of value ... [so that] the price may vary with respect to value, every gap between the two magnitudes being *purely nominal*' (Schmitt 1985: 35; our translation). In the case of inflation, it is therefore neither the value of produced output nor that of the monetary 'mass' that varies, but the nominal expression of value and, therefore, of every single unit of money. It is because the same value is carried by an increased number of money units that each single unit loses part of its value. As already maintained by Adam Smith, (nominal) money must be kept distinct from the value of money. While nominal money simply expresses the *numerical* quantity of money issued by banks, the value of money is the result of the integration between the units issued and current output. 'A nation is rich, not according to the abundance of its money, nor to the high money value at which its commodities circulate, but according to the abundance of its commodities, contributing to its comforts and enjoyments' (Ricardo 1951, Vol. IV: 22).

It is thus reaffirmed by Smith and Ricardo that money's value or purchasing power does not result from the ratio between nominal money and the level of prices but from its integration with output. In the case of inflation, we are faced with a situation where, the amount of nominal money being greater than the value of money, the numerical expression of produced goods and services is proportionally increased. First elaborated along the same line as was later followed by the quantity theory of money, Ricardo's analysis develops soon in a much more promising direction that, highlighting the concept of absolute value, differentiates it substantially from the neoclassical approach. By gradually separating bank money from gold, Ricardo opens the way to its definition as a 'form of value', later to be developed by Marx. 'Money is not a thing but a particular form of value' (Marx 1981: 1003). Issued by banks at the public's request, money's first task is that of monetising production by becoming one with current output. The inflationary overemission that a central bank could carry out to the benefit of the State is thus averted if the monetary system is made to work in accordance with the rule that nominal money be equal to the value of money. 'If Government wanted money, it should be obliged to raise it in the legitimate way; by taxing the people; by the issue and sale of exchequer bills, by funded loans, or by borrowing from any of the numerous banks which might exist in the country; but in no case should it be allowed to borrow from those, who have the power of creating money' (Ricardo 1951, Vol. IV: 283). Ricardo's advice is therefore to steer clear of every possible gap between the banks' monetary emission and the financial intermediation that they operate in favour of the public. This may be implemented only if central bankers are denied the possibility of acting irrespective of the logical laws governing the monetary system. 'In the present state of the law, they [central bankers] have the power, without any control whatever, of increasing or reducing the circulation in any degree they may think proper: a power which should neither be entrusted to the state itself, nor to any body in it; as there can be no security for the uniformity in the value of the currency, when its augmentation or diminution depends solely on the will of the issuers' (ibid.: 69). If every monetary emission is a financial intermediation, all the money issued finds its *raison d'être* in current output and is therefore 'endogenously' determined by the public. Under these conditions, a nominal overemission would no longer be possible and our monetary systems would be freed from inflation forever. This is the message that we can derive from the analysis proposed by Ricardo (1951–5) in his last monetary publications, particularly in his *Proposals for an Economical and Secure Currency*, published in February 1816, and in his *Plan for the Establishment of a National Bank*, published in February 1824.

In terms of modern monetary analysis, we would say that inflation is avoided on condition that no 'empty' money is added to that currently associated with produced output. This would never result from banks' credit activity so long as the sums that they lend to the public are derived from their deposits of money income, i.e. from the amount of real money generated by production. As claimed by Ricardo, central banks (as well as commercial banks) act as both monetary and financial intermediaries since they issue nominal money and lend real money. 'The Bank of England performs two operations of banking, which are quite distinct, and have no necessary connection with each other: it issues a paper currency as a substitute for a metallic one; and it advances money in the way of loan, to merchants and others' (ibid.: 276). Now, this functional distinction can be accounted for by separating the monetary from the financial department, thus providing bankers with a book-keeping instrument telling them the exact amount they can lend at each moment in time. If this were done, Ricardo's suggestion to keep nominal money at equality with the value of money would have been followed through to its end to the great benefit of monetary stability. Yet, inflation is not only caused by the possible deviation of nominal credit from income deposits. As a matter of fact, this possibility is only a minor cause of a disorder whose explanation requires Ricardo's analysis to be applied to the process of capital accumulation. The 'Prince' of economists has provided the foundations; it is up to us to make the best possible use of them to increase our understanding of our monetary systems and the causes that still hamper their stable development.

Now, Ricardo's analysis is rich in fruitful suggestions also with respect to the problems of crisis and unemployment. In particular, it is worth mentioning his reflections upon the possibility of saving to reduce income expenditure, thus decreasing global demand relative to global supply. Ricardo's claim about hoarding must not be misunderstood. As stressed by Schmitt, hoarding would reduce neither the value of money (that would remain stable despite the nominal decrease of money units) nor its circulation. 'Hoarded money is still present both within the monetary "mass" and within circulation. Hoarding is an *action*, a movement and not, as is ingenuously believed, an abstention, that is, inertia' (Schmitt 1985: 45; our translation). But there is more to it. Schmitt observes, in fact, that Ricardo had already clearly understood that every income is necessarily spent. 'Is not this assuming that what is not spent is hoarded? The revenue is in all cases spent, but in one case the objects on which it is expended are consumed, and nothing reproduced, in the other those objects form a new capital tending to increased production' (Ricardo 1951, Vol. III: 299). What Ricardo is telling us is that income is not a real commodity that may be stocked or hoarded according to the decision taken by its owners. The very concept of hoarding is misleading, of course, for it denotes the formation of a treasure (that is the origin of the Italian word *tesorizzazione*). Yet, Ricardo has not been led astray. Income is monetary, and like money it cannot be identified with any real object. True, output is necessary if a positive income is to exist at all. Money (the form) and output (the real content) are the two complementary aspects of income. Nevertheless, income is a monetary 'object', so that it cannot survive beyond the moment of its expenditure. This means that it does not survive beyond its very formation, or, in other words, that it is spent as soon as it is formed. Startling as it may appear, this conclusion is the only one compatible with the *flow* nature of bank money. Correctly understood, it means that income is immediately transformed into capital, i.e. into a claim on a bank deposit whose object is the physical output stocked with firms.

Ricardo did not elaborate his analysis to the point of maintaining that income is immediately spent. However, his concept of circulating capital is not far from that of Schmitt's capital-time, and his claim that income is necessarily spent clearly shows how close it was to the modern conception of bank money, income and capital. If we abstract from the immediate and temporary expenditure of income (which transforms it into capital-time) to switch to its final expenditure (which implies the reverse transformation of capital-time into income), we see that Ricardo's analysis is to the point. In fact, income can either be spent for the final purchase of current output or invested in the production of capital goods. In the first case, it is literally destroyed together with the stock of real goods, which subsist only in the form of use values. In the second case, income is spent on the factors market and reappears as a claim over the real stock of consumption goods still unsold.

The author of the *Principles* (Ricardo 1951) is perfectly aware of the fact that income holders may decide to save part of their income and that their decision is not necessarily matched by that of borrowers. In this case, is it not true that income may be partially saved simply by not being spent? Let us first note that if a gap is to be found it cannot come from savers being unwilling to lend their savings.

Ricardo is straight: whether directly or through the intermediation of banks, part of current savings is lent to be definitively spent by its borrowers. '[T]he greatest part [of savings] has realised itself in goods which are in the hands of those who have borrowed the money saved. It makes no difference whether those who saved it lent it themselves or by depositing it with a banker enabled him to do it' (ibid.: 280). Firms must be included among the possible borrowers. Through the sale of shares and securities they can form a (circulating) capital and invest it in their productive activity. Here again, the matching between savers and borrowers takes place through the financial intermediation of banks. The only difficulty seems therefore to be related to a situation in which the amount saved is greater than the amount that households and firms are actually willing to borrow. How can we reconcile this particular case with Ricardo's claim that '[t]he revenue is in all cases spent' (ibid.: 299)? In Ricardo's notes on Bentham's *Sur les prix* (already quoted above), we find a precious piece of information. Referring to that part of income that is saved but not explicitly borrowed, he claims that '[i]n no case can a pecuniary revenue be realised in the form of money but by hoarding' (ibid.: 280). If we take the term 'hoarding' in its literal sense, we can interpret Ricardo's statement as indicating that income can be saved only in its real form, i.e. in the form of real goods. Neither money nor money income can be hoarded; real goods can. But this means that also the part of savings that is not explicitly borrowed is spent, notably for the purchase of the goods accumulated by firms in their unsold stock of current output. As is clearly shown by double-entry book-keeping, unspent income defines a bank deposit that is immediately lent to firms in order to finance their current stock (the very object of their debt to banks). Once this 'implicit' lending is taken into account, it appears that the totality of income is spent, either finally (in which case it is destroyed) or temporarily (in which case it is transformed into capital-time).

Ricardo's analysis of hoarding establishes with great clarity the logical impossibility of imputing the origin of crisis to the behaviour of income holders. Global demand is not in the least modified by changes in the propensity to save because the totality of income is necessarily spent. Moreover, since money creation does not add anything to the stock of capital, 'it is a vain hope to believe that a crisis can be countered by banks' money creation' (Schmitt 1985: 18; our translation). As in the analysis of inflation, Ricardo's contribution to the understanding of deflation passes through a rigorous investigation of the nature of money as well as of its relationship with income and capital. Even though he has not provided us with a complete theory of monetary disorders, his heritage is of the utmost importance, for it lays down the principles that can indeed lead us to such a theory.

Marx's contribution

As we already know, Marx's contribution to monetary economics starts with an in-depth analysis of money and of its definition as the form of value. What we shall concern ourselves with in this section is his further enquiry into the nature of the process of capital reproduction and accumulation expounded in Book II of his main work. Having critically analysed the theories of his predecessors, Marx adds to the distinction between circulating and fixed capital – which he attributes to the process of circulation – the distinction between constant and variable capital – which pertains to the process of valorisation. His whole analysis is then continued, placing particular emphasis on the role played by labour power, the only 'commodity' whose consumption creates value. Unfortunately, the difficulties arising from Marx's distinction between labour and labour power – the logical impossibility of realising surplus value monetarily and the still unsolved transformation problem – have seriously undermined the heuristic value of his investigation. As we shall attempt to show, labour power notwithstanding, Marx's analysis deserves all our attention, for it provides one of the deepest insights into the pathological working of our monetary systems.

The problem is very clearly stated by Marx at the beginning of his chapter on simple reproduction: 'How is the *capital* consumed in production replaced [physically and] in its value out of the annual product, and how is the movement of this replacement intertwined with consumption of surplus-value by the capitalists and of wages by the workers?' (Marx 1978: 469). Now, it is in the analysis of capital reproduction (simple and enlarged) that we find the explanation of the anomalous process leading to monetary disorders.

Marx analyses first the process of simple reproduction. Referring to Adam Smith's distinction between *means of production* and *means of consumption*, he first notes that, for workers producing means of production, '[t]he money they receive as wages forms revenue for them, and yet their labour has not produced consumable products, either for themselves or for others' (ibid.: 441–2). On the contrary, as this quotation clearly shows, Marx is perfectly aware of the fact that, independently of physical considerations, the production of capital goods is substantially different from that of consumption goods. We might even go so far as claiming that, financed out of profit, the production of instrumental goods does not allow workers to get a positive purchasing power over their own output, their wages being 'emptied' of (their) real content. In his analysis, Marx maintains that while fixed capital used in the production of instrumental goods 'always functions as capital, and never as revenue' (ibid.: 444), the other parts of the value of the annual social output consisting in means of production 'do indeed form at the same time *revenues for all agents involved in this production*, i.e. wages for the workers, profits and rents for the capitalists. For the *society*, however, they do not form revenue, but *capital*' (ibid.: 444–5). Formed as social capital, instrumental goods are definitively purchased by firms from the moment of their production. Wages paid to workers still define their income, of course. Yet, the means of production that should have defined the real content of this income are no longer available for workers to purchase (and exchange with consumption goods). This is not surprising, indeed, since capital goods can be accumulated only if households are prepared to sacrifice part of their current consumption. The crucial point is to establish whether this accumulation takes place to the benefit of households or not. In other words, we have to verify whether the means of production are a *social* capital because they are collectively owned or because they are subtracted from households – through a process of alienation that is the mark of a serious disorder in capital accumulation.

In his analysis, Marx is led to divide total production in two sectors, one defining the production of capital goods and the other that of consumption goods.

> The society's total product, and thus its total production process, breaks down into two great departments:
>
> I.   *Means of production*: commodities that possess a form in which they either have to enter productive consumption, or at least can enter this.
> II.   *Means of consumption*: commodities that possess a form in which they enter the individual consumption of the capitalist and working classes.
>
> (ibid.: 471)

Let us look at Marx's numerical example. In the first sector – where instrumental goods are produced – capital is made up of 4,000 units of constant capital and 1,000 units of variable capital so that, assuming a rate of surplus value equal to 100 per cent, the total value of produced means of production amounts to:

$$4,000_c + 1,000_v + 1,000_s = 6,000$$

On the same assumption, in the second sector – where consumption goods are produced – 2000 units of constant capital and 500 units of variable capital give rise to a total value of:

$$2,000_c + 500_v + 500_s = 3,000$$

If we leave the problem of surplus value aside and we suppose that both v and s define the income actually available in the system, we verify that the totality of the second sector's income (1,000 units) is spent within this sector for the purchase of an equivalent value of consumption goods. 'The wages and surplus-value in department II are thus converted within department II into the product of department II' (ibid.: 473). As for the 2,000 units of income of the first sector, they are also spent in the second sector for the purchase of the remaining 2,000 units of consumption goods. 'The $1,000_v + 1,000_s$ in department I must likewise be spent on means of consumption, i.e. on the products of department II' (ibid.: 473). Thus, 4,000 units of constant capital used in sector I cannot be sold, the totality of available income having already been spent in sector II. Now, Marx tells us that these 4,000 units 'consist of means of production that can only be used in department I and serve to replace the constant capital consumed there; they are therefore disposed of by mutual exchange among the individual capitalists of department I' (ibid.: 474). Independently of the nature of profit, Marx thus obtains a result very similar to that conveyed by modern monetary macroeconomics. The output of the first sector's workers is directly purchased by their firms at the very moment that wages are paid. The interesting thing is that Marx resists the temptation to reduce the entire phenomenon to a direct appropriation of capital goods by the firms producing them. He claims instead that the process takes place through the intermediary of money, which brings the problem much closer to reality but also makes it much harder to grasp. 'This mutual exchange is brought about by a money circulation, which both mediates it and makes it harder to comprehend, even though it is of decisive importance, since the component of variable capital must always reappear in the money form, as money capital which is converted from the money form into labour-power' (ibid.: 474).

Consistent with Marx's simple reproduction scheme, we may therefore maintain that the production of instrumental goods takes place in the first sector through the investment of the profit realised in sector II. It is therefore firms that, having momentarily spent their profit for the purchase of the stock of consumption goods built up in sector II, transform it into fixed capital by investing it in the payment of wages to workers of sector I. By doing so, firms acquire the productive activity of these workers, taking hold of the very result of this activity: capital goods. 'The individual capitalist, however, effects this advance [of fixed capital] only by acting as buyer, *spending* money on the purchase of means of consumption or *advancing* money on the purchase of elements of his productive capital, either labour-power or means of production' (ibid.: 497).

The analysis develops further when Marx switches from the study of simple reproduction to that of enlarged reproduction, i.e. when he incorporates the amortisation of fixed capital in the process of capital accumulation.

> One portion of the constant capital value, that which consists of means of labour in the strict sense (as a distinct division of the means of production), is transferred from the means of labour to the product of labour (the commodity) while these means of labour still continue to function as elements of the productive capital, and moreover in their old natural form; what is transferred from the instrument to the product of labour, and reappears as an element of the value of the commodities, that these means of labour produce, is their wear and tear, the loss of value that they suffer bit by bit in the course of their function over a certain period.
>
> (ibid.: 524–5)

The amortisation of fixed capital must not be confused with wear and tear, physical or technological, which is merely its cause. As noted by Marx, amortisation requires the accumulation of a fund aimed at financing it, i.e. at financing the reproduction of worn-out fixed capital. 'If a part of its [fixed capital's] value has circulated with the product, according to the average wear and tear, and been transformed into money, then this forms an element of the money reserve fund for the replacement of the capital when its reproduction in kind falls due' (ibid.: 251). Now, Marx is confronted with a serious problem as to the monetary realisation of the value transferred by fixed capital to final output. Let us go back to his two-sector scheme again. In the process of simple reproduction, the exchange between the 2,000 units of income formed in the production of instrumental goods and the 2,000 units of value of the constant capital used up in the production of consumption goods does not raise any difficulty. In that of enlarged reproduction, on the contrary, this exchange does not allow the second sector's firms to build up a monetary reserve enabling them to amortise their fixed capital.

> The exchange between $I(1,000_v + 1000_s)$ and $2,000\ II_c$ thus immediately presents the apparent difficulty that the means of production I, the natural form in which the $2,000_{(v + s)}$ exists, have to be replaced to the entire amount of their value of 2,000 by an equivalent in means of consumption II, whereas the means of consumption $2,000\ II_c$ cannot be exchanged to their full value for the means of production $I(1,000_v + 1,000_s)$.
>
> (ibid.: 529)

In fact, 'the money through which the element of wear and tear contained in the commodity value of $2,000\ II_c$ is realised can derive only from department I' (ibid.: 529), but the exchange between equivalents seems to prevent sector II from obtaining from sector I a greater sum than it gives. With great lucidity, Marx rejects the hypothesis of II, selling consumption goods for an amount of 2,000 units and purchasing means of production up to a sum of 1,800 because, if this were the case, sector II would obtain the monetary funds necessary to finance amortisation only to the detriment of its means of production, which would decrease by 200 units (since II would purchase only 1,800 units of them instead of 2,000). If, from the value point of view, the problem can be solved by recurring to Marx's idea that a positive value is transferred from fixed capital to final output because of wear and tear – so that the product of II has actually a value of 2,200 instead of 2,000 – no satisfactory solution emerges from the point of view of monetary realisation. Where do the 200 units of extra income that are required for the purchase of the output of sector II come from? 'Capitalist society spends more of its disposable annual labour on the production of means of production (therefore of constant capital), which cannot be resolved into revenue in the form of wages or of surplus-value' (ibid.: 514). To maintain that there is direct appropriation (without the intervention of money) of the means of production will not do. Every produced good must be expressed in monetary terms if it is to be part of national output.

The solution to Marx's problem can be found once the production of amortisation or replacement goods is also taken into account. In this case, in fact, the income necessary to the monetary realisation of the means of production is derived from the payment of the costs of production of replacement goods, i.e. new capital goods produced in order to replace those used up by wear and tear. This does not mean, however, that the problem of fixed capital amortisation has no other implications for the process of capital accumulation. Once the production of replacement goods has been taken into consideration, it remains to be determined whether or not the pathological purchase operated by firms of sector I in the case of simple reproduction also occurs when reproduction is enlarged through an increasing process of capital accumulation. Now, as far as we can see, there are no elements in Marx's analysis that may induce us to believe that, when fixed capital amortisation is accounted for, workers are no longer deprived of part of their real income accumulated by firms in the form of new capital goods.

> [T]he portion of the annually produced means of production equal in value to the means of production functioning within this sphere of production – the means of production with which means of production are made – and therefore a portion equal in value to the constant capital applied here is absolutely excluded, not only by the natural form in which it exists, but also by its capital function, from being any component of value that constitutes revenue.
>
> (ibid.: 442)

The anomaly we have observed in Marx's simple reproduction scheme is deeply rooted in the workings of our monetary systems, too deeply to be easily disposed of or removed simply by extending the process of capital accumulation. Indeed, the introduction of fixed capital amortisation into Marx's reproduction schemes implies the division of productive activity into three sectors: one relative to the production of consumption goods, the second to that of capital or instrumental goods and the third to that of replacement goods. As shown by modern monetary economics, this threefold division is caused by the lack of structural distinction – at the level of banks' book-keeping – among monetary, income and capital transactions. At the time, i.e. 130 years ago, Marx could not have reached a perfect understanding of the monetary origin of this pathology and of its consequences for monetary and real disorders. It is only fair to recognise, however, that his contribution to our present understanding of these problems is, together with Smith's, Ricardo's and Keynes's, among the most enlightening.

Keynes's contribution revisited

As is well known, in Keynes's analysis inflation is an anomalous state of the economy in which total demand is nominally greater than total supply. Since this difference is also expressed as that between saving and investment, it is worth considering how Keynes interpreted inflation in terms of saving and investment. As testified by the great number of letters, memoranda and articles published in Vol. XIII of *The Collected Writings of John Maynard Keynes* edited by Moggridge, the debate between Keynes and Robertson on the relationship between saving and investment lasted until Keynes decided to define income as the sum of consumption and investment, and saving as the excess of income over consumption, so 'that, for the community as a whole, investment and saving are necessarily, and by definition, equal' (Keynes 1973b: 476). In this respect, the main difference between the *Treatise* and the *General Theory* lies in Keynes's choice to incorporate windfall profits into his definition of income. This may be explained by the difficulties that he encountered after publication of the *Treatise*, and by the need to find an easier way to convey his new ideas about the principles of a monetary economy of production. Whatever the reasons that pushed Keynes to put aside his analysis of windfall profits, it is worth observing that he did not repudiate it.

He merely recognised 'that investment *plus* profits (as there defined) was necessarily equal to saving' (ibid.: 476), claiming that the transition from the definition of income in the *Treatise* to that in the *General Theory* was 'a change of terminology and not a change of view' (ibid.: 476). Now, the best way to stick with Keynes's claim and to account for the substantial coherence of the theories he put forth in his two most famous books is to consider windfall profits as the result of an anomalous state of affairs. Hence, in an orderly system – as the one described in the *General Theory* – profits are that part of current income transferred to firms by consumers, and it is thus logical to include them in the macroeconomic definition of income. In a pathological system, on the other hand, normal profits are increased by a sum of windfall profits, which, precisely because of their anomalous origin, cannot be included in the measure of current income. If we choose this particular reading of Keynes's work, we can maintain – as I did in *Money, Income and Time* – that the *General Theory* logically comes before the *Treatise*, the aim of the latter being to explain how windfall profits may be added to normal profits as a consequence of an inflationary state of the economic system.

The crucial point at stake, of course, is not whether our interpretation of Keynes's true intentions is correct. Even if substantiated by the space devoted in the *Treatise* to the analysis of inflation, it could well be dismissed on purely exegetical grounds. What really matters is whether Keynes's analysis may be reinterpreted along a new line of thought consistent with the results of modern monetary macroeconomics, and whether his intuitions may lead us to a better understanding of our economic systems. Let us suppose, therefore, that windfall profits stand for inflationary profits. Keynes's analysis teaches us that inflation allows firms to realise an amount of extra profits that cannot be considered as part of national income. Moreover, it highlights the fact that these extra profits may not be entirely reinvested, in which case they would increase saving with respect to investment. Even though saving and investment are always necessarily equal, they can differ (nominally) in a situation characterised by an inflationary increase of money units and by a pathological process of capital accumulation. 'We may have a rise or fall of Q, the total profits above or below zero, due to an inequality between saving and the value of investment. We shall call this *profit inflation* (or *deflation*)' (Keynes 1971: 140).

Before investigating the notion of windfall profits further, let us remind the reader that there is no contradiction in claiming that saving and investment are always necessarily at equality and that they may differ from one another only if we refer to their nominal or numerical expression. It would be logically unacceptable to maintain that, despite their identity, saving and investment may vary relative to one another in *value* terms. Identity is too strong a relationship to be transformed into a condition of equilibrium without incurring any serious contradiction. This is not what happens when saving differs numerically from investment – or total demand from total supply. The two terms of the identity remain unchanged in terms of value; what varies is only their numerical expression. And it is precisely because their logical identity tells us that their value is unchanged that their numerical inequality defines a monetary disorder. For example, if total demand is numerically greater than total supply, we can immediately infer that an inflationary gap has occurred, which has caused a decrease in the purchasing power of each money unit (the same value being now carried by an increased number of money units). It is in this sense that Keynes's inequalities must be interpreted if we want our investigation of his theory to be consistent with the fundamental identities on which it is based. This means that the concept of windfall profits – to which we thus revert – finds its *raison d'être* in the numerical gap between total demand and total supply that is opened up by inflation.

Hence, according to Keynes's analysis, the nominal difference between total demand and total supply leads to the formation of profit inflation, i.e. of an anomalous profit whose expenditure is the undepleted source of a new profit. This is the meaning conveyed by Keynes's notion of the widow's cruse. The definition of profit he gives in his *Treatise* may be the source of some confusion, it is true. Yet, his claim that profits 'must be regarded not as part of the earnings of the community ... but as increasing (or, if negative as diminishing) the value of the accumulated wealth of the entrepreneurs' (ibid.: 112) may be interpreted only as meaning that, besides normal profits, there is another category of earnings that firms do not derive from the income of the community. Normal profit is an income that firms derive from the expenditure of households. It is an income that, first formed as a bank deposit owned by workers, is then transferred to firms through the sale of output. On the contrary, windfall profit is not part of the income formed by production. It does not derive from a transfer from households to firms, but from an inflationary increase in money units. Thus, whereas the formation of normal profit is logically referred to as the expenditure of an income that is not itself a profit – a logical requirement if we are to avoid the vicious circle of explaining profit by profit – that of windfall profit requires the expenditure of an inflationary income only initially. Once formed, windfall profits are a permanently renewed source of other (inflationary) profits, the exuberant units of nominal money defining a (nominal) bank deposit that can repeatedly be injected into the economy. The claim that 'profits, as a source of capital increment for entrepreneurs, are a widow's cruse which remains undepleted however much of them may be devoted to riotous living' (ibid.: 125) makes sense only if it refers to inflationary (or windfall) profits. It is in this sense that Keynes's mythological image can be introduced into economic analysis. And it is only in this case that the condition of zero profits becomes a plausible requirement for the stability of money's purchasing power. 'The essential characteristic of the entity which we call *profits* is that its having a zero value is the usual condition in the actual economic world of today for the equilibrium of the purchasing power of money' (ibid.: 141).

The 'actual economic world of today' that Keynes refers to is characterised by the presence of monetary disorders such as inflation and deflation. To have understood that both of these disorders can be defined only once the laws of monetary economics have rigorously been established is one of the great merits of the Cambridge economist. 'In my opinion the main reason why the problem of crises is unsolved, or at any rate why this theory is so unsatisfactory, is to be found in the lack of what might be termed a *monetary theory of production*' (Keynes

1973b: 408). Heeding his intuitions, Keynes did not limit his contribution to the analysis of the logical identity between supply and demand. He also showed that the purchasing power of money, deriving from this identity, is modified each time a transaction alters the relationship between money (form) and current output (real content). This is the case whenever normal profits are spent on the labour market to finance the production of capital goods. Thus spent, in fact, profits give rise to a new bank deposit, starting the process represented by Keynes as a widow's cruse and leading eventually to both inflation and deflation.

A further important step towards a better understanding of the genesis of monetary disorders is taken by Keynes when he extends his analysis to the problem of amortisation. The subject of the appendix to the sixth chapter of his *General Theory*, this problem had not been seriously tackled from a macroeconomic point of view since the works of Marx. Although Keynes's own approach is essentially microeconomic, it provides some deep insights into the relationship between amortisation and global output. It would be unfair, however, to deny that these insights are somehow difficult to spot. For example, his claim that 'it may be occasionally convenient in dealing with *output as a whole* to deduct user cost' (Keynes 1973a: 67) could be interpreted as meaning that replacement goods do not enter global net output or that wear and tear does not increase the value of total output. It is not surprising, therefore, to find that in a recent article on user cost the author – 'writing as J.M. Keynes' – maintains that 'user cost has one foot resting in microeconomics and the other in macroeconomics' (Torr 1997: 133), and adds that 'at the macro level, user cost must also be subtracted from total sales, since it is the cost of the items used up in the production process and as such must not be included in the total of final consumption and investment goods' (ibid.: 133). Only apparently consistent with Keynes's approach, this claim is altogether misleading. If it is true that used up capital is not the source of any new value, it is also true that no positive amortisation occurs as long as this capital is not replaced. Wear and tear does not increase the value of currently produced consumption and investment goods. In this respect, Keynes is right in claiming that labour alone is the original factor of production. Yet, if the items used up in the production process are not replaced by new ones, is it correct to take the concept of user cost to mean the 'disinvestment in equipment due to the production of output' (Keynes 1973a: 67)? Of course, it is extremely important to reiterate the fact that economic value is determined by labour alone, and that capital is not productive in terms of value. But it is also necessary to understand properly that 'disinvestment' does not simply mean wear and tear. Keynes's choice of this term is not arbitrary. To the extent that capital goods are used up in the production of other goods, their depreciation reduces investment. 'I understand user cost to be that part of depreciation which arises from the equipment *being used*, to the exclusion of the loss of value (whether from deterioration or from obsolescence or any other cause) which would equally occur if it were not used' (Keynes 1973b: 570). Wear and tear of used up instrumental goods is thus a sort of negative investment, which clearly means that, if no new equipment were produced to replace the one used up, user cost would decrease global investment. The fact that, despite positive user costs, consumption and investment are not diminished proves that amortisation implies – as a new investment – the positive production of new capital goods.

If capital used up in the production process were not replaced by an equivalent new one, wear and tear would still be positive but amortisation would not. The decrease in capital would reduce wealth until disinvestment zeroes the value of total capital. This can be avoided only if a new investment matches the loss due to disinvestment. Now, properly defined, this new investment is an amortisation. To amortise capital means to produce a new amount of capital goods that is to replace that part lost through wear and tear. Hence, as already stated by Ricardo in his *Principles*, the measure of amortisation is given by the labour required to keep fixed capital constant.

> If I had a machine worth 20,000 l. which with very little labour was efficient to the production of commodities, and if the wear and tear of such machine were of trifling amount, and the general rate of profit 10 per cent., I should not require much more than 2000 l. to be added to the price of the goods, on account of the employment of my machine; but if the wear and tear of the machine were great, if the quantity of labour requisite to keep it in an efficient state were that of fifty men annually, I should require an additional price of my goods, equal to that which would be obtained by any other manufacturer who employed fifty men in the production of other goods, and who used no machinery at all.
>
> (Ricardo 1951: 39)

Although it may cause confusion, it is perfectly legitimate to include amortisation in investment and to maintain 'that our measure of total output does not include goods used up in the production process' (Torr 1997: 134). Goods used up in the production process are not included in the measure of total output – this is correct – but amortisation goods are because they are part of the production of new investment goods. Used up capital does not increase the value of global current output as no value is transferred from capital to finished goods (or, as the Classics would put it, no value is transferred to final output from 'dead labour'). Yet, the production of amortisation goods does increase the value of current output.

The analysis of amortisation that we have only briefly sketched here is fundamental in giving us a complete picture of a system of production based on capital accumulation. What remains to be done is to show how this analysis is related to that of windfall profits, and how they both concur to explain the onset of monetary disorders. This is what we shall attempt to do in the next, and last, section.

Unemployment, capital accumulation and interest rates

Wicksell's contribution

In his comment on Mr Brand's memorandum regarding the need for a bridging chapter between the two major sections of the *Committee on Finance and Industry Report*, Keynes is explicit in stressing the role played by the rate of interest in his analysis of economic recession. In particular, he maintains that '[w]e cannot possibly recover normal prosperity ... until the market rate of interest and the natural rate (meaning by this the rate at which the world's savings would be just absorbed) are brought together instead of standing a long way apart' (Keynes 1981: 272–3). The British economist is thus taking over the central elements of the analysis developed more than 30 years earlier by Wicksell and whose origin may be traced back to Ricardo. The main idea is that price stability rests on the convergence between money and the natural rate of interest, the latter being determined by the ratio between 'the amount by which the total product (or its equivalent in other commodities) exceeds the sum of the wages, rents, etc., that have to be paid out' (Wicksell 1965: 103) and the total amount of capital invested in production. Wicksell's problem is how to explain monetary disorder in a system in which 'there is no apparent reason for any alteration in the general level of *money* prices' (ibid.: 105). His analysis is based on a solid grasp of the banking system and on the clear understanding that '[m]oney is continually becoming more fluid, and the supply of money is more and more inclined to accommodate itself to the level of demand' (ibid.: 110). But, if monetary disorders are not caused by money supply being distinct from the demand for money, can we nevertheless explain the existence of a positive gap between total demand and total supply? In the case of deflation, for example, how can a fall in the general level of prices be brought about, 'it being assumed that money is obtainable in any desired quantity on terms which correspond to the real advantages entailed in the use of credit' (ibid.: 105)?

Wicksell's argument is that equilibrium is disturbed if 'banks and other lenders of money lend at a different rate of interest ... from that which corresponds to the current value of the natural rate of interest on capital' (ibid.: 105). Emphasis is thus switched from the quantity of money to the rate of interest, with particular reference to the natural rate of interest on capital and, therefore, to the process of capital accumulation. As long as the natural interest rate is higher than the money interest rate, capital accumulation is carried on intensively, productive investments being more profitable than financial lending and entrepreneurs being 'inevitably induced to extend their businesses in order to exploit to the maximum extent the favourable turn of events' (ibid.: 106). As observed by Keynes, for years market rates have remained below natural rates, thus allowing for a sustained process of capital accumulation. 'I incline to believe that during the period of the economic construction of the modern world we have enjoyed, generally speaking, market rates if anything *below* the natural rate, and this has been a necessary condition of the accumulation of wealth' (Keynes 1981: 273). Things change and economic recession rears its head when market rates are higher than natural rates. In fact, capital accumulation cannot increase endlessly. On the contrary, since profits tend to increase at a lesser pace than capital, the time will come when the natural interest rate on capital falls below the money interest rate. When this happens, entrepreneurs no longer find it worth investing the totality of their net profits in the production of new capital goods. The limit of accumulation having been reached, capital cannot go on growing as before: '[t]he demand for goods and services falls off, or at any rate lags behind the supply' (Wicksell 1965: 106) and unemployment increases. As observed by Wicksell, the problem does not lie in the absolute level of the money rate of interest. What matters is the level reached by the natural rate and the gap existing between that and the money rate: 'a further datum must be supplied, namely, the level of the *natural* rate, before it is possible to determine whether any particular rate of interest is to be regarded as high or as low' (ibid.: 107). Now, although the Swedish economist intuits that the reasons for this divergence must be looked for at the banking level, he openly admits that he is unable 'to assess the importance in actual banking practice of the various factors' (ibid.: 118) influencing the natural or the money rate of interest. He correctly notes that 'it is practically certain that the lending rate of interest never follows directly on movements of the natural rate, and usually follows them only very slowly and with considerable hesitation' (ibid.: 119), but he partially misses the point that what causes the pathological divergence between the two rates is the anomalous process of capital accumulation lying at the core of our monetary systems.

As a matter of fact, it must be recognised that Wicksell came very close to the modern interpretation provided by quantum monetary macroeconomics. In the example introduced at the end of Chapter 9 of *Interest and Prices*, he shows how moving from circulating to fixed capital implies a positive investment of money income on the labour market.

> Our imaginary procedure is then as follows: At the beginning of the year the entrepreneurs borrow their capital from the banks, in the form of a sum of money K. This is equal to the value of the total amount of available real capital, that is to say, of the total amount of consumption goods completed during the previous year *minus* the interest drawn in the previous year by the capitalist. This money capital is now paid to the workers and to the landlords .... With the aid of this money, the whole of the available commodity capital is now bought up by the consumers, and the money capital K returns once again to the banks in the shape of deposits made by the capitalist dealers.
>
> (ibid.: 138)

As this long quotation shows, according to Wicksell's analysis, fixed capital accumulation is a process requiring the previous formation of a circulating capital and its corresponding stock of consumption goods. The investment of this monetary capital leads to the formation of a fixed capital, directly appropriated by firms, and of an income spent by workers on the purchase of the previously accumulated stock of consumption goods. Of course, firms own the newly produced capital goods only insofar as they can repay their banks the money capital initially borrowed from them. This they can do only on condition that they realise a profit through the sale of their stock of consumption goods. The amount of fixed capital actually produced is thus determined by the amount of profits invested by firms. 'The rest of the goods, which at the existing price level amount to K in value, are available as real capital for the coming year' (ibid.: 141). It is because of this investment on the labour market that fixed capital is directly appropriated by firms. And it is because a positive money income is spent in the payment of wages that production takes place in two distinct sectors. If no positive expenditure were included in the payment of wages, produced goods and services would all be owned by the whole of income holders and production would not be partially appropriated by firms: only one sector would exist, the distinction between consumption and capital goods being consistent with the orderly working of the banking system. As shown by Schmitt, this result can be achieved only if the distinction between sectors is replaced by that among monetary, financial and fixed capital departments introduced at the banking level. It is only in this case, in fact, that every transaction takes place according to the logical distinctions between money, income and capital.

Disorder and the structure of national payment systems

In line with the tradition of Smith, Ricardo, Marx, Wicksell and Keynes, new monetary macroeconomics shows that a monetary disorder manifests itself as a *nominal* (or numerical) unbalance between total supply and total demand – whose substantial identity is never challenged – and has its origin in a pathological transaction that deprives income holders from a part of current output. It is in this sense that the distinction of the economic activity into sectors must be understood, and not in the trivial sense that output consists of different kinds of goods and services. To say that production is split between two sectors means that wage-earners work only in part for the benefit of households (income holders), part of their activity being directly appropriated by what Schmitt calls the set of 'disembodied firms' (Schmitt 1984b: 208; our translation). As the reader already knows, the anomaly lies in the fact that a positive income (profit) is spent to pay wages for workers producing capital goods. Taking place on the labour market, this positive expenditure implies the purchase of labour, which is thus pathologically transformed into a commodity. 'Or, le profit est investi dans une opération tout à fait originale; il achète le travail; il en est la rémunération. Cette fois, le travail est lui-même une marchandise; il est acheté par la transformation des profits en nouveaux salaires' (ibid.: 204). Since 'the purchase of labour is identical to the purchase of its product' (ibid.: 204; our translation), firms get hold of fixed capital goods from the very moment that they are produced, i.e. from the instant that wages are paid out to workers. This does not mean, however, that, deprived of the real content of their wages, workers producing capital goods have no economic right whatever over produced output. Although their wages do not define any positive purchasing power – which can result only from the association of wages with their real content (directly appropriated here by firms) – workers benefit from the right to collect the real goods stocked by firms when profits were formed. It must be remembered, in fact, that the formation of profits defines that of a circulating capital, whose real content is stocked and transformed into a 'wage fund' at the moment profits are invested.

As claimed by Jevons (1911: 223) in his *Theory of Political Economy*, '[c]apital, as I regard it, consists merely in the *aggregate of these commodities which are required for sustaining labourers of any kind or class engaged in work*'. This kind of capital is what Jevons calls '*capital in its free or uninvested form*' (ibid.: 223). It is circulating capital or capital-time whose function is to support labourers engaged in the production of fixed capital. Once fixed capital goods are produced, they are appropriated by firms, and workers are given a financial claim on the 'aggregate of commodities' previously stocked. Hence, despite the fact that the investment of profits 'empties' wages of their real content, it does not immediately lead to a monetary disorder. 'It is true that production of p^+ [the period in which profits are invested] implies an empty emission, but it is harmless since the capital goods instantaneously subtracted from real wages ... are exactly compensated by saved-up wage goods' (Schmitt 1984b: 206–7; our translation). The consequence of the pathological investment of profits (i.e. of the expenditure of a positive income within the payment of wages) consists therefore in the creation of the set of disembodied firms and in the splitting of production into two distinct sectors.

Now, things get dramatically worse as soon as instrumental goods are being used and new capital (amortisation) goods are produced to repair the loss due to wear and tear. The whole process is described in detail by Schmitt in his 1984 book *Inflation, chômage et malformations du capital*. Referring the reader back to it, we shall simply observe that the introduction of a third sector corresponding to the production of replacement goods is a direct consequence of capital goods being formed in the second sector. Capital goods being appropriated by the set of disembodied firms, the production of replacement goods generates an income that is bound to be spent for the purchase of consumption goods, thus leading to the formation of a surplus profit whose investment increases (numerically) total demand without modifying total supply. This time, no stock of real goods is available to compensate the loss of workers, whose wages remain hopelessly empty. The presence of this empty money is the mark of inflation, a situation in which the investment of the firms' extra profits generates a process of capital overaccumulation. Thus, amortisation, i.e. the production of replacement goods, allows firms to earn an extra profit, the investment of which brings them a new measure of capital goods defining an equivalent increase of the sum total of fixed capital. 'En chaque période, les émissions vides produisent du capital fixe dans la mesure exacte où elles produisent du capital instrumental' (ibid.: 231). Hence, inflation and capital overaccumulation are the joint consequences of the pathological process of fixed capital formation and amortisation in the whole period of time that the natural rate of interest is higher than the money rate.

Capital overaccumulation has of course the positive effect of increasing physical productivity, thus limiting psychologically the negative impact of inflation: money units lose part of their purchasing power, but physical output increases in quality and quantity. Yet, because of the present pathological system of payments, the increase in productivity has very high costs. As we have seen, one element of these costs is inflation, the other is the necessity to pay capital an increasing amount of profits. This second cost derives from the cumulative nature of the pathological process of capitalisation. The more fixed capital is accumulated, the more it must be remunerated, which means that an increasing part of current output must be sacrificed to pathological capital. 'Comme la suraccumulation est cumulative dans le temps, les profits doivent se former en une proportion sans cesse croissante du produit' (ibid.: 231). The consequence of this increase in the sum of interest that must be paid to capital is that the natural rate of interest tends to decrease with respect to the exponential growth of fixed capital. When the process of capital accumulation and overaccumulation has reached its limit, the natural interest rate falls below the money rate and – as suggested by Wicksell and Keynes – investment is restrained. Unemployment is thus the last, unavoidable consequence of a pathological process that has its origin in the lack of an operative book-keeping distinction between money, income and capital.

As shown by Schmitt, both inflation and involuntary unemployment can be avoided by introducing at the banking level this threefold distinction, i.e. by asking banks to organise their activity in three departments: the monetary, the financial and the fixed capital departments. Whereas the first two departments are needed to account for the logical distinction between money and income, the third is required to avoid profits already invested in the production of capital goods still being available on the financial market.

> If wages transformed into profits are not withdrawn from the financial market (represented by the second department), they make up a loanable fund that will nourish *a second measure of final expenditures*. Borrowers will spend an income already spent by households in the operation forming profits. The second expenditure of the (same) income is an *empty emission*, root of such disorders as inflation and unemployment.
>
> (ibid.: 323; our translation)

The introduction of the third department thus averts the very formation of disembodied firms. Invested profits being transferred from the second to the third department, wages are no longer paid out of a positive income. The set of income holders remains the unique owner of the whole product – consumption and investment goods – and no empty money is created that modifies the relationship between total demand and total supply. 'En fin de compte, *l'investissement sera financé par l'épargne et non plus par les émissions vides*' (ibid.: 328).

Our economic systems being monetary and bank money being of a book-keeping nature, it is not surprising that the origin of disorder has to be looked for at the banking level. Once its genesis has been discovered, it appears that, acting as monetary and financial intermediaries, banks may make use of double-entry book-keeping in two different ways. Either they can keep entering transactions as they do today – without articulating their book-keeping by introducing the distinction between money, financial and fixed capital departments – or they can operate in conformity with the logical nature of bank money and therefore introduce this distinction. In the first case, the investment of profits leads to the pathological re-emission of wages – the same wages already spent by firms for the purchase of capital goods still available on the financial market – and to an excess demand that defines the first step of a process that, through inflation, leads to capital overaccumulation and unemployment. 'Excess demand is the precise action defining the unique source of the capitalist mode of production: the expenditure of false wages attracts and fixes instrumental capital in the patrimony of [disembodied] firms, households being deprived of it' (ibid.: 330; our translation). In the second case, profits are transferred to the third department, the production of fixed capital goods defining the final transformation of savings into capital. Since in this case incomes already definitively saved can no longer be spent, 'invested profits are the indelible savings of households' (ibid.: 330; our translation), which are the final owners of fixed capital.

To the extent that profits are invested in the production of instrumental goods, part of current income is definitively saved and transformed into fixed capital; this is the logical rule of sound capital accumulation. By transferring invested profits to the third department, banks act in conformity with this principle. As a consequence, the fixed capital accumulated through the initial income holders' sacrifice (i.e. saving) of part of their current earnings is still owned by the undifferentiated set of households. From then on, capital accumulation will take place according to the logical nature of bank money and the threefold distinction between money as such, income and capital. Capital goods will be produced without being appropriated by disembodied firms and their amortisation will no longer lead to the creation of empty money and to the pathological process of capital overaccumulation. The world will thus benefit from a coherent monetary structure and be forever freed from inflation and involuntary unemployment. Until then, it is our scientific and ethical duty to do our best to contribute to a better understanding of monetary economics. This is what we have attempted to do throughout this book, in the hope of raising the reader's interest in a new approach to monetary macroeconomics. This approach, in my opinion, can provide a way out of the present impasse in which our science is struggling in vain.

Conclusion

My purpose here is not really to draw a clear-cut, definitive conclusion or to provide the expected summing up. In fact, the subjects analysed in this book are far too complex to justify either of these attempts. Furthermore, I am inclined to believe that the reader who has followed me this far will have already reached his own conclusions. It might therefore be more useful to spend a few words tracing the possible implications of the macroeconomic analysis of monetary economies that I have been advocating throughout the book. In particular, I would like to emphasise how Schmitt's quantum theoretical approach may contribute to the most recent debates about the concept of time.

If we take Price's latest book on the arrow of time, for example, we observe that physicists and philosophers are still puzzled by the lack of consistency between physical theories – which are largely time symmetric – and physical phenomena involving radiation, thermodynamics and cosmology – which seem to be time asymmetric. 'In all these cases, what is puzzling is why the physical world should be asymmetric in time at all, given that the underlying physical laws seem to be very largely symmetric' (Price 1996: 6). In the words of Feynman, the American Nobel Prize winner for physics in 1965, 'in all the laws of physics that we have found so far there does not seem to be any distinction between the past and the future. The moving picture should work the same going both ways, and the physicist who looks at it should not laugh' (Feynman 1992: 109). As recognised by such famous scientists and philosophers as Prigogine, Penrose and Davies, Price's thoughtful analysis of the time asymmetry problem in physics throws a new light on the controversial claim that time's arrow could reverse, physical events being submitted to both forward and backward causation. Price's suggestive thesis is that the past may depend on the future, and not only the future on the past as is usually claimed. His attempt to support the case for advanced action is thought provoking and cannot be discarded a priori. Why should we discard the possibility that what will happen in the future will modify what happens in the present? Of course, this sounds contrary to common sense and to our everyday perception of reality. Yet, as observed by Price, the temporal asymmetry inherent in human experience does not necessarily reflect the taxonomy of the objects in themselves.

[O]ur taxonomy reflects our own temporal asymmetry as *knowers*, in much the same way that our use of causal notions reflects our own temporal asymmetry as *agents*. But once we notice this, why should we continue to think that the taxonomy of the objects in themselves is governed by this asymmetry? Why shouldn't we suppose, instead, that the real taxonomy is from our standpoint teleological: that is, that there are real distinctions between objects which turn on what is to happen to them in the future?

(Price 1996: 189)

As is clearly apparent from this quotation and indeed from the whole of Price's book, authors in such a complex field as physics are not afraid of going against widespread beliefs. The case for advanced action has not yet been accepted by the great majority of physicists, true, but this is not really surprising given the difficulty of the argument and its apparent inconsistency with factual observation. Now, if it is hard to accept that the taxonomy of physical objects in themselves may be time symmetric and thus allow for backward causation, it is possible to show that there are economic events taking place today whose results may be modified, retroactively, by what will take place tomorrow.

Schmitt's quantum approach affects the entire body of monetary economics and calls for a new paradigm in which time is no longer considered as a unidirectional flow influencing income and capital through production functions. From an economic point of view, production is not a (continuous or discontinuous) function of time. As clearly shown today by double-entry book-keeping, the nature of money is such that payments are instantaneous events. Hence, production is also an instantaneous event since it takes place at the very instant that labour costs are paid for. Now, production has a real component, too. It is undeniable in fact that the costs that are paid for refer to a period of activity covering a positive span of continuous time. During this period of continuous time, matter and energy are transformed into physical goods and services that make up the real object of production. What happens at the instant, t_0, when the costs of production are paid for is that the physical output resulting from this process of transformation is instantaneously given its monetary form. In the space of a mere instant, physical output is thus changed into a set of economic goods and services. This means that the emission of money has the twofold result of defining production in its corpuscular and wave-like aspects. The corpuscular aspect of production results from the fact that at t_0 matter and energy are given a new utility-form through a transaction – the payment of wages – that quantises the period of time corresponding to their physical transformation and leads to the emission of the product as a *quantum of time*. The wave-like aspect is the instantaneous covering of this same lapse of time, both backwards and forwards. In Schmitt's words, the product 'is neither matter nor materialised labour: it is a quantum of time. Since production is the action of instantaneously "covering" in a circular movement the time of preparation of the product, the latter is created and destroyed by the same wave' (Schmitt 1984b: 94; our translation). According to quantum macro-economics, production defines only half of the real emission, the other half being represented by consumption. At t_0, output is literally created as a positive sum of money income. At t_1, when it is finally purchased, it is destroyed as such, and commodities lose their economic (monetary) form. Now, like the payment of wages, the final expenditure of income defines the emission of the product as a quantum of time. The product being the same, the two emissions are twin-like, albeit of opposite sign. Since they quantise the same period of time, they are thus simultaneous in quantum time, t_1 being retroactively made to coincide with t_0. 'The identity of the two halves of the transaction means their *simultaneity*: following the payment of wages (on the factor market), the expenditure of wages (on the commodity market) is logically subjected to the *law of retroactivity*, and is effective from the very instant workers are paid' (ibid.: 85; our translation). Hence, if at t_1 the expenditure of wages leads to the formation of a positive amount of profit, backward causation results in an instantaneous change in the payment of wages that took place at t_0. Formed at t_1 (on the commodity market), profit appears to have been spent at t_0 (on the factor market). Before t_1, output consists of wage goods only, and no expenditure occurs within the payment of wages. As soon as wages are spent and a profit is formed, output turns out to be partially made up of profit goods and a positive expenditure of profit is spotted on the factor market. 'Workers' expenditure on the commodity market is the necessary retroactive sanction of a final purchase included in the emission of wages' (Schmitt and Cencini 1982: 144). The perfect symmetry between the formation of profit within the expenditure of wages and the expenditure of profit within the payment of wages goes to show that retroactivity does not alter the relationship between money and output (contrary to what happens today when profits are invested on the factor market) and that monetary macroeconomics allows for backward causation.

As production takes place the moment that wages are paid out, economic output is formed at this very instant, t_0, and is entirely made up of wage goods. This is necessarily so because at t_0 no final purchase has yet occurred and wages are the only income available. Let us now suppose that at t_1 only a part of total output, say 80 out of 100 units of value, is purchased by wage-earners, the remaining 20 units being formed as profit. This means that at t_1 the same output of t_0 is now made up of wage *and* profit goods. The novelty of Schmitt's approach is that it shows that what happens at t_1 – chronologically later than t_0 – modifies what happened at t_0. If the payment of wages is the only event that has taken place so far, we can only know the total amount of produced output and its temporary form of wage goods. After t_1, our knowledge is increased also with respect to what happened at t_0. The two instants being simultaneous in quantum time, the result of t_1 modifies retroactively that of t_0. Since a profit is formed at t_1, we now know that at t_0 part of produced output was in fact made up of profit goods. This is not to say that this distinction between wage and profit goods was already present at t_0, before income was actually spent and profit formed. What occurs at t_0 is modified only by what occurs at t_1. If instead of 20 units of profit only 10 units were formed at t_1, what happened at t_0 would have to be reinterpreted accordingly, 10 out of 100 units of product being now made up of profit goods.

Of course, what is modified by the final purchase taking place at t_1 is not the physical form of produced output. Whatever is produced at t_0, its physical peculiarities do not change because of what happens at t_1. The problem is economic. It is the economic taxonomy of produced output that varies according to the profit formed at t_1. If the consumers' purchase of current output gives rise to a positive profit, the product of t_0 is modified in that only part of it consists of wage goods. What is new here is the fact that the distinction between wage and profit goods resulting from t_1 has a backward effect and applies since t_0.

This is also what happens in the case of interest. When a positive interest is paid to capital lenders, the result of the initial payment of wages must be reinterpreted. What presented itself as a production of 100 units of wage goods appears to be a production of wage *and* interest goods. Even if the use of capital does not directly increase the value of final output, the increase in productivity that labour derives from its working with the aid of instrumental goods takes the form of a re-emission of wages measured by the amount of interest. The payment of interest taking place at t_1 gives us a better understanding of what happened at t_0, namely that the goods produced have a total value of 110 wage units and that part of them (10 wage units in value terms) are interest goods. In this particular case, retroactivity modifies both the taxonomy of the produced output of t_0 and its value. Labour remains the unique factor of production, and wages are the definition of current output. Yet, what happens at t_1 has a retroactive effect on what happened at t_0. Retrospectively, we become aware of the fact that, backed by fixed capital, labour has indeed created a total value of 110 units, 10 units of which define the production of interest goods.

Retroactivity is perhaps the most astonishing implication of quantum analysis and the one that may interest most those who have never been entirely satisfied with the traditional approach to time and economics. The conception of production as an instantaneous event that quantises time is not easy to grasp and is almost beyond our reach if we think of production only as a physical process. The introduction of bank money changes things radically. Its numerical, non-dimensional nature turns bank money into a flow whose existence is instantaneous. Destroyed at the very moment that it is created, money is nevertheless capable of giving its numerical form to produced output. Bank deposits result from this association between output and numbers, and define the outcome of an instantaneous process called economic production. Hence, from an economic viewpoint, production is an emission because by defining output money quantises the period of time required for its physical manufacture. The emission of time as a finite and indivisible period is a direct consequence of the fact that money exists only for the space of an instant and that an instant is just what is needed to give output its numerical form.

As a matter of fact, production would be an emission even if it were not defined monetarily. As claimed by Schmitt, labour quantises time and hence gives rise to the product independently of its measure in terms of money. *'The quantisation of time is not a measuring process: it brings about the product and not its measure'* (Schmitt 1984b: 59; our translation). Yet, it is plain that with the introduction of bank money the real emission of labour finds its numerical expression through its association with the nominal emission of banks. Our monetary systems endow real emissions with their most developed form and provide a privileged insight into the realm of quantum analysis. It would not be surprising, therefore, if the new conception of time required to account for temporal symmetry stemmed from the quantum theoretical approach to money and production. Apart from economics, the way opened by Schmitt's work on the theory of emissions might prove fruitful in other fields. I shall leave to other, better equipped researchers the task of investigating any implications of his analysis in the domain of physics or in philosophy. My aim was much less ambitious and confined to the realm of economics. I hope, nevertheless, to have succeeded in raising the reader's interest in the quantum approach to monetary macroeconomics and in the way that the concept of quantum time calls into question firmly held beliefs, opening new horizons to scientific knowledge.

Bibliography

Ahmad, S. (1991) *Capital in Economic Theory*, Aldershot: Elgar.

Arestis, P., Palma, G. and Sawyer, M. (eds) (1997) *Capital Controversy, Post-Keynesian Economics and the History of Economics*, London: Routledge.

Balasko, Y. and Shell, K. (1981) 'The overlapping-generation model. II. The case of pure exchange with money', *Journal of Economic Theory* 24, 112–42.

Baranzini, M. (ed.) (1982) *Advances in Economic Theory*, Oxford: Blackwell.

Baranzini, M. and Cencini, A. (eds) (1987) *Contributi di analisi economica*, Bellinzona: Casagrande.

Baranzini, M. and Scazzieri, R. (eds) (1986) *Foundations of Economics*, Oxford: Blackwell.

Barro, R. (1988) 'The persistence of unemployment', *American Economic Review* 78 (2), 32–7.

Barro, R. and Grossman, H. (1976) *Money, Employment and Inflation*, Cambridge: Cambridge University Press.

Begg, D. (1983) *The Rational Expectations Revolution in Macroeconomics*, Baltimore: Johns Hopkins University Press.

Black, S.W. (1989) 'Transaction costs and vehicle currencies', *International Monetary Fund Working Paper No. 89/96*, November, Washington: International Monetary Fund.

Bliss, C.J. (1975) *Capital Theory and the Distribution of Income*, Amsterdam: North-Holland/Elsevier.

Böhm-Bawerk, E. (1959a) *Capital and Interest*. Vol. I. *History and Critique of Interest Theories*, South Holland: Libertarian Press (first published 1884).

—— (1959b) *Capital and Interest*. Vol. II. *Positive Theory of Capital*, South Holland: Libertarian Press (first published 1889).

—— (1959c) *Capital and Interest*. Vol. III. *Further Essays on Capital and Interest*, South Holland: Libertarian Press (first published 1909).

Bradford, W. and Harcourt, G.C. (1997) 'Units and definitions', in Harcourt, G.C. and Riach, P.A. (eds) *A 'Second Edition' of The General Theory*, Vol. I, London: Routledge.

Bradley, X. and Gnos, C. (1991) 'Définition de l'inflation: actualité de la problématique keynésienne des unités de salaire', *Economies et Sociétés* 25, 173–89.

Brunner, K. and Meltzer, A.H. (1990) 'Money supply', in Friedman, B.M. and Hahn, F.H. (eds) *Handbook of Monetary Economics*, Vol. I, Amsterdam: North-Holland/Elsevier.

Burmeister, E. (1974) 'Synthesizing the neo-Austrian and alternative approaches to capital theory. A survey', *Journal of Economic Literature* 12, 413–56.

Cass, D. and Shell, K. (1980) 'In defense of a basic approach', in Kareken, J.H. and Wallace, N. (eds) *Models of Monetary Economies*, Minneapolis: Federal Reserve Bank of Minneapolis.

Cencini, A. (1982) 'The logical indeterminacy of relative prices', in Baranzini, M. (ed.) *Advances in Economic Theory*, Oxford: Blackwell.

—— (1984) *Time and the Macroeconomic Analysis of Income*, London: Pinter Publishers; New York: St Martin's Press.

—— (1988) *Money, Income and Time*, London: Pinter Publishers.

—— (1994) 'L'inflation: une approche théorique', in *Encyclopaedia Universalis*, Paris: Encyclopaedia Universalis.

—— (1995) *Monetary Theory. National and International*, London: Routledge.

—— (1999) *Capitoli di teoria monetaria*, Bellinzona: Meta-Edizioni.

Cencini, A. and Baranzini, B. (eds) (1996) *Inflation and Unemployment*, London: Routledge.

Champernowe, D.G. (1953–4) 'The production function and the theory of capital: a comment', *Review of Economic Studies* 55 (21), 112–35.

Clower, R.W. and Howitt, P.W. (1978) 'The transactions theory of the demand for money: a reconsideration', *Journal of Political Economy* 86, 449–66.

Collins, M. (ed.) (1993) *Central Banking in History*, Aldershot: Elgar.

Debreu, G. (1959) *Theory of Value*, New Haven: Yale University Press.

Deleplace, G. and Nell, E.J. (eds) (1996) *Money in Motion*, London: Macmillan; New York: St Martin's Press.

Desai, M. (1987) 'Endogenous and exogenous money', in Eatwell, J., Milgate, M. and Newman, P. (eds) *The New Palgrave. A Dictionary of Economics*, Vol. II, London: Macmillan.

—— (1995) *The Selected Essays of Meghnad Desai. Vol. I. Macroeconomics and Monetary Theory*, Aldershot: Elgar.

Faber, M. (ed.) (1986) *Studies in Austrian Capital Theory, Investment and Time*, New York: Springer.

Fama, E.F. (1980) 'Banking in the theory of finance', *Journal of Monetary Economics* 6, 39–57.

Feynman, R.P. (1992) *The Character of Physical Law*, Harmondsworth: Penguin Books.

Fisher, F.M. (1969) 'The existence of aggregate production functions', *Econometrica* 37, 553–77.

—— (1993) 'Aggregation: aggregate production functions and related topics', in Monz, J. (ed.) *Collected Papers by Franklin M. Fisher*, Cambridge, MA: MIT Press.

Fisher, I. (1930) *The Theory of Interest*, New York: Macmillan.

—— (1965) *The Nature of Capital and Income*, New York: A.M. Kelley (first published 1906).

Fontaine, P. and Jolink, A. (eds) (1998) *Historical Perspectives on Macroeconomics*, London: Routledge.

Friedman, B.M. and Hahn, F.H. (eds) (1990) *Handbook of Monetary Economics*, 2 vols, Amsterdam: North-Holland/Elsevier.

Friedman, M. (1953) *Essays in Positive Economics*, Chicago: Chicago University Press.

—— (ed.) (1956) *Studies in the Quantity Theory of Money*, Chicago: Chicago University Press.

—— (1968) 'The role of monetary policy', *American Economic Review* 58, 1–17.

—— (1970) *The Counter-Revolution in Monetary Theory*, London: The Institute of Economic Affairs.

—— (1987) 'Quantity theory of money', in Eatwell, J., Milgate, M. and Newman, P. (eds) *The New Palgrave. A Dictionary of Economics*, Vol. IV, London: Macmillan.

Frisch, H. (ed.) (1982) *Schumpeterian Economics*, Eastbourne: Praeger.

Garegnani, P. (1972) *Il capitale nelle teorie della distribuzione*, Milan: A. Giuffré.

Gnos, C. (1992) *Production, répartition et monnaie*, Dijon: Editions Universitaires de Dijon.

—— (1998) 'The Keynesian identity of income and output', in Fontaine, P. and Jolink, A. (eds) *Historical Perspectives on Macroeconomics*, London: Routledge.

Gnos, C. and Rasera, J.-B. (1985) 'Circuit et circulation: une fausse analogie', in *Cahiers de la Revue d' économie politique*, Paris: Sirey.

Goodhart, C.A.E. (1975) *Money, Information and Uncertainty*, London: Macmillan.

Grandmont, J.-M. and Younès, Y. (1972) 'On the role of money and the existence of a monetary equilibrium', *Review of Economic Studies* 39, 355–72.

Guitton, H. (1984) 'Préface', in Schmitt, B. *Inflation, chômage et malformations du capital*, Paris: Economica and Castella.

Gurley, J.G. and Shaw, E.S. (1960) *Money in a Theory of Finance*, Washington: The Brookings Institution.

Hahn, F.H. (1982) *Money and Inflation*, Oxford: Blackwell.

—— (1989) 'On some problems of proving the existence of an equilibrium in a monetary economy', in Starr, R.M. (ed.) *General Equilibrium Models of Monetary Economies*, San Diego: Academic Press.

Hahn, F.H. and Brechling, F.P.R. (eds) (1965) *The Theory of Interest Rates*, London: Macmillan.

Hahn, F.H. and Solow, R.M. (1995) *A Critical Essay on Modern Macroeconomic Theory*, Cambridge, MA: MIT Press.

Handa, J. (2000) *Monetary Economics*, London: Routledge.

Harcourt, G.C. (1972) *Some Cambridge Controversies in the Theory of Capital*, Cambridge: Cambridge University Press.

Harcourt, G.C. and Riach, P.A. (eds) (1997) *A 'Second Edition' of The General Theory*, 2 vols, London: Routledge.

Heller, W.P. and Starr, R.M. (1989) 'Equilibrium with non-convex transactions costs: monetary and non-monetary economies', in Starr, R.M. (ed.) *General Equilibrium Models of Monetary Economies*, San Diego: Academic Press.

Hicks, J.R. (1935) 'A suggestion for simplifying the theory of money', *Economica* 2 (5), 1–19, reprinted in Hicks, J.R. (1967) *Critical Essays in Monetary Theory*, Oxford: Clarendon Press.

—— (1965) *Capital and Growth*, Oxford: Clarendon Press.

—— (1973) *Capital and Time*, Oxford: Clarendon Press.

—— (1977) *Economic Perspectives, Further Essays on Money and Growth*, Oxford: Clarendon Press.

—— (1978) *Value and Capital*, Oxford: Clarendon Press (first published 1939).

—— (1982) *Money, Interest and Wages*, Oxford: Blackwell.

Hume, D. (1826) *The Philosophical Works*, Vol. III, reprinted in Rotwein, E. (ed.) (1955) *David Hume. Writings on Economics*, Edinburgh: T. Nelson & Sons.

Jaffee, D. and Stiglitz, J. (1990) 'Credit rationing', in Friedman, B.M. and Hahn, F.H. (eds) *Handbook of Monetary Economics*, Vol. II, Amsterdam: North-Holland/Elsevier.

Jevons, W.S. (1871) *The Theory of Political Economy*, London: Macmillan.

—— (1875) *Money and the Mechanism of Exchange*, London: Appleton & Co.

—— (1911) *The Theory of Political Economy*, London: Macmillan (first published 1871; second edition, revised and enlarged, 1879).

Johnson, H.G. (1969) 'Inside money, outside money, income, wealth, and welfare in monetary theory', *Journal of Money, Credit and Banking* 1, 30–45.

—— (1972) *Further Essays in Monetary Economics*, London: Allen & Unwin.

Kalecki, M. (1944) 'Professor Pigou on "The Classical Stationary State" – a comment', *Economic Journal* 54, 131–2.

Kareken, J.H. and Wallace, N. (eds) (1980) *Models of Monetary Economies*, Minneapolis: Federal Reserve Bank of Minneapolis.

Keynes, J.M. (1938) 'Mr Keynes and "finance"', *Economic Journal* 48, 318–22 (reprinted in *The Collected Writings of John Maynard Keynes*, Vol. XIV, London: Macmillan).

—— (1971) *A Treatise on Money*, Vol. V and VI of *The Collected Writings of John Maynard Keynes*, London: Macmillan (first published 1930).

—— (1973a) *The General Theory of Employment, Interest and Money*, Vol. VII of *The Collected Writings of John Maynard Keynes*, London: Macmillan (first published 1936).

—— (1973b) *The General Theory and After. Part I, Preparation*, Vol. XIII of *The Collected Writings of John Maynard Keynes*, London: Macmillan.

—— (1973c) *The General Theory and After. Part II, Defence and Development*, Vol. XIV of *The Collected Writings of John Maynard Keynes*, London: Macmillan.

—— (1981) *Activities 1929–1931. Rethinking Employment and Unemployment Policies*, Vol. XX of *The Collected Writings of John Maynard Keynes*, London: Macmillan.

Kirzner, I.M. (1996) *Essays on Capital and Interest*, Cheltenham: Elgar.

Kohn, M. (1981) 'In defense of the finance constraint', *Economic Inquiry* 19, 177–95.

Kuczynski, M. and Meek, R.L. (eds) (1972) *Quesnay's Tableau économique*, London: Macmillan; New York: A.M. Kelley.

Leontief, W.W. (1951) *The Structure of American Economy, 1919–1939*, New York: Oxford University Press.

Lindahl, E.R. (1939) *Studies in the Theory of Money and Capital*, London: Allen & Unwin.

Lutz, F.A. and Hague, D.C. (eds) (1961) *The Theory of Capital*, London: Macmillan; New York: St Martin's Press.

McCallum, B.T. (1990) 'Inflation: theory and evidence', in Friedman, B.M. and Hahn, F.H. (eds) *Handbook of Monetary Economics*, Vol. II, Amsterdam: North-Holland/Elsevier.

McCandless Jr, G.T. (1991) *Introduction to Dynamic Macroeconomic Theory, An Overlapping-Generation Approach*, Cambridge, MA: Harvard University Press.

Malinvaud, E. (1953) 'Capital accumulation and efficient allocation of resources', *Econometrica* 21, 233–68.

—— (1977) *The Theory of Unemployment Reconsidered*, Oxford: Blackwell.

—— (1981) *Profitability and Unemployment*, Oxford: Blackwell.

Marty, A.L. (1969) 'Inside money, outside money, and the wealth effect: a review essay', *Journal of Money, Credit and Banking* 1, 101–11.

Marx, K. (1969) *Theories of Surplus Value*, 3 vols, London: Lawrence & Wishart (first published 1905–10).

—— (1973) *Grundrisse*, Harmondsworth: Penguin (first published 1939).

—— (1976) *Capital, Vol. I*, Harmondsworth: Penguin (first published 1867).

—— (1978) *Capital, Vol. II*, Harmondsworth: Penguin (first published 1885).

—— (1981) *Capital, Vol. III*, Harmondsworth: Penguin (first published 1894).

Mill, J.S. (1893) *Principles of Political Economy*, 5th edn, New York: Appleton.

Mishkin, F.S. (1993) *Money, Interest Rates and Inflation*, Aldershot: Elgar.

Morishima, M. (1992) *Capital and Credit. A New Formulation of General Equilibrium Theory*, Cambridge: Cambridge University Press.

Ono, Y. (1994) *Money, Interest and Stagnation*, Oxford: Clarendon Press.

Orphanides, A. and Solow, R. (1990) 'Money, inflation and growth', in Friedman, B.M. and Hahn, F.H. (eds) *Handbook of Monetary Economics*, Vol. I. Amsterdam: North-Holland/Elsevier.

Ostroy, J.M. (1989) 'The international efficiency of monetary exchange', in Starr, R.M. (ed.) *General Equilibrium Models of Monetary Economies*, San Diego: Academic Press.

Ostroy, J.M. and Starr, R.M. (1989) 'Money and the decentralization of exchange', in Starr, R.M. (ed.) *General Equilibrium Models of Monetary Economies*, San Diego: Academic Press.

Papademos, L. and Modigliani, F. (1990) 'The supply of money and the control of nominal income', in Friedman, B.M. and Hahn, F.H. (eds) *Handbook of Monetary Economics*, Vol. I, Amsterdam: North-Holland/Elsevier.

Pasinetti, L.L. (1977) *Lectures on the Theory of Production*, New York: Columbia University Press.

—— (1981) *Structural Change and Economic Growth*, Cambridge: Cambridge University Press.

—— (1993) *Structural Economic Dynamics*, Cambridge: Cambridge University Press.

—— (1997) 'The marginal efficiency of investment', in Harcourt, G.C. and Riach, P.A. (eds) *A 'Second Edition' of The General Theory*, Vol. I, London: Routledge.

Patinkin, D. (1965) *Money, Interest, and Prices*, New York: Harper & Row.

—— (1972) *Studies in Monetary Economics*, New York: Harper & Row.

—— (1989) 'Neutrality of money', in Eatwell, J., Milgate, M. and Newman, P. (eds) *The New Palgrave. A Dictionary of Economics*, Vol. III, London: Macmillan.

Pesek, B.P. and Saving, T.R. (1967) *Money, Wealth and Economic Theory*, New York: Macmillan.

Piffaretti, N. (1994) 'L'origine de l'intérêt du capital. De la période de production au temps quantique', unpublished B.Sc. dissertation, University of Fribourg.

Poulon, F. (ed.) (1985) *Les écrits de Keynes*, Paris: Dunod.

Price, H. (1996) *Time's Arrow and Archimedes' Point*, Oxford: Oxford University Press.

Ricardo, D. (1810) *The High Price of Bullion. A Proof of the Depreciation of Bank Notes* (reprinted in *The Works and Correspondence of David Ricardo*, Vol. III, Cambridge: Cambridge University Press).

—— (1951) *On the Principles of Political Economy and Taxation*, Cambridge: Cambridge University Press (first published 1817, second edition 1819).

—— (1951–5) *The Works and Correspondence of David Ricardo*, edited by P. Sraffa, Cambridge: Cambridge University Press.

—— (1985) *Scritti monetari*, Rome: Istituto della Enciclopedia Italiana, Bibliotheca Biographica.

Robinson, J. (1953–4) 'The production function and the theory of capital', *Review of Economic Studies* 55 (21), 81–106.

—— (1970) 'Capital theory up to date', *Canadian Journal of Economics* 3, 309–17.

Rogers, C. and Rymes, T.K. (1997) 'Keynes's monetary theory of value and modern banking', in Harcourt, G.C. and Riach, P.A. (eds) *A 'Second Edition' of The General Theory*, Vol. I, London: Routledge.

Rueff, J. (1979) *Oeuvres complètes*, Paris: Plon.

Samuelson, P.A. (1962) 'Parable and realism in capital theory: the surrogate production function', *Review of Economic Studies* 29 (80), 193–206.

—— (1966) 'Paradoxes in capital theory: a symposium. A summing up', *Quarterly Journal of Economics* 80, 568–83.

—— (1982) 'Schumpeter as an economic theorist', in Frisch, H. (ed.) *Schumpeterian Economics*, Eastbourne: Praeger.

Sayers, R.S. (1957) *Central Banking After Bagehot*, Oxford: Oxford University Press.

—— (1958) *Modern Banking*, Oxford: Oxford University Press.

Scazzieri, R. (1993) *A Theory of Production*, Oxford: Oxford University Press.

Schmitt, B. (1966) *Monnaie, salaires et profits*, Paris: Presses Universitaires de France.

—— (1972) *Macroeconomic Theory. A Fundamental Revision*, Albeuve: Castella.

—— (1975) *Théorie unitaire de la monnaie, nationale et internationale*, Albeuve: Castella.

—— (1984a) *La France souveraine de sa monnaie*, Paris: Economica and Castella.

—— (1984b) *Inflation, chômage et malformations du capital*, Paris: Economica and Castella.

—— (1985) *Introduzione agli scritti monetari di David Ricardo*, Rome: Istituto della Enciclopedia Italiana, Bibliotheca Biographica.

—— (1986) 'The process of formation of economics in relation to other sciences', in Baranzini, M. and Scazzieri, R. (eds) *Foundations of Economics*, Oxford: Blackwell.

—— (1996) 'A new paradigm for the determination of money prices', in Deleplace, G. and Nell, E.J. (eds) *Money in Motion*, London: Macmillan; New York: St Martin's Press.

—— (1998) *Le chômage et son éradication*, mimeograph, University of Fribourg.

Schmitt, B. and Cencini, A. (1982) 'Wages and profits in a theory of emissions', in Baranzini, M. (ed.) *Advances in Economic Theory*, Oxford: Blackwell.

Schumpeter, J.A. (1955) *The Theory of Economic Development*, Cambridge, MA: Harvard University Press (first published 1912).

—— (1994) *History of Economic Analysis*, London: Routledge (first published 1954).

Senior, N.W. (1854) *Political Economy*, London: R. Griffin and Co.

Shackle, G.L.S. (1967) *The Years of High Theory*, Cambridge: Cambridge University Press.

Smith, A. (1974) *The Wealth of Nations*, Harmondsworth: Penguin Classics (first published 1776).

Solow, R.M. (1955–6) 'The production function and the theory of capital', *Review of Economic Studies* 23 (2), 101–8.

—— (1957) 'Technical progress and aggregate production function', *Review of Economics and Statistics* 39, 312–20.

—— (1958) 'Technical progress and the production function', *Review of Economics and Statistics* 40, 411–13.

—— (1963) *Capital Theory and the Rate of Return*, Amsterdam: North-Holland.

Sraffa, P. (1960) *Production of Commodities by Means of Commodities*, Cambridge: Cambridge University Press.

Starr, R.M. (ed.) (1989) *General Equilibrium Models of Monetary Economies*, San Diego: Academic Press.

Starrett, D. (1989) 'Inefficiency and the demand for "money" in a sequence economy', in Starr, R.M. (ed.) *General Equilibrium Models of Monetary Economies*, San Diego: Academic Press.

Stephan, G. (1995) *Introduction into Capital Theory*, Berlin: Springer.

Stiglitz, J.E. (1997) *Economics*, New York: Norton & Co.

Thornton, H. (1965) *An Enquiry into the Nature and Effects of the Paper Credit of Great Britain*, New York: Kelly (first published 1939).

Tobin, J. (1965) 'Money and economic growth', *Econometrica* 33, 671–84.

—— (1967) 'The neutrality of money in growth models. A comment', *Economica* 47 (133), 69–72.

—— (1971) *Essays in Economics*, Vol. I. *Macroeconomics*, Amsterdam: North-Holland.

—— (1972) 'Inflation and unemployment', *American Economic Review* 62, 1–19.

—— (1980) 'Discussion of overlapping generations models', in Kareken, J.H. and Wallace, N. (eds) *Models of Monetary Economies*, Minneapolis: Federal Reserve Bank of Minneapolis.

Torr, C. (1997) 'User cost', in Harcourt, G.C. and Riach, P.A. (eds) *A 'Second Edition' of The General Theory*, Vol. I, London: Routledge.

von Neumann, J. (1945–6) 'A model of general economic equilibrium', *Review of Economic Studies* 13, 1–9.

Wallace, N. (1980) 'The overlapping generations model of fiat money', in Kareken, J.H. and Wallace, N. (eds) *Models of Monetary Economies*, Minneapolis: Federal Reserve Bank of Minneapolis.

Walras, L. (1984) *Elements of Pure Economics*, London: Allen & Unwin (first published 1874).

Wicksell, K. (1934) *Lectures on Political Economy*, London: Routledge.

—— (1954) *Value, Capital and Rent*, London: Allen & Unwin.

—— (1965) *Interest and Prices*, New York: Kelley (first published 1898).

—— (1997) *Selected Essays in Economics*, edited by B. Sandelin, London: Routledge (first published in 1912).

Woodford, M. (1990) 'The optimum quantity of money', in Friedman, B.M. and Hahn, F.H. (eds) *Handbook of Monetary Economics*, Vol. II, Amsterdam: North-Holland/ Elsevier.

Wrigley, E.A. and Souden, D. (eds) (1986) *The Works of Thomas Robert Malthus*, London: Pickering.

Author index

Subject index